California
Economic
Growth

1999 Edition

CENTER FOR CONTINUING STUDY OF THE CALIFORNIA ECONOMY

California Economic Growth—1999 Edition was prepared as part of the research program of the Center for Continuing Study of the California Economy (CCSCE). The project was directed by Stephen Levy, Senior Economist, who was the report's principal author. Adrienne Mills and Nancy Levy prepared the graphs and text and handled the report production. CCSCE appreciates the valuable assistance of Robert K. Arnold in formulating the issues section and providing conceptual guidance to the overall project.

CCSCE staff specializes in analysis and long term projections of economic and demographic variables in California and subareas of the state. **California Economic Growth—1999 Edition** is the product of an internally financed, ongoing program of CCSCE to provide business and government decision makers with an independent assessment of the future growth of California and subareas of the state.

Other publications in the CCSCE annual report series:

CALIFORNIA POPULATION CHARACTERISTICS

CALIFORNIA COUNTY PROJECTIONS

Table of Contents

Appendix A: Basic Industries by SIC Category

INTRODUCTION

INTRODUCTION

California Economic Growth has been the cornerstone of the CCSCE publication series, the report in which CCSCE outlines its analysis of the state's economy, and alerts subscribers to the early signs of future trends.

Now that the California economy has turned the corner, the long term strengths CCSCE has been talking about throughout the recession are becoming apparent to all. The theme of this year's report is meeting the challenges of renewed economic growth. How can California's growing prosperity reach more people? And how can the pressures of job and population growth on California's physical and environmental resources be reduced?

The 1999 edition of **California Economic Growth** covers the same topics emphasized last year – 1) a review of the 1998 economy and outlook for 1999; 2) the outlook for the national economy; 3) a detailed analysis of California's economic base; 4) projections of jobs, population, households, income and spending; 5) a review of construction trends; and 6) an analysis of each major regional economy in California.

The estimates and projections of California's economic characteristics published in this report are part of an ongoing research program of the Center for Continuing Study of the California Economy (CCSCE). Except where noted, all the detailed estimates and projections in this report were prepared by CCSCE.

Our work benefited greatly from the continuing assistance of many dedicated people working for local, state and federal agencies involved in data collection and analysis. CCSCE wishes to acknowledge the special assistance of:

Ted Gibson, Chief Economist of the California Department of Finance; Mary Heim of the Demographic Research Unit of the California Department of Finance; Jeff Reynolds and Joe Fitz of the California Board of Equalization; Ben Bartolotto, Research Director of the Construction Industry Research Board; Bill Kolarik of the International Trade Administration; Elizabeth Hill and Brad Williams of the Legislative Analyst's Office; Brian Bugsch of the California World Trade Commission; Charles Bowman, Richard Holden, Dick Hagaman and the entire staffs of the U.S. Bureau of Labor Statistics and California Employment Development Department who have responded graciously to numerous requests for data and assistance.

CCSCE also wishes to acknowledge the ongoing support of the many private and public sector clients who have long term relationships with CCSCE. We also wish to acknowledge our loyal subscribers who have affirmed the value of having an independent perspective on the California economy.

MAJOR ECONOMIC REGIONS
OF CALIFORNIA

1. LOS ANGELES BASIN
2. SAN FRANCISCO BAY AREA
3. SAN DIEGO REGION
4. SACRAMENTO REGION
5. REST OF STATE

About California

California is the world's seventh largest economic power with a Gross State Product that exceeds $1 trillion. With more than 33 million residents and 11 million households California is by far the nation's largest state market. Major regions of the state – the Los Angeles Basin, San Francisco Bay Area, Sacramento and San Diego – are among the nation's largest metropolitan market areas.

The need for credible information about California is well recognized. Private investors worldwide are constantly comparing California's economic environment to other locations. Financial institutions must assess the security of public and private debt and investments in the state. Public agencies must plan to meet the public service demands of more than 500,000 new residents each year.

Many of the nation's future challenges will first be met in California: maintaining competitiveness in high technology industries, capitalizing on the state's ethnic diversity, responding to defense cutbacks, expanding into Asian markets and combining environmental protection with economic growth. What happens in California will influence national policy in these and other areas.

ABOUT CCSCE

The Center for Continuing Study of the California Economy (CCSCE) has become the recognized source of independent information about long term trends in California. CCSCE was founded as an independent, private economic research organization specializing in the analysis and study of California. CCSCE focuses on long term economic and demographic trends in the state and its major economic regions.

CCSCE works with private companies and public institutions that require an explanation and analysis of the growth process as well as detailed quantitative projections. CCSCE has developed a proprietary model to project long term economic trends in California based on a detailed analysis of the prospects of California industries within the framework of national and global trends.

CCSCE uses its findings to help decision makers in both the private and public sector make long term strategic plans regarding business decisions and public policy.

CCSCE was established in 1969 by Robert K. Arnold and Stephen Levy. It has been a source of reliable information on California for investors, businesses, and public agencies for over a quarter of a century.

EXECUTIVE SUMMARY

EXECUTIVE SUMMARY

The decade of the 1990s began with an unexpectedly long and deep recession. Defense spending cuts and a decline of more than 50% in new construction were followed by a sharp drop in confidence and retail spending. Some residents and leaders thought that the best days of the California economy were behind us.

The next four years showed that the underlying strength of California's economic base had remained intact throughout the long recession. The performance of California's entrepreneurs and workers clearly demonstrated that the state is still the leading center for development of new products and services.

For the period from 1994 through 1998 California's job growth solidly outpaced the nation – 11.3% versus 9.2%.

It is these middle years of the decade, and not the 1990-1994 experience, which tell the story of where the California economy is headed. The California economy faces **substantial future opportunities**. CCSCE projects that California will outpace the nation in job, population, household, income and spending growth in the decade ahead.

New products and technologies in advanced telecommunications, multimedia, and the use of the Internet symbolize the state's leadership position in future growth industries. California already has the economic base that other regions and nations are striving to create.

Past and Future Job Growth
California

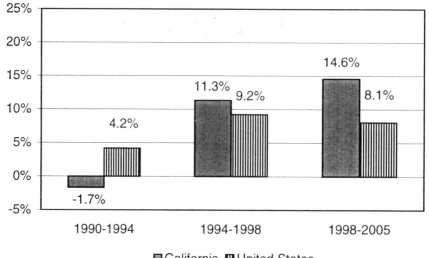

■ California ▥ United States

The California economy still faces major challenges. **Abundant opportunity does not equal guaranteed success.** Though most of the hard work will be performed by California's entrepreneurs and workers, there is a significant role for public policy – a role that is in danger of going unmet.

The facts that support these themes – **recovery, opportunity, and challenge** – are set forth in the 300 pages that follow.

The California Economy Surges Ahead

California added more than 400,000 jobs in 1998. As a result, the state unemployment rate fell to 5.7% in November 1998 – the lowest level since before the 1990 recession.

Since January 1997 the state has gained nearly 840,000 jobs. California's 6.5% increase in job levels far outpaces the very robust 4.6% nationwide gain. Job levels in California are up 1.7 million from the recession low and 1.2 million above the pre-recession peak.

Nonfarm Wage and Salary Jobs (Thousands)				
	Jan. 1997	Nov. 1998	Change	Percent Change
California	12,907.4	13,743.8	836.4	6.5%
United States	12,146.0	126,775.0	5,629.0	4.6%

Source: EDD (Interim Series) and U.S. Bureau of Labor Statistics

Nonfarm Wage and Salary Jobs
California
July 1990-November 1998

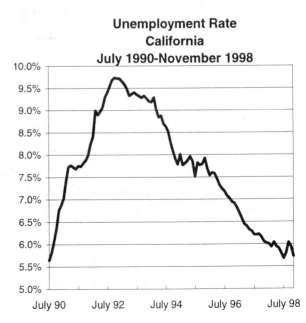

Unemployment Rate
California
July 1990-November 1998

Job growth brought strong gains in income and spending. Total personal income is on a pace to rise 6.8% in 1998. These gains will far outpace the 2.1% gain in California consumer prices.

Spending gains also outpaced inflation. Taxable sales rose 5.7% for the first three quarters of 1998.

Construction spending grew at double digit rates in 1998. Nonresidential construction reached nearly $15 billion in 1998 – up 20% following a 25% increase in 1997.

Housing markets continued to improve moderately in 1998. Resale prices and volumes hit record levels in many regions of California. New home construction increased to 125,000 units – still less than half of mid 80s building levels.

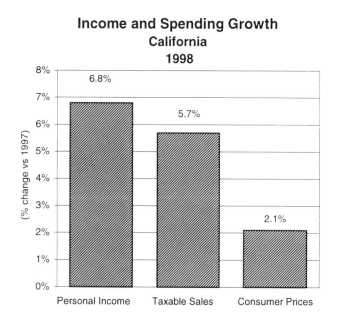

Southern California Roars Back

The Los Angeles Basin and San Diego regions were the economic growth leaders in California in 1998. Jobs increased by 3.3% in the Basin led by strong gains in Orange County and the Riverside - San Bernardino metro area. Los Angeles County also added 100,000 jobs in 1998. San Diego posted a 3.1% job gain.

Both regions were helped by growth in Mexico's economy and by gains in the non high tech manufacturing sectors. In addition both Los Angeles and San Diego had substantial gains in construction spending.

Nonfarm Wage and Salary Jobs (Thousands)			
Region	Jan-Nov 1997	Jan-Nov 1998	% Change
Los Angeles Basin	6,174	6,375	3.3%
San Francisco Bay Area	3,172	3,259	2.7%
San Diego	1,047	1,079	3.1%
Sacramento	700	717	2.5%
San Joaquin Valley (1)	756	769	1.7%
California	13,147	13,572	3.2%
United States	122,530	125,092	2.6%

Source: California Employment Development Department; U.S. Bureau of Labor Statistics; (1) Fresno, Kern, San Joaquin, Stanislaus counties

The Bay Area, California's growth leader in 1995, 1996, and 1997, slowed last year. The region's strong position in high tech trade with Asia restrained Bay Area job growth in 1998 as Silicon Valley went from being the growth leader in 1997 to just average job gains last year.

Jobs grew by 2.5% in the Sacramento region – near the national average – while the San Joaquin Valley had job increases of just 1.7%.

California's Economic Base — Current Strength and Future Potential

California's economic recovery was led by **future** high growth sectors. The growth potential in these sectors provides the foundation for CCSCE's projections of continued above average growth in the California economy.

The recovery was led by four sectors with strong long term growth potential – high tech manufacturing, foreign trade, entertainment & tourism and professional services. In addition, Southern California re-emerged as the diversified manufacturing capital of the nation with firms carving out growth niches in traditional markets such as textiles, apparel, furniture, and toys.

High Technology

High tech manufacturing will grow three times as fast as other manufacturing industries in the United States during the next ten years. California has more than 20% of nationwide production and jobs. Recent high tech highlights include:

- Silicon Valley posted its 9th consecutive annual record level of new venture capital funding. More than $4 billion will be invested in Silicon

Valley startups in 1998 and California will receive more than 1/3 of national venture capital funding.

- California firms have recovered all the share losses of the early 1990s and captured a **record high 20.7% of U.S. high tech manufacturing jobs in 1998**.

- Exports of high tech manufacturing products from $29.7 billion in 1990 to $68.0 billion in 1997 – a gain of 129% – before a temporary leveling off in 1998 as a result of declines in Asian sales.

- California is the leading center for biotech research and development (home to industry leaders like Genentech and Amgen) with more than 1/3 of the nation's public companies and more than 50% of R & D expenditures. California is also a leading center for advanced telecommunications product development.

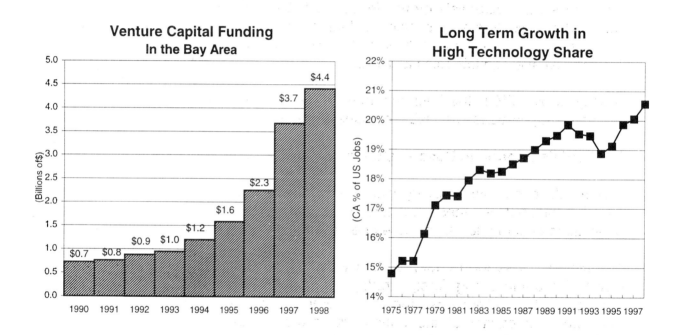

California companies like Intel, Applied Materials, Silicon Graphics, Beckman Instruments, and Hewlett Packard represent leadership positions in their markets. Newer companies like Qualcomm (advanced telecommunications) and Netscape (making the Internet accessible) symbolize California's leadership in emerging technology markets.

Successive records in venture capital funding underscore the fact that California remains the world's leader in technology innovation. California continued to receive one-third of the nation's new venture capital funding which will lead to future growth in jobs, production and exports.

Foreign Trade

The volume of foreign trade is growing more than twice as fast as the overall economy. Exports are growing even faster led by technology industries and entertainment.

The Asian economic downturn in 1998 caused a temporary decline in exports, total trade volume, and California's share of U.S. trade. However, trade with Mexico and Europe grew at double digit rates and the long term prospects for Asian trade remain bright.

- Exports of goods produced in California rose 88% between 1990 and 1997 and remain above $100 billion in 1998. Total exports of California products including services and agriculture are near $160 billion.

- Exports to Mexico have tripled since 1990 to top $14 billion in 1998 – nearly as much as California exports to Japan.

- Trade volumes handled by California ports and airports grew by 10% annually in the past decade and exceeded $300 billion in 1997 and 1998.

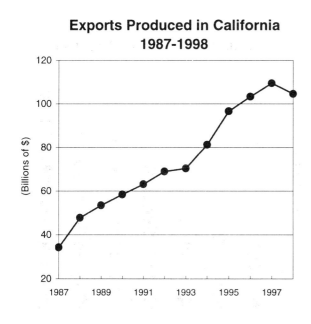

**Exports Produced in California
1987-1998**

**Long Term Growth in
Foreign Trade Share**

Ports and airports throughout the state are investing billions in expansions which will accommodate future growth. These investments from the Alameda Corridor to port expansions in Long Beach and Oakland and airport expansions in San

Diego, Los Angeles, and San Francisco are critical to keeping California as a world class trading center.

Entertainment & Tourism

Entertainment and tourism jobs will grow twice as fast as the total economy in the decade ahead. California is the world's leading center for the development of entertainment products and a premier tourist site for state, national and world visitors.

- The number of film starts produced in California has tripled to more than 600 in 1997. Moreover, California's participation in U.S. film starts is now above 60%.

- U.S. film exports more than tripled between 1991 and 1997 to exceed $6 billion. These gains symbolize the strong worldwide demand for U.S. entertainment products with California representing the largest centers of design and production.

- Motion picture production jobs (with an average wage of more than $65,000) are up 60% since 1990 and newly revised job estimates show that 1998 brought another 10,000 jobs in the industry.

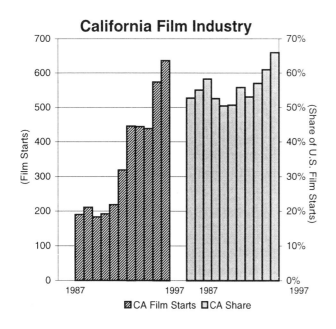

- Tourism is on the rebound and major expansions are planned in amusement, sports and entertainment facilities throughout California.

Hotel rates and occupancy are rising and new hotel proposals are being developed in major tourist centers.

The continued rise in disposable income in the United States and worldwide lays a solid foundation for the long term growth of California's entertainment and tourism sector.

Professional Services

Professional services like software and engineering and management services are the fastest growing sector of the nation's economic base and pay wages more than 50% above the national average. Average California wages in the 1st quarter of 1998 were $71,000 in software and $52,000 in engineering and management services compared to the average wage nationally of $31,000.

Computer services including software development and Internet access tools is California's leading high wage growth sector.

- Job levels doubled between 1993 and 1998 ending with 250,000 jobs in California's computer services sector.

- California is home to world leading firms like Netscape, Yahoo, Excite (Internet services); Pixar and Lucas Arts (animation); and E-Trade (on-line brokerage service).

- California is also the leading auto design center with design facilities for General Motors, Ford, and Chrysler as well as Toyota, Honda, Nissan, Mitsubishi, Isuzu and Mazda.

Computer Services

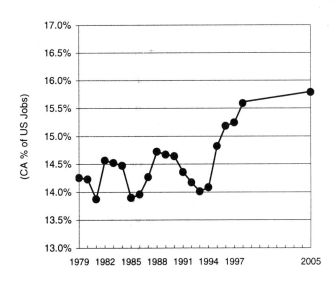

California's engineering and management services sector has more than 450,000 jobs – many oriented to providing services to national and worldwide markets. California firms provide design, construction, management, legal and financial services to fast growing Asian markets where recent international treaties will broaden the access of U.S. firms.

Diversified Manufacturing

Diversified manufacturing is the largest sector in California's economic base in 1998 – with $150+ billion in sales (more than high tech manufacturing) and over 1,000,000 jobs. **In 1998 California's diversified manufacturing industries reached record levels for jobs, production and national market share.**

California firms have added jobs in industries where job levels are stagnant or in rapid decline in the nation. This has been achieved through the application of design, creativity and entrepreneurship to create growth niches in older manufacturing markets.

- California has added 50,000 jobs in the apparel industry while the nation has lost 500,000 jobs. As a result California's share of national production has increased from 7% to near 20% in the past two decades largely based on a competitive advantage in design for women's apparel

- California firms have added jobs and shown rapid share gains in other diversified manufacturing sectors such as beverages, textiles, special industry machinery and toys. As a result in 1998 California firms accounted for a record high 8.4% of the nation's diversified manufacturing sector – despite the loss of many defense industry jobs.

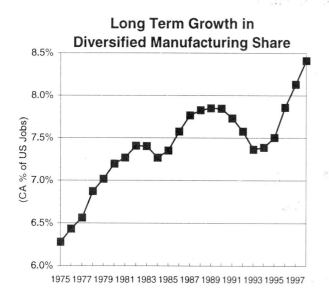

Quantitative Implications for California Growth

CCSCE's analysis of California's economic base concludes that the state will continue to experience substantial economic and demographic growth.

California will add 2.2 million jobs, 1.5 million households and 4.2 million residents by 2005. Total income will grow by 3.5% per year faster than the rate of inflation and reach $1.2 trillion (in 1998$) by the year 2005.

California Major Growth Trends			Percent Change	
	1998	2005	California	U.S.
Total Jobs (Thousands)	15,503.5	17,766.9	14.6%	8.1%
Income (Billions of 98$)	$905.2	$1,151.1	27.2%	19.7%
Households (Thousands)	11,127.6	12,682.6	14.0%	7.5%
Population (Thousands)	33,550.0	37,800.0	12.7%	5.9%

California will outpace the nation in jobs, income, household and population growth.

The growth in California's economic base will bring new workers and their families to California. These residents will require goods and services which, in turn, will create jobs to serve the growing population. These population serving jobs, for example, in retail trade and services, will be an important part of the state's future job growth.

All regions of the state will grow faster than the nation. The Southern California economic recovery will continue and lead to the state's largest numerical gains in jobs, population, and households. The smaller regions will post the highest growth rates but California's job, population, and household base will remain concentrated in the Los Angeles Basin and San Francisco Bay Area.

Challenges

Abundant opportunities do not mean guaranteed success.

Governor Davis and his administration will inherit several challenges related to California's eocnomy. Three continuing challenges are highlighted below and, in more detail, in Section 6:

1. The state policy role in creating the foundations for economic growth – a long term economic strategy for California

2. The paradox whereby economic growth puts pressure on California's land and environment but a high quality of life is critical to attract entrepreneurs and workers

3. The long term challenge of providing access and opportunity to individuals who are not fully participating in California's prosperity

Challenge One: Developing a Long Term Economic Strategy for California

Abundant opportunity does not equal guaranteed success. California will need to work hard to convert opportunities into gains in real wages, income, and profits.

California does start with an advantage. The state's economic base is already well positioned in future growth sectors. California's challenge is not to create a new economic base but, rather, to nurture and expand the state's leadership position in key industries.

The actions of California's firms and workers will be the primary determinant of the pace of economic growth. Private sector investment and management decision will be critical for converting opportunity into prosperity.

Public policy has a significant role to play in creating a positive environment for private investment.

Public policy affects the economy in many ways as shown on the accompanying chart. The new administration will have a chance to develop a new set of priorities for the state's role in supporting economic growth.

Some themes in California now are gaining momentum because they simultaneously address business and residents' perspectives:

- The economy depends on California's education system

- A strategic infrastructure plan is needed for the economy and for quality of life

- A high quality of life is a competitive asset for California businesses

An ongoing challenge is to find a balance between **reform** and **resources**. Both are desired as current education dialogues show clearly.

Attracting Private Investment Requires Public Investment

A Diverse Economy Requires A Diverse Economic Strategy

Business Costs & Regulatory Environment
Workers' Compensation
Taxes and Fees
Housing Prices
Tort Reform
Capital Access
Streamlined Permitting
Market Based Environmental Regulations

Education and Training
K-12
Higher Education
School to Work Transitions
Reform of Public Sector Training Programs

Infrastructure
Highways & Public Transportation
Ports
Airports
Water Systems & Solid Waste Disposal

Quality of Life
Good Schools
Low Crime
Air Quality
World Class Amenities

Helping Industries Organize for Success
Reducing Trade Barriers
Increased R&D and Technology Support
Fostering Industry Networks and Collaboration
Linking Industry with Government and Schools
Regional Economic Initiatives

For example, meeting California's infrastructure challenges will require a mix of reform and resources. Increasing infrastructure **capacity** doesn't always mean more building although plenty of new construction will be required. For example, conservation has been an important tool in providing "new" water and electricity for residents and businesses.

School and transportation construction will pose challenges to our creativity in expanding capacity to meet the requirements of growth. Reforms in construction practices and how schools and roads are used can be important tools in making the large upcoming public investments effective in terms of outcomes and cost.

There is hope that 1999 will bring the development of a long term capital planning strategy in California as more and more groups are realizing its importance to both economic growth and quality of life.

Challenge Two: Combining Economic Growth and Quality of Life: A Growth Management Strategy for California

In 1998 CCSCE prepared a report on the connections between land use decisions, quality of life and the California economy. The report **Land Use and the California Economy: Principles for Prosperity and Quality of Life** was sponsored by California business and community foundations and is available at no charge from Californians and the Land at (415) 281-0415.

The report identifies the paradox of economic growth in California:

1. California's strong economy and resulting job and population gains put pressure on California's land, environment and quality of life. These pressures will intensify under the growth expected by CCSCE and others.

2. California business leaders increasingly identify a high quality of life as critical for attracting talented people. **High housing prices, long commutes and environmental pressures are a business problem as well as of great concern to residents**.

The elements of a solution – a strategy to manage California's growth – are well known. So too are the difficulties in reaching agreement on specifics. The CCSCE report identified five principles for simultaneously achieving economic growth, environmental and quality of life goals.

Principle One: Regional Perspectives Are Required

Regions are the correct geography for doing the critical thinking about growth. While state policies may be necessary to provide the right incentives, the actual housing, job transportation and open space connections occur at the regional level. Likewise, while most Californians want local land use decision making, everyone recognizes that city decisions must be connected in some way to achieve good regional outcomes.

Principle Two: Land Must be Used More Efficiently

The essence of this principle is that the only way to minimize sprawl is to increase housing in existing urban areas. This will require major changes in state-local fiscal incentives, a commitment to maintain California's large cities as attractive places to live, and policies to make land recycling and infill development easier.

Principle Three: Public Investment is Required

California faces more than $100 billion in infrastructure investments in the next ten years. The need for substantial increases in public investment – in schools, transportation, airports, and water – has been documented again and again in analyses of California's economic competitiveness. These same investments are also needed to support smart land use planning and maintain a high quality of life for all Californians.

Principle Four: Fiscal Reform is Essential

Current fiscal rules give the wrong land use planning incentives. Current fiscal rules make infrastructure funding difficult. Current fiscal rules prevent local governments from providing high quality public services for California's growing number of businesses and residents.

The long-standing problems documented by many groups – disincentives for housing, competition for retail development, and the inability of local sales and property tax bases to keep pace with job and population growth – require a change in existing state and local fiscal structures. Economic growth alone will not change the fiscal disincentives for smart land use.

Principle Five: Equity Considerations Must Be Included

Smart land use planning must include job and housing opportunities for all Californian's, as well as open space and preservation of the state's unique land resources. Californians share the same land, the same economy, and the same environment. The challenge is to ensure that increases in economic prosperity and quality of life reach all residents.

Challenge Three: Broadening Access to Economic Prosperity

Four years of economic growth **have** made a difference to many Californians. Average wages and income are up strongly reaching record levels and far outpacing consumer price increases. Moreover, in 1997 and 1998 low income Californians finally shared in the wage growth.

A strong economy had a substantial impact on reducing unemployment and raising incomes. Economic growth remains the most important tool for raising incomes and reducing poverty.

However, active public sector policies on workforce preparation – education, training and related services – are also required – both to help individuals unable to fit into today's economy and to meet the growing demands of California businesses for more skilled workers.

The legislature will address workforce issues in 1999 – both in response to new federal workforce program rules and to the **California Integrated Workforce Development Plan** led by the Secretaries of Education and Trade and Commerce, the Superintendent of Schools and Chancellor of the California Community Colleges. CCSCE's research continues to support the finding that the different parts of California's labor force are connected. Future public policy should build on these connections with a universal workforce approach that addresses the multiple challenges in a unified framework:

- recognizing the growing similarity of former welfare recipients and working poor Californians in their personal goals and workforce requirements

- recognizing that many middle level workers will need to upgrade skills and change careers to maintain a rising standard of living

- recognizing that workforce preparation (with a stress on upgrading K-12 education) is the number one public policy issue of California businesses and that private sector expertise can enhance the usefullness of public workforce strategies

California's health foundations are becoming a new voice on workforce issues. The California Wellness Foundation and others are developing research and action programs around the connections between work and health.

There are strong connections between the work and health status of Californians. Income, job satisfaction, and related issues like work schedules and job security all show strong connections to health status. A good job and, therefore, the requirements for getting a good job, are one of California's best health promotion policies.

KEY CONCEPTS IN UNDERSTANDING THE CALIFORNIA ECONOMY

KEY CONCEPTS IN UNDERSTANDING
THE CALIFORNIA ECONOMY

There are four important concepts that are helpful in understanding how the California economy operates. These concepts are helpful both in explaining recent trends and in discussing the long term outlook for the California economy.

The four concepts are:

- The distinction between growth in **numbers** and growth in **prosperity**

- The importance of the state's **economic base** in determining future growth

- How the **pool** of new opportunities in the nation and the state's **share** of U.S. job and output growth combine to determine how fast California will grow in the number of added jobs, population and households.

- The distinction between the determinants of **long term** versus **short term** economic growth in a state like California

Growth in Numbers Versus Growth in Prosperity

This report addresses two major questions about the California economy:

How California is Related to the U.S. Economy

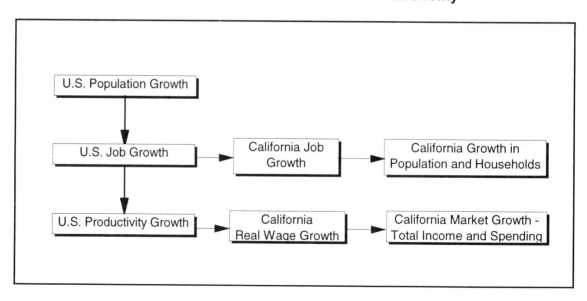

- How will California grow in **numbers**? How many more jobs, people and households will be added in California in the years ahead?

- How much will the state improve in terms of the **prosperity** of California's residents? What will the trends be for real income and spending?

The questions about numerical growth are answered by examining the **prospects for job growth** in California. The growth rate of a region like California is dependent on the decisions of individual firms to locate new facilities or expand existing ones. The growth in California's **economic base** (export industries) will determine the rate of overall job growth.

Population and household growth in California are related to job growth. California will gain new residents and require new housing units roughly in proportion to the state's job growth.

The growth in numbers in California is largely determined by the growth in numbers in the nation. Given the substantial projected growth in population and jobs in the nation, there is no doubt about the findings that California will grow significantly in terms of total jobs, population, and households.

The nation will add nearly 16 million residents between 1998 and 2005 and another 100 million people after that by 2050. If CCSCE's numerical growth projections are not met in 2005, they will be met and surpassed shortly thereafter. California will remain the nation's largest market by a significant degree (and with the largest projected growth in numbers) for any conceivable future planning period.

Despite the recent slowdown in job, population, and household growth, **public and private decision makers in California should continue to anticipate large numerical growth**.

Growth in **prosperity** – real income and spending – has quite different determinants. The principal factor driving gains in real income and spending is **productivity growth** – increases in the productive capability of the workforce.

Productivity growth has been a problem and a mystery in recent years. Low productivity growth has constrained the growth in real wages in the state and nation since the early 1970s.

There are mixed results in terms of increasing prosperity for California residents. Difficult challenges remain ahead.

- Average income and wage levels are **rising** and should continue to grow. However, average wage and income gains are modest by comparison to the 1950s and 1960s because productivity growth has remained low.

- A rising tide has not lifted all boats. There are at least two major problem areas:

  - Many people remain without a job or even basic skills. How to get all people (now including welfare recipients) ready for the first step into the labor market remains a difficult challenge.

  - Many workers in middle class jobs are, indeed, working harder for less. Perhaps the major economic challenge in the decade ahead is to understand what is necessary for middle level workers to look forward to a lifetime of productive employment and rising living standards.

California's Economic Base is the Key Factor in Relative Job Growth

How fast or slowly California adds jobs compared to other areas is determined by growth in the state's **economic base**. Basic industries – the industries included in California's economic base – make a substantial share of their sales to customers outside the state. Basic industries export goods and services to areas elsewhere in the nation or worldwide.

Basic industries produce both goods and services. Major goods producing basic industries in California include computer equipment, electronic components, apparel, aircraft, and instruments.

Services are also an important component of California's economic base. Major service producing basic industries include motion pictures, computer services, engineering and design services, and tourism.

Basic industries are an important focus for public policy.

- *Exportable goods and services are subject to intense competition. A state competitiveness strategy means being competitive in basic industries.* Growth in jobs and sales in the state depends on how well the state's firms and workers compete – often with locations throughout the world. People involved in basic industries – whether in manufacturing apparel, filming a motion picture, or deciding where to vacation – have a choice of location.

- *Growth in the economic base will determine the opportunities for job growth and increases in income in the rest of the economy.* Prospects for employment growth in supporting activities like retail trade, medical services, construction and local education depend on employment expansion in basic industries. States with the fastest growing economic bases have the highest rates of overall employment growth.

The Pool of New Opportunities and California's Share

California's future job growth will be determined by:

- How many and what kind of jobs are created in the nation – the **pool** of new jobs.

- What **share** of new jobs will locate in the state.

The **pool** of new jobs has two important characteristics – size and composition. The size of the pool is discussed in Section 4 – the U.S. will gain substantial numbers of new residents and new jobs in the years ahead.

The composition of those jobs is also important in analyzing California's growth. Where new jobs will be (in what industries) makes a difference to the state's future economic prospects.

The finding of CCSCE's analysis is that the composition of U.S. job growth is favorable to California's economic base. The fastest sales and job growth in basic industries is occurring in industries where California has a large base of activity and a strong competitive position.

Recently, the question of California's future share of national jobs and production has received a great deal of attention. CCSCE devotes a major part of this report to reviewing recent share trends and analyzing two related issues:

- What are the likely future trends in California's share of key basic industries?

- What are the factors most likely to affect California's competitive position (i.e., share) in the future?

There is agreement that California will have the opportunity to participate in emerging growth markets.

There is agreement that California faces challenges in converting these opportunities into job and income gains. There is little agreement yet, however, on what are the most important areas of challenge or on what public policies are critical for success.

CCSCE hopes that the analysis in **California Economic Growth** will help focus these questions and provide some answers.

The Relationship of Total Job Growth to Changes in California's Economic Base – Economists look at three kinds of impacts when assessing the impact of an addition (or reduction) to the state's economic base. These are

- Direct impacts

- Indirect (or supplier) impacts

- Induced (or consumption) impacts

The **direct** impacts are the sales and income (wages and profits) created directly by the activity. For example, an increase in medical instruments or apparel sales creates additional income and jobs.

The directly affected industry buys inputs (supplies) from many other industries. For example, medical instrument and apparel manufacturers buy additional supplies when they receive new orders. Their purchases create additional sales, income and jobs. These activities are called the **indirect** impacts of changes in basic industry sales.

A portion (often large) of the purchases occur outside California. Therefore, the indirect impacts in California of changes in basic industry sales are usually modest.

Direct, Indirect, and Total Economic Impacts

The direct and indirect (supplier) sales create **a pool of income and profits** for residents in the state. Residents spend the income on consumer purchases and create additional sales and jobs. These jobs are **"induced"** by the impacts of the income and jobs from the direct and indirect activities.

The consumption **multiplier** is another name for induced spending and jobs.

The distinctions between direct, indirect and induced spending explain how changes in basic industry activity can cause much larger changes in total jobs. The linkage explains why basic industries are critical in determining regional growth rates even though most new jobs are not in the economic base.

Long Term Versus Short Term Outlook and Issues

For the most part the explanation of short term trends in the California economy depends on different factors than the key determinants of the State's long term economic prospects. Similarly, the policy choices, especially the policy choices facing state government, vary between the short and long term context.

Here are some examples of the difference between short term and long term economic determinants. In the long term residential building is determined by population growth and affordability factors. Yet between 1989 and 1993 California experienced a 64% drop in residential building while the state added more than 2 million residents and both mortgage rates and home prices declined. As the cyclical factors diminish (as they are doing now) the construction market will again be determined by long term job and population growth.

Long Term Versus Short Term Economic Growth in California		
Determinants and Issues	Short Term	Long Term
Job Growth	National and world economic cycles, cyclical fluctuations in key industries	Long term growth trends for key industries in economic base
Housing Construction	Fluctuations in prices and buyer confidence	Household growth
Spending	Fluctuations in income **and** variations in consumer confidence	Growth in personal income
Principal Public Policy Tools	National fiscal and monetary policy; policies that affect consumer confidence	National policies in support of productivity and key industry growth. State policies to attract and retain key basic industries.

In the long run spending and consumption related jobs are related to the growth in total jobs and income. In the short term, however, fluctuations in income and in consumer confidence can distort the spending/income ratio. For example, a sharp (and temporary) drop in spending relative to income restrained job growth in California in the early 1990s.

In the long term job growth depends on the pool of new jobs created in the U.S. and the share that will locate in California. In the short term, however, job levels fluctuate in response to world events (e.g., economic turmoil in Asia), national economic cycles (e.g., the high levels of recent U.S. job growth), and region specific factors (e.g., the importance of technology manufacturing in California's economy and state specific cycles in construction and consumer confidence).

As a result of the difference between short and long term growth determinants, California can face significant long run growth prospects even though the state may now be entering a period of slowing growth. In the short term, many of the continuing areas of strength – foreign trade, high tech, tourism & entertainment – may be outweighed by the negative impacts of slowing economic growth outside the United States.

As a result both cyclical and permanent factors can contribute to job losses during a recession. The important points for policy analysis are 1) to keep separate the analyses of short and long term factors and 2) to develop **separate** policy responses to short and long term job and income growth determinants.

The distinction between long term and short term economic growth is especially important in the policy arena. State governments have no significant short term economic tools. They cannot influence the world economy or the national business cycle. They cannot significantly change the confidence of home buyers or consumers. States cannot influence cycles in key markets like aerospace.

State government policies are rarely the principal cause of cyclical fluctuations in state economies nor can state government policies do much to reverse short term cycles.

State governments, however, have a much more significant role in long term economic growth. State governments have a key role in **some** areas – like education, infrastructure, quality of life, and rules and regulations – which do affect the state's attractiveness for business investment.

CCSCE's views on California's long term policy agenda to promote economic growth are included in the section, *Key Issues Facing California*.

THE CALIFORNIA ECONOMY
IN 1998 AND 1999

THE CALIFORNIA ECONOMY IN 1998 AND 1999

The California economy produced substantial job and income gains in 1998 and monthly job gains continued above 30,000 in September, October and November. The large job and income gains came despite a downturn in California exports.

Income gains raced ahead of consumer price increases allowing California residents to experience a fourth straight year of rising living standards. Consumers, with rising incomes and confidence, pushed taxable sales nearly 6% higher in 1998 compared with a 2.1% increase in consumer prices.

Construction continued a strong rebound in 1998. Residential building rose more than 10% although new construction is still well below previous highs. Resale housing activity surged with median prices reaching all time highs in some regional markets. Nonresidential building valuation rose by another 20% following gains of more than 25% in 1997.

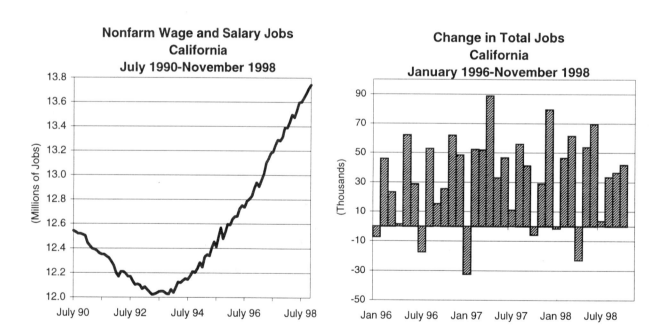

All regions participated in 1998 gains but the focus of growth shifted to Southern California. The Los Angeles Basin and San Diego regions posted the strongest job growth while the Bay Area and Sacramento regions slowed down and the San Joaquin Valley lagged in 1998 job growth.

Last year at this time the consensus forecast for 1998 looked for slower growth with rising prices and interest rates. All three parts of the forecast were in the wrong direction despite the deepening of international economic and financial turmoil. The same puzzle faces forecasters for 1999. CCSCE's analysis of today's short term economic forecasts appears at the end of Section 3 following a review of current economic data and trends.

California Had Strong Job Growth in 1998

California added more than 400,000 jobs in 1998. Between January 1997 and November 1998 state job levels surged – adding nearly 840,000 jobs for a 6.5% job increase in the past 23 months. In comparison the national economy had a 4.6% job gain during the same period.

Nonfarm Wage and Salary Jobs (Thousands)				
	Jan. 1997	Nov. 1998	Change	Percent Change
California	12,907.4	13,743.8	836.4	6.5%
United States	12,146.0	126,775.0	5,629.0	4.6%

Source: EDD (Interim Series) and U.S. Bureau of Labor Statistics

California has added 1.7 million jobs since the recession lows and has 1.2 million more jobs than before the recession started. As a result California's unemployment rate fell to 5.7% in November 1998 – the lowest level since before the 1990 recession.

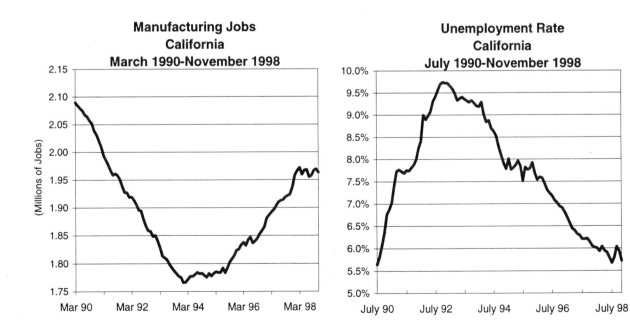

Construction, Finance, and Services Lead The State's Job Growth

Services led the California economy in 1997 and 1998 with a gain of 326,000 jobs (8.2%) led by gains in high wage sectors like software and engineering services. Construction jobs had the highest growth rate (+19.4%) and the sector has now recovered all the 1989-93 job losses.

Finance, Insurance and Real Estate posted an 8.9% job gain and, like Construction, finally recovered the job losses incurred from the recession and industry consolidations. Finance is another high wage sector with strong long term growth potential.

California Nonfarm Wage & Salary Jobs (Thousands; Seasonally Adjusted)				
	January 1997	November 1998	Change	% Change
Mining	29.2	24.0	-5.2	-17.8%
Construction	523.4	624.7	101.3	19.4%
Manufacturing	1,880.8	1,963.2	82.4	4.4%
Transportation, Public Utilities	650.8	700.7	49.9	7.7%
Wholesale Trade	759.8	802.4	42.6	5.6%
Retail Trade	2,239.0	2,335.0	96.0	4.3%
Finance, Insurance, Real Estate	740.7	806.6	65.9	8.9%
Services	3,954.3	4,280.3	321.0	8.2%
Government	2,129.4	2,206.9	77.5	3.6%
Total Nonfarm Jobs	12,907.4	13,743.8	836.4	6.5%

Source: California Employment Development; Interim Series

Manufacturing and Wholesale Trade continued to post jobs gains despite the export slowdown. Manufacturing job levels rose 4.4% (+82,400) between January 1997 and November 1998. As a result, nearly 2/3 of the manufacturing jobs lost during the aerospace decline have been regained in other manufacturing sectors.

High tech manufacturing sectors added jobs in 1997 and 1998 led by electronic components (+9,800), and measuring and control instruments (+7,000). Apparel and textiles recorded job gains of 6,100 despite continued sharp declines in national job levels. Miscellaneous manufacturing (including toys) added 7,000 jobs between January 1997 and November 1998.

Construction related manufacturing job levels rose led by furniture (+6,100). Aircraft posted a gain of 4,900 jobs and fabricated metal products added 9,100 jobs.

California Manufacturing Job Trends (Thousands)			
	January 1997	November 1998	Change
Apparel and Textiles	175.0	181.1	6.1
Drugs	28.9	31.4	2.5
Miscellaneous Manufacturing (incl. Toys)	43.1	50.1	7.0
Furniture	52.7	58.8	6.1
Fabricated Metal Products	119.6	128.7	9.1
Computers	91.6	91.9	0.3
Electronic Components	144.5	154.3	9.8
Aircraft	82.6	87.5	4.9
Search and Navigation Equipment	57.4	56.9	-0.5
Measuring and Control Instruments	64.7	71.7	7.0

Source: California Employment Development; Interim Series

Southern California Roars Back

The Los Angeles Basin and San Diego Regions were the economic growth leaders in California in 1998. Southern California outpaced Northern California for the first time in the 1990s based on strong construction gains, proximity to Mexico where trade is still growing rapidly and regional manufacturing gains.

The Los Angeles Basin led California with a 3.3% job gain (more than 200,000 jobs) during the first eleven months of 1998. Los Angeles County had a respectable 2.6% gain (+102,000 jobs) and passed the 4 million job level in November for the first time since 1990.

The Inland Empire (Riverside and San Bernardino counties) posted a 4.8% job gain to lead all metro areas in California. Orange County added 50,000 jobs in 1998 for the 2nd straight year for a 4.1% job gain.

The Bay Area, growth leader for most of the 1990s, slowed to near the national growth rate in 1998 constrained by declines in high tech exports. Though Silicon Valley will end the year with a 3% job gain (down from 5% in 1996 and 97), all of the job gains were in the first half of 1998. East Bay and San Francisco job gains continued throughout the end of 1998.

Nonfarm Wage and Salary Jobs
(Thousands)

Region	Jan-Nov 1997	Jan-Nov 1998	% Change
Los Angeles Basin	6,174	6,375	3.3%
L.A. County	3,864	3,966	2.6%
Orange County	1,226	1,277	4.1%
Riv-San Bern Metro Area	841	881	4.8%
San Francisco Bay Area	3,172	3,259	2.7%
Oakland Metro Area	949	975	2.8%
San Fran Metro Area	983	1,003	2.0%
San Jose (Silicon Valley)	926	954	3.1%
San Diego	1,047	1,079	3.1%
Sacramento	700	717	2.5%
San Joaquin Valley (1)	756	769	1.7%
California	13,147	13,572	3.2%
United States	122,530	125,092	2.6%

Source: California Employment Development Department; U.S. Bureau of Labor Statistics; (1) Fresno, Kern, San Joaquin, Stanislaus counties

San Diego had a 3.1% job gain and was the only region to record an increase in foreign trade. San Diego had gains in construction, telecommunications, and trade related jobs as well as continued gains in maquiladora related activities.

Nonfarm Wage and Salary Jobs
Los Angeles Basin
March 1990-November 1998

Nonfarm Wage and Salary Jobs
San Francisco Bay Area
March 1990-November 1998

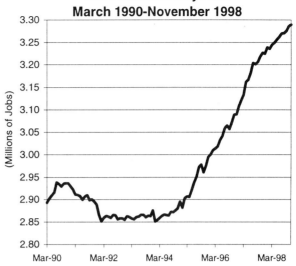

Nonfarm Wage and Salary Jobs
San Diego
March 1990-November 1998

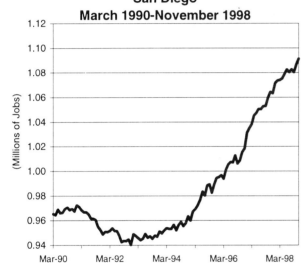

Nonfarm Wage and Salary Jobs
Sacramento Region
March 1990-November 1998

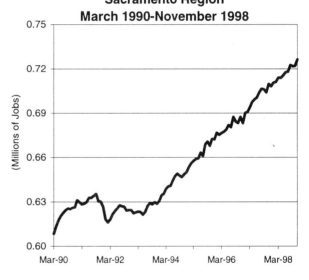

Nonfarm Wage and Salary Jobs
San Joaquin Valley
March 1990-November 1998

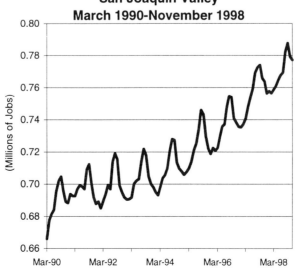

Job Growth and Wage Gains Push Incomes Higher

Total personal income in California grew by 6.8% in the first half of 1998 following a 6.0% gain in 1997. Consumer prices were up by approximately 2% in each year. As a result, California residents experienced substantial gains in real income.

Income gains were led by large increases in total wages and salaries. Wage and salary income was up 9.0% in the first half of 1998 following a 7.9% gain in 1997. Average wages probably rose by 10% for the two years combined.

Gains in California's average wage had three major determinants:

1. The nation had strong productivity gains in 1997 and 1998, partially reflecting the better use of the nation's large investment in computing technology.

California Personal Income (Percent Change)	1996-97	1st Half 1997-98
Total Personal Income	6.0%	6.8%
Wages and Salaries	7.9%	9.0%
Other Labor Income (Benefits)	2.0%	9.3%
Proprietors Income	5.3%	10.1%
Property Income	4.9%	3.2%
Transfer Payments	2.8%	0.5%

Source: California Department of Finance

These productivity gains, if continued, will mark a new era of prosperity in the United States. Productivity gains remain the fundamental determinant of long term increases in real income and living standards.

2. California had continuing job gains in high wage industries like software, engineering services, motion pictures, manufacturing and finance and also strong gains in many above average wage industries like construction and wholesale trade.

3. Lower income workers finally achieved wage gains in 1997 and 1998 driven by strong labor demand and helped by an increase in the minimum wage.

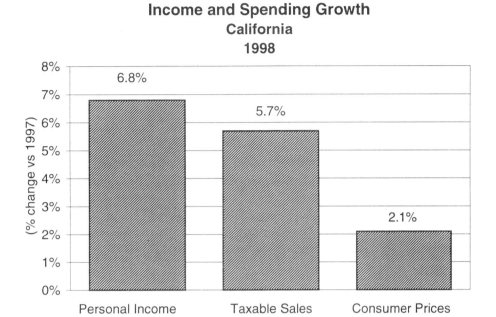

Income and Spending Growth
California
1998

Retail Spending Outpaces Inflation in 1998

Retail spending is continuing to outpace inflation in California. Taxable sales were up 5.7% in the first three quarters of 1998 – far outpacing the 2.1% rise in consumer prices.

California Taxable Sales in 1998 ($Billions)				
	First Quarter	**Second Quarter**	**Third Quarter**	**First 3Q**
1998	$81.1	$90.6	$91.2	$262.8
1997	77.1	85.0	86.6	248.7
% Change	5.2%	6.7%	5.4%	5.7%

Source: California Board of Equalization; percentages calculated from unrounded data.

Construction and Foreign Trade – Two Big Sectors to Determine How California Fares in 1999

Construction and foreign trade are two large sectors in the California economy which went in different directions in 1998. Whether California achieves another year of double digit construction increases and whether and when foreign trade rebounds from the recent decline will be critical determinants in how the California economy performs in 1999.

Construction

Both residential and nonresidential construction posted double digit dollar gains in 1998. Nonresidential construction was up 20.8% in the first ten months of 1998. Industrial and "other" nonresidential construction (e.g., stores, hotels, and amusement facilities) posted the largest dollar gains.

California Nonresidential Construction ($Millions)			
	Jan-Oct 1997	Jan-Oct 1998	Percent Change
Industrial	$1,404.8	$2,145.1	52.7%
Office	1,472.4	1,602.6	8.8%
Alterations & Additions	4,161.8	4,515.2	8.5%
Other	3,406.6	4,353.9	27.8%
Total Nonresidential	**$10,445.6**	**$12,616.8**	**20.8%**

Source: Construction Industry Research Board

Industrial building rose more than 45% to exceed $2 billion – outpacing 1997's 40% gain. Alterations and additions grew by 8.5% but remained the largest category of nonresidential construction at $4.5 billion for the ten month period. Office building increased by approximately 10% after doubling in 1997.

Los Angeles County joined the nonresidential building surge with a 41.6% increase in the first 10 months of 1998. Other large gains were posted in Orange (+45.3%), San Bernardino (+29.6%), San Diego (+24.9%), and Alameda (+21.2%). Nonresidential building was up 35% in Southern California but only 3.7% in the Bay Area where Silicon Valley construction leveled off after doubling between 1995 and 1997.

California
Construction Trends
(Billions of 1998$)

	New Building Construction			Residential Permits (Thousands)		
	1989	1993	1998	1989	1993	1998
Los Angeles Basin	$26.4	$9.1	$14.2	116.4	28.8	43.1
San Francisco Bay Area	8.7	5.3	10.0	35.6	15.1	23.5
San Diego	4.5	1.7	3.5	18.7	5.6	12.5
Sacramento	3.6	1.8	3.0	20.8	8.8	15.1
San Joaquin Valley	3.6	2.5	2.8	27.3	16.4	15.9
Other	3.2	2.0	2.8	18.8	9.9	12.0
California	**$49.9**	**$22.4**	**$36.3**	**237.7**	**84.6**	**124.7**

Source: Construction Industry Research Board; 1998 estimates by CCSCE based on Jan-Oct CIRB data.

Despite the strong year in 1998 Southern California remains far below peak levels in total construction. While the Bay Area's 1998 construction spending ($10 billion) is above 1989 levels, the Los Angeles Basin with $14.2 billion in new construction was barely over 50% of 1989 spending levels. The San Diego, Sacramento and San Joaquin Valley regions also remain 20-30% below 1989 construction levels despite posting record job levels in 1997 and 1998.

Resale Housing Market Heats Up

The resale housing market in California set price and volume records in 1998.

Average resale volume has stayed above 600,000 units per year throughout 1998 as shown on page 3-12. Resale volumes remained near record levels even during the financial volatility of the fall months.

The combination of strong job growth and low levels of new residential construction in the 1990s are putting pressure on resale markets throughout California. Market tightness, which started in Silicon Valley and Orange County, spread to more regional markets in 1998.

Median resale housing prices exceeded $210,000 in California in the summer of 1998 for the first time since 1991. Median resale prices reached record levels throughout the Bay Area and in Orange and San Diego counties.

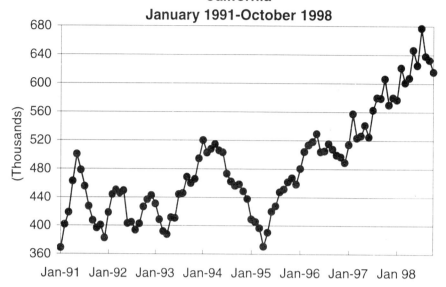

Annual Existing Home Sales Volume
California
January 1991-October 1998

Median prices are far outpacing inflation now in most California markets with the largest gains in the high job growth regions.

Median Resale Home Prices			
	October 1996	October 1998	Percent Change
California	$174,100	$197,230	13.3%
Central Valley	105,300	114,950	9.2%
Los Angeles County	171,320	190,300	11.1%
Orange County	213,460	265,210	24.2%
Riv-San Bern Metro Area	110,410	124,050	12.4%
Sacramento	115,000	125,000	8.7%
San Diego County	172,600	208,090	20.7%
San Francisco Bay Area	264,890	318,410	20.6%
Santa Clara County	275,510	356,990	29.6%

Source: California Association of Realtors

Median resale prices were up nearly 30% in Santa Clara County during the past two years and are the highest median prices for any metro area in the nation. The Bay Area, Orange County and San Diego County also posted price gains of more than 20% to reach record levels in 1998.

Median Existing Home Sales Price
California
January 1991-October 1998

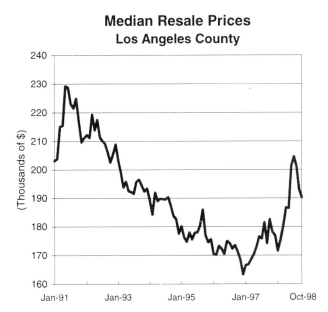

Median Resale Prices
Los Angeles County

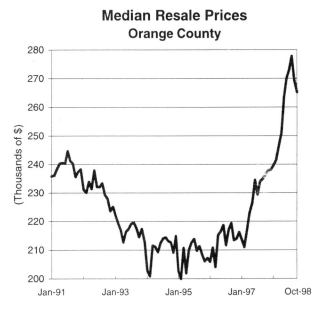

Median Resale Prices
Orange County

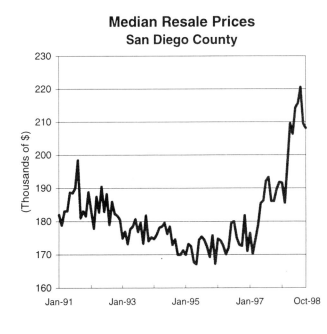

Median Resale Prices
San Diego County

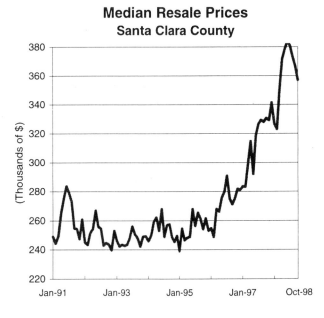

Median Resale Prices
Santa Clara County

3-13

Other markets were up but with much more modest gains. Prices remain particularly depressed in the Central Valley, Sacramento and Riverside – San Bernardino markets – previously the high growth, low housing cost centers of California.

Foreign Trade – A Decline in 1998

Exports of goods produced in California declined in 1998 – driven down by large declines in exports to Asia. For the first 3 quarters of 1998 California exports were down 3.3% – worse than the 1.1% national decline.

The declines were centered in exports to Asian countries and exports of high tech goods.

Exports of California Firms
($Billions)

Country	1997	1st 3 Q 1997-98 % Change	Industry	1997	1st 3 Q 1997-98 % Change
Japan	$17.4	-15.9%	Electronics	$30.4	-3.4%
Mexico	12.1	14.9%	Ind Mach, Computers	28.5	-6.3%
Canada	11.4	12.3%	Transp Equip	11.2	-0.2%
Korea	7.0	-40.6%	Instruments	9.1	2.6%
Europe	23.7	17.3%	Food Products	5.5	-2.3%
Other Asia	27.5	-18.9%	Chemicals	4.5	-1.9%
Total	**$109.5**	**-3.3%**	**Total**	**$109.5**	**-3.3%**

Source: California World Trade Commission

Exports to Asia could fall as much as $11 billion in 1998 – down nearly 20% from 1997 levels. These losses are mostly offset by gains in other markets. European exports were up approximately $4 billion or 17.3%. Both Mexican and Canadian purchases of California goods were up more than 10%.

Based on the statewide data it is likely that Silicon Valley and Bay Area exports led the decline in 1998 while exports from Los Angeles Basin firms were down slightly and San Diego firms posted an export gain based on increased trade with Mexico.

California Exports 1997-98

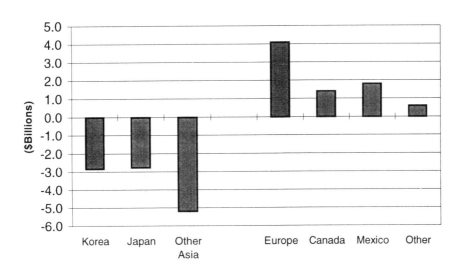

Foreign Trade by Customs District

The total volume of trade through California customs districts (imports and exports) also declined in 1998. Based on data for the first 9 months of 1998 total trade volume through California ports and airports could be down by more than 2% to $308.4 billion for the full year.

Foreign Trade by Customs District ($Billions)			
	1997	**1998**	**Percent Change**
Los Angeles	$185.8	$182.0	-2.1%
San Francisco	107.0	99.8	-6.7%
San Deigo	23.0	26.6	15.7%
California	315.8	308.4	-2.3%
United States	$1,550.0	$1,581.0	2.0%

Source: U.S. Department of Commerce; 1998 estimates based on Jan-Sept. data.

San Diego continues to show double digit trade growth. For the first nine months of 1998 trade volume was up 15.7% in San Diego.

The Bay Area had the largest trade decline (6.7%) driven by declines in exports to Asia. The Los Angeles region had gains in import volume and an overall 2.1% decline in total trade.

The United States Outlook for 1999

The fundamental determinants of United States economic growth are in good position as 1999 begins. Investment, productivity, inflation and interest rates performed well in 1998 and the long term trends are more favorable than at any point in the 1990s.

Unless international economic problems escalate, any slowdown in the U.S. economy in 1999 should be mild and temporary.

The U.S. economy is always subject to two short term threats to stable economic growth:

- The threat of recession
- The threat of escalation inflation

The U.S. economy has avoided both threats for more than seven consecutive years. Gross domestic product grew by more than 3% again last year despite the year earlier consensus forecast of a 1998 slowdown.

Inflation declined again with consumer prices growing by 1.5% and producer prices **falling** by 1%. Interest rates – long term and short term – fell throughout the year contradicting year earlier forecasts of price and interest rate increases.

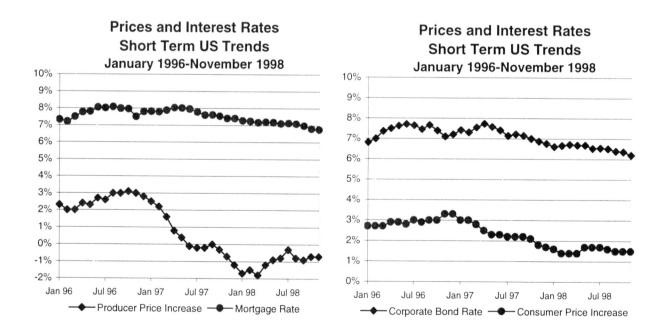

The U.S. economy posted a third straight year of strong productivity gains with 1998 productivity growth exceeding 2%. These gains in worker productivity combined with a 30 year low in unemployment rates (4.5%) have pushed incomes and spending up sharply.

Federal Reserve Bank policy shifted course in midyear in what may be viewed years from now as a major new direction for the Fed.

- Federal Reserve Chairman, Alan Greenspan, has long felt that the U.S. economy may be entering a new period of long term productivity gains. The evidence in 1997 and 1998 bolsters his case. As a result the Fed has not seen continuing strong economic growth as a threat to inflation because the economic gains reflect real increases in productivity and output.

  Productivity gains of more than 2% have occurred for three consecutive years twice before in the past 25 years. Accordingly it is too early to say that the United States has definitely entered an era of sustained productivity. 1999 will provide a test when we see how well productivity gains are maintained if the anticipated slowdown in U.S. economic growth occurs.

U. S. Productivity Gains 1990-1998

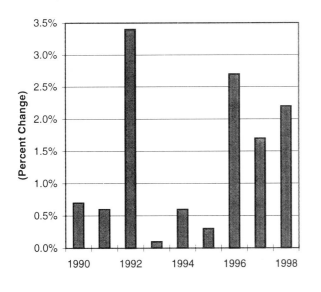

U. S. GDP Growth 1990-1998

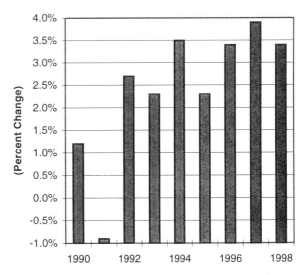

- In midyear the Fed began a policy of short term interest rate reductions. The reason was to insulate the U.S. economy from international financial and economic turmoil.

  The effect was to place the Fed on record as recognizing the threat of an economic slowdown in the U.S. and making the Fed an active participant in trying to maintain economic growth.

The results were a sharp drop in interest rates. Long term treasury bond rates are at 5% – down from 7% two years ago. Mortgage rates are near 6.75% and long term corporate bond rates are near 6.2%.

Short term interest rates are down also with the federal funds rate at 4.7%, 3 month treasuries near 4.5%, and the bank prime lending rate at 7.75%.

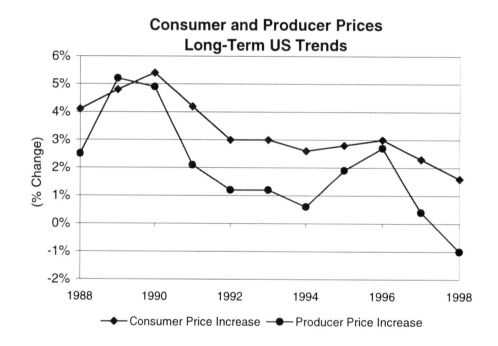

Consumer and Producer Prices Long-Term US Trends

The California Outlook for 1999

There is a broad consensus that the California economy will grow in 1999 but at a slower rate than in 1998. A similar forecast was reported last year for 1998 – that forecast proved conservative as California economic growth did not slow despite international economic and financial turmoil.

California Economic Forecast for 1999 (% Growth)		1999		
	1998	**Low**	**High**	**Average**
Jobs	3.3%	2.2%	2.9%	2.3%
Personal Income	6.8%	4.7%	6.6%	5.8%
Retail Sales	5.7%	4.7%	6.7%	5.6%
Residential Permits	11.7%	-4.7%	26.9%	14.0%

Source: 1998-CCSCE; 1999 – CCSCE review of existing forecasts

The slowdown in California is based on an expected slowdown in the U.S. economy. The California economy follows national economic trends, except in rare instances, as shown by the comparison of California and U.S. unemployment rate trends shown below.

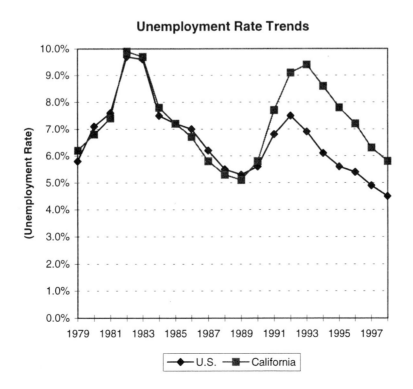

Unemployment Rate Trends

The arguments for a U.S. economic slowdown are by no means certain. Arguments in favor of a slowdown include:

- There has been some slowing in monthly job gains. In the first half of 1998 average monthly job gains were 270,000, while in the next five months they averaged near 240,000.

- Profit growth has slowed. Corporate profits were up 11.6% in 1996, 9.0% in 1997 and may be only 1.2% in 1998.

- The rate of investment growth has slowed.

- The stock market has been volatile, rising by 16% through July then falling by 17% in early October then recovering nearly all the summer losses in November and December

- There is still a risk of further export declines related to global economic slowing

On the other hand many sectors remain strong:

- Consumption spending (2/3 of GDP) has remained strong in the 3rd quarter of 1998 growing by 4.1% after adjusting for inflation. Holiday spending was robust in November and December.

- Interest rates (including mortgage rates) fell sharply during the 4th quarter of 1998 and ended the year at historically low levels. Most economists expect additional rate cuts by the Federal Reserve Bank in early 1999.

- The trade deficit, while high, has stopped rising.

The Impact of Foreign Trade and Construction in California's 1999 Outlook

Residential construction has the potential to provide a boost to the California economy. Resale housing markets tightened in more regions of California in 1998. Unless there is an anticipated fall in consumer confidence, another increase in new residential building is expected in 1999 given continued population and income gains and low mortgage rates.

Nonresidential construction is expected to increase but at a slower pace than in 1997 and 1998. Nonresidential construction will be very sensitive to how the overall economy performs.

Foreign trade should be a small positive for the California economy in 1999 – a turnaround from the 1998 impact. Last year CCSCE wrote:

"It is likely that 1997 exports from California will end up near the 1996 level of $105 billion (they were $109 billion). If exports to Asia declined by as much as $10 billion in 1998 (looking on target), it is possible that total exports might decline by as much as $5 billion (also looking on target). This could make as much as a 0.5% difference in California's rate of growth."

The 1999 outlook is more positive:

- Non Asian exports should continue to rise – perhaps by 10% (less than 1998's 15%)

- Asian exports should not decline further. Economists expect a small rebound in Japan's economy and the yen/dollar exchange rate is favorable again for U.S. exports. While exports to other Asian countries may not recover much in 1999, there is no reason to expect additional declines because there is no underlying reason for Asian economic growth to be lower than in 1998.

- One likely scenario is for Asian exports to be flat and other exports up $5 billion thus producing a $10 billion turnaround from the 1998 performance.

THE U.S. ECONOMY IN
THE DECADE AHEAD

THE U.S. ECONOMY IN THE DECADE AHEAD

National trends in job and income growth create the opportunities and context for job and income gains in California. The number and kind of jobs that are added in the nation will shape the amount and pattern of job growth in California.

Productivity trends (i.e. how fast real output per worker is changing) are the principal determinant of income growth in both the nation and California. The prospects for real income gains (i.e. sustained improvement in average living standards) will be determined by how fast worker productivity can be increased.

A new set of long term national projections were published by the United States Bureau of Labor Statistics (BLS) in November 1997.[1] These projections describe the broad trends in jobs, occupations, and income that will shape the context in which the California economy functions in the decade ahead.

Population and Labor Force

Population growth will average 2.3 million per year for the 1996-2006 decade. The projected growth rate (0.8% per year) is below recent levels while the amount of population growth has been relatively stable for the past five decades.

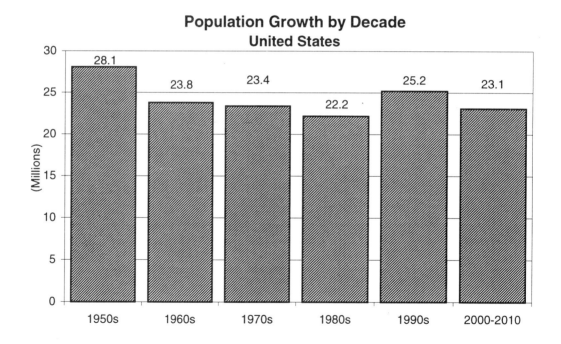

Population Growth by Decade
United States

---

[1] The projections are presented in the November 1997 edition of the **Monthly Labor Review.**

Birth levels will remain relatively stable because the number of women of childbearing ages will not change much in the next ten years and no major changes in fertility rates are expected. The number of deaths annually will begin to increase as the population ages.

Immigration is projected to continue at approximately 800,000 per year. Immigration will account for one-third of the nation's population growth in the decade ahead.

Population will not increase equally among all age groups. The pattern of population growth remains heavily influenced by the aging of the baby boom generation.

Most (18.4 million) of the nation's population gains will occur in the 45-64 age group. Three other trends are noteworthy:

- Growth in the 65+ age group will be modest. The baby boomers will not begin reaching age 65 until 2012 and the preceding (depression) cohort was relatively small.

- The 16-24 age group will grow again adding nearly 6 million persons to the college and entry level labor force cohort.

- The young adult population (ages 25-44) will decline by 5.4 million. This trend will reduce competition for younger workers and may help in reversing the declines in real wages experienced by younger workers in recent years.

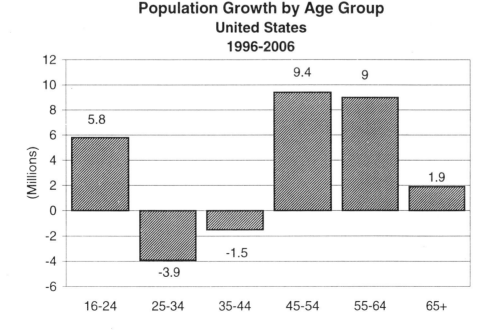

Population Growth by Age Group
United States
1996-2006

BLS projected that labor force growth would average 1.1% per year between 1996 and 2006. The U.S. labor force would grow from 134 million in 1996 to 149 million in 2006. The strong economic growth of 1997 and 1998 has pushed labor force growth slightly ahead of BLS projections.

United States Total Labor Force 1986-2006 (Millions)				Annual Percent Change	
1986	1996	1998	2006	1986-96	1996-2006
117.8	133.9	137.4	148.8	1.3%	1.1%

Source: Bureau of Labor Statistics

In the 1970s and 1980s labor force participation rates soared in the United States as women poured into the labor force. This substantial increase in female labor force participation rates was one of the most profound social and economic trends of the postwar period.

Future increases in labor force participation rates are expected to be much smaller. The total labor force participation rate is projected to increase from 66.8% to 67.6% in 2006. Although recent trends (the welfare to work mandate and the lower than expected unemployment rates) may push participation rates slightly above the BLS projections, future increases are limited by the following trends.

—   The aging of the labor force will push more workers into age groups with lower participation rates (e.g. from illness or early retirement).

—   Female participation rates are now close to male rates in the younger age groups.

—   Male participation rates have shown no reversal of the slow downward trend except in the older age groups.

United States
Labor Force Participation Rates
1986-2006

		1986	1996	2006
Total		65.3%	66.8%	67.6%
Men		76.3%	74.9%	73.6%
	25-54	93.8%	91.8%	90.8%
	55+	40.4%	38.3%	43.8%
Women		55.3%	59.3%	61.4%
	25-54	70.8%	76.1%	79.3%
	55+	22.1%	23.9%	29.9%

Source: Bureau of Labor Statistics

It is unlikely that the U.S. labor force will be much larger than projected in 2006. Everyone who will be of working age is already born. With the movement of the baby boomers past 45 any upward movement in the labor force would have to come from a substantial re-entry into the labor force of older males or a massive change in male retirement patterns in the decade ahead.

Because the growth in labor force participation rates is slowing substantially, future gains in real income will depend significantly on improvements in worker productivity and not, as in previous decades, on an increase in the average hours of work per family.

U.S. Productivity Growth

One of the most dramatic economic changes in the United States in the past two decades is the decline in productivity growth. Between 1947 and 1973 productivity, defined as output per worker, grew by 3.0% annually. From 1973 through 1992 productivity growth fell to just 0.8% per year. This decline occurred for many reasons, but its persistence ranks as one of the major disappointments of the U.S. economy since 1970.

The last 3 years bring hope that the U.S. economy is entering a new period of higher productivity gains. This is a very important trend if it continues.

Why is Productivity Important?

Productivity growth is the principal determinant of growth in real income. Growth in productivity – the ability to produce more goods and services per hour of work – is the key to rising real wages and a rising standard of living.

In the 1950s and 1960s the productivity of the average worker rose by 3% a year on the average. With 3% annual growth, living standards double every 23 years.

After 1973 there was a sharp decline in the overall rate of productivity gains to just 0.8% per year on average. With that rate of growth, living standards double every 87 years.

However, recent trends suggest that productivity growth may rise to 1.4% annually, less than in the 50s and 60s, but enough to reduce the doubling time for living standards to 50 years.

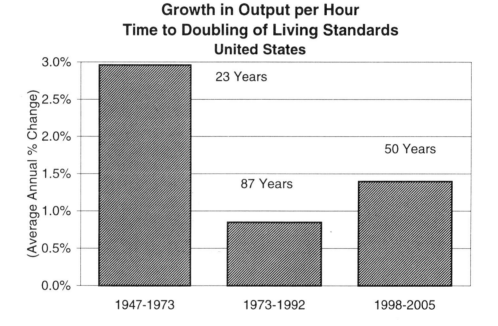

Growth in Output per Hour
Time to Doubling of Living Standards
United States

What is the Outlook for Productivity Growth

There are three major paths to raising productivity:

- Increasing the skill and experience of the U.S. workforce

- Raising investment in plant and equipment

- Reorganizing the workplace to achieve greater efficiency

All three paths have been reflected in the national policy debate over raising U.S. growth rates. The nation is debating proposals to 1) encourage college attendance, 2) reform K-12 education, 3) restructure workforce preparation programs and 4) modify various regulatory policies.

The capital gains tax was recently reduced and proposals to tax consumption as a way to raise savings and investment are under discussion. Private companies are exploring ways to reorganize workplace practices and motivate workers.

Economists are uncertain about recent productivity trends. Productivity growth, as measured by government economic statistics, shows a pattern of low annual productivity gains in the 1990s. Measured productivity gains in the 1990s until 1996 were less than 1% per year. The productivity improvement sensed by many economists did not show up in official statistics.

In 1996, however, reported productivity growth surged to 2.7% which was followed by a 1.7% gain in 1997. Productivity gains continued in the first half of 1998 at nearly a 2% growth rate.

Many economists believe that the nation's huge investment in technology is finally paying off. Federal Reserve Bank Chairman Alan Greenspan has been a leading spokesperson for the idea that the strong productivity gains in 1996 and 1997 can be continued. Recent fed policy of lowering interest rates is based, in part, on the belief that strong economic growth without inflation is possible as a result of stronger productivity growth.

There are several reasons to believe that productivity gains should be stronger in the decade ahead.

- Private capital investment has been high for several years. Much of the investment has been in computers and related equipment. Spending on durable equipment rose from $386 billion in 1990 to $661 billion in 1997. It is reasonable to assume that the nation's massive investment in computers will eventually translate into productivity gains.

- Restructuring, corporate downsizing and development of new work practices (such as at the NUMMI auto plant in Fremont, California) should also lead to productivity gains.

- Average education levels have still been increasing, although slowly.

A Range of Productivity and GDP Projections

CCSCE used a range of productivity projections in developing the income and spending projections reported in **California Economic Growth.** These projections reflect the wide range of possible futures for U.S. productivity growth. Moreover, the projections reveal the substantial payoff to living standards from even modest sustained increases in productivity growth.

U.S. Productivity Growth 1998-2005	
Low	0.9% per year
Middle	1.4% per year
High	2.0% per year

The low projection (0.9% per year) represents a very slight improvement from the 1973-92 experience. The middle projection represents our estimate of a reasonable rate of long term productivity gains given the favorable trends cited above. The high projection represents a mid point between the high productivity gains in the 1947-73 period and the low gains after 1973.

The middle projection of 1.4% productivity growth per year is used in developing the baseline income and spending projections in later sections.

Implications for GDP Growth

Productivity growth will be the principal determinant of how well the U.S. economy does in the decade from 1998 to 2005. There is also a reversal of the long term decline in the average work week. It is now likely that the average hours worked per week may remain level or even increase slightly.

- Under the low scenario, gross domestic product (GDP) would grow by 2.1% annually – a sharp decline from the 2.6% gains of the 1980s and the 2.5% average GDP increase in the 1990s.

- In the middle case GDP grows at 2.6% per year. This is higher than the 2.1% annual growth projection by BLS.

- With high productivity gains GDP grows by 3.2% a year – above the growth experienced in the 1970s and 1980s.

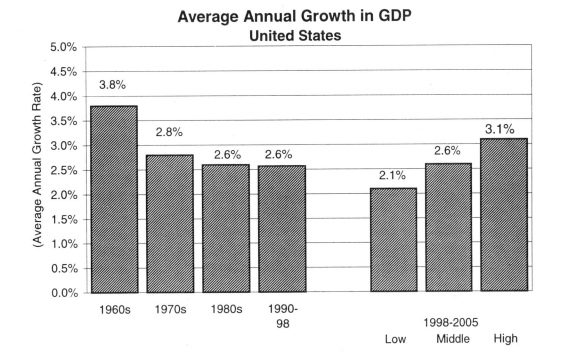

Average Annual Growth in GDP
United States

The differences in economic growth are substantial.

Gross Domestic Product	
(Trillions of 1998$)	
1998	$8.5
2005	
Low	$9.8
Middle	$10.2
High	$10.6

With 1.4% annual productivity gains the U.S. economy would be **more than $300 billion larger** in 2005 compared with the low growth alternative – **a difference of more than $1,000 each year for every person in the nation.**

Jobs and Occupations

Total jobs are projected to increase at 1.3% annually between 1996 and 2006. This annual growth is lower than in the previous decade but higher than the projected population and labor force increases.

The BLS projections imply continuing growth in the percent of workers who hold more than one job. The number of multiple job holders is expected to increase from 7.8% million in 1996 (5.8% of the labor force) to 11.4 million in 2006 or 7.7% of the 2006 labor force.

Job growth will be led by service industries. Manufacturing jobs are projected to remain relatively constant at just over 18.1 million in 2006. Thus, all of the projected jobs gains will be in other sectors. There are no major changes from the trends of the 1986-96 period.

United States Jobs By Major Industry Group 1986-2006 (Thousands)					
				Change	
	1986	1996	2006	1986-96	1996-2006
Agriculture	2,938.7	3,028.3	2,615.0	89.6	-413.3
Mining	777.8	573.9	443.4	-203.9	-130.5
Construction	4,810.0	5,400.0	5,899.9	590.0	499.9
Manufacturing	18,950.5	18,457.4	18,107.8	-493.1	-349.6
Transp., Pub. Utilities	5,246.7	6,260.2	71,10.7	1,013.5	850.5
Trade	23,628.7	28,108.0	31,103.1	4,479.3	2,995.1
Fin., Ins., & Real Estate	6,274.6	6,899.2	7,651.0	624.6	751.8
Services	22,736.3	34,099.0	45,729.9	11,362.7	11,630.9
Government	16,693.0	19,447.0	21,150.2	2,754.0	1,703.2
Self Employed	9,320.0	9,979.0	11,116.0	659.0	1,137.0
Total Jobs	**111,374.4**	**132,252.0**	**150,927.0**	**20,877.6**	**18,675.0**

Source: Bureau of Labor Statistics

The fastest growing industries are mostly in computer/professional services, health care, social services, and entertainment. They include industries with high, average, and low wage levels.

United States Fast Growing Industries 1996-2006 (Millions of Jobs)			
	1996	2006	Average Annual Growth Rate
Computer Services	1.2	2.5	7.6%
Mngmt. & Public Relations	.9	1.4	4.8%
Travel Services	.2	.3	4.8%
Residential Care	.7	1.1	4.8%
Personnel Supply	2.6	4.0	4.3%
Misc. Social Services	2.6	1.3	4.1%
Health Care Practitioners	2.8	4.0	3.9%
Amusements	1.1	1.6	3.5%
Auto Repair	.9	1.2	3.3%
Nursing Facilities	1.7	2.4	3.2%

Source: Bureau of Labor Statistics

While there are no manufacturing industries on the leading job growth list, manufacturing leads the list for projected gains in production. The leading industries, measured by projected average annual change in output levels, are computer equipment (14.9%), computer services (9.3%), auto rentals (8.3%), electronic components (7.3%), brokers (5.6%), personnel supply (5.5%), communications equipment (4.8%), child care services (4.6%), and plastic products (4.5% per year).

Occupational Change

All major occupational categories are expected to grow in the decade ahead. Moreover, when job openings from retirements and occupational changes are counted, even blue collar occupations will show growth in the period to 2006.

United States
Occupational Change
1996-2006
(Millions)

	1996	2000	Percent Change	Total Openings
Exec. Admin., Managerial	13.5	15.6	17.2%	5.2
Prof. Specialty	18.2	23.0	26.6%	8.3
Technicians	4.6	5.6	20.4%	1.9
Marketing Sales	14.6	16.9	15.5%	6.5
Admin. Support	24.0	25.8	7.5%	6.9
Service	21.3	25.1	16.1%	10.4
Craft	14.4	15.4	6.9%	4.4
Laborers	17.8	19.4	8.5%	5.9
Agriculture	3.8	3.8	1.0%	1.1
Total Jobs	**132.4**	**150.9**	**14.0%**	**50.6**

Source: Bureau of Labor Statistics

Occupations which require high skills and education are growing faster than the average as shown above. Professional specialty and technical occupations have the fastest growth rates among the major categories.

However, occupations are expanding at all skill levels. As noted above there are openings in blue collar occupations and the largest occupational growth will occur in occupations with relatively low training requirements.

United States
Occupations with Fastest Growth
1996-2006
(Percent)

Computer Scientists	118%	Occup. Therapy Aides	69%
Computer Engineers	108%	Paralegals	68%
Systems Analysts	103%	Occup Therapists	66%
Home Care Aides	85%	Teachers	59%
Physical Therapy Assts.	79%	Human Service Workers	55%
Medical Assistants	74%	Data Equip. Repairers	52%
Desktop Pub. Spec.	74%	Speech Pathologists	51%
Physical Therapists	71%		

Source: Bureau of Labor Statistics

THE CALIFORNIA ECONOMY TO 2005

THE CALIFORNIA ECONOMY TO 2005

The California economy has added more than 1.5 million jobs during the past four years. The economy has emerged from the defense downsizing and sharp construction decline with a strong leadership position in many key growth industries.

California's future opportunities are reflected in a set of industry records set in 1997 and 1998:

- Record levels of exports and foreign trade

- Record levels of venture capital funding and high tech sales, profits and exports

- Record levels of motion picture production and exports

- Record levels of sales and jobs in diverse manufacturing sectors such as apparel, toys, and semiconductor equipment manufacturing

California firms and workers possess leadership positions in many new and exciting 21st century growth industries — Internet products and services, multimedia, biotech — as well as California's long standing growth sectors in technology, foreign trade, and entertainment.

While economic growth may be slowing temporarily as 1999 begins, CCSCE expects that the long term trends discussed below will determine California's economic growth prospects in the decade ahead.

There is a difference between opportunities and success. Great opportunity does not guarantee great success. California faces economic challenges — in education, business climate, infrastructure, and quality of life. Whether California's opportunities can be converted to growth and prosperity will depend on the skill of the state's entrepreneurs and workers and on whether public policy responds to the great challenges facing the state.

The opportunities are explored below. The challenges are discussed in Section 6.

California's Economic Base In Transition

The world economy is constantly changing. Older industries face slower growth or even decline. Newer industries are created and enter periods of rapid growth.

California Economic Base in Transition

(Thousands of Jobs)

—●— Metal Products —◆— Computer Services

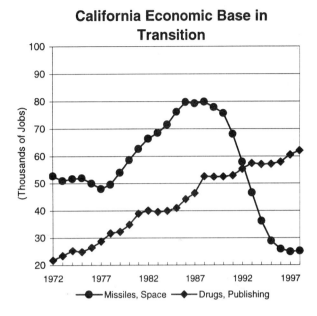

California Economic Base in Transition

(Thousands of Jobs)

—●— Missiles, Space —◆— Drugs, Publishing

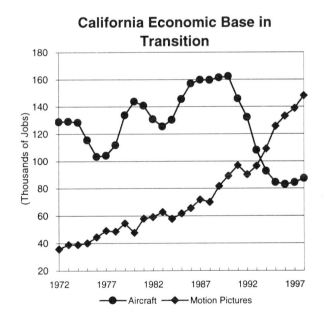

California Economic Base in Transition

(Thousands of Jobs)

—●— Aircraft —◆— Motion Pictures

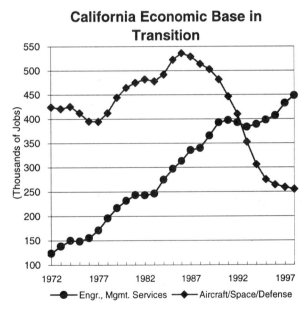

California Economic Base in Transition

(Thousands of Jobs)

—●— Engr., Mgmt. Services —◆— Aircraft/Space/Defense

The California economy has historically benefited from change even though the transitions are often painful. California remains a favored site for the creation of new ideas, new technologies, new firms, and new industries. California's large existing technology base, tolerance for diverse life styles, great physical attractiveness, and world class higher education system have attracted talent and capital.

The California economy has experienced substantial change in the past 25 years. Some dramatic examples are shown on the accompanying graphs.

In 1972 there were more than ten jobs in metal products for every job in computer services. In the past three years traditional software, multimedia, and Internet products have led to a surge in computer service jobs which now far outnumber jobs in metal products. Computer service jobs actually pay more on average than the metal products manufacturing jobs. In 1997 the average wage in computer services in California was $68,700; in metal products it was $35,000.

In 1972 there were more than twice as many jobs in missiles and space production as in the drug and publishing industries. In 1998 there were 2½ times more jobs in drugs and publishing — sectors with continuing growth prospects.

In 1972 there were three jobs in the aircraft industry for every job in motion picture production. In 1998 there were 55,000 more jobs in motion picture production, which in 1997 had an average salary of $64,900 compared to $56,400 in aircraft.

In 1972 there were three jobs in the aircraft, space, defense complex for each job in engineering and management services. Since then the number of jobs in engineering and management services has tripled — growing by more than 300,000 jobs. These jobs paid $52,600 on average in 1997.

The Economic Base is the Key to Assessing Growth Prospects

Basic industries sell primarily to markets outside the state — markets in other states and other countries. Because basic industries do not depend on local markets, firms have a choice of where to locate production facilities. As a result, regions in the states "compete" for the location of firms in basic industries. The location decisions of these firms determine how fast a state like California will grow relative to other states in the nation.

CCSCE examines trends in 80 basic industries as shown on Appendix Table A-1. In 1998 the industries in California's economic base accounted for nearly 4.2 million (27%) of California's 15.5 million total jobs.

California
Major Sectors in Economic Base
1998

	Jobs (Thousands)	Change Since 1990
High Tech Manufacturing	418.5	27.7
Computers	95.8	-5.0
Communication Equipment	37.8	7.3
Electronic Components	159.0	20.1
High Tech Instruments	125.9	5.3
Diversified Manufacturing	1,001.5	84.0
Textiles	24.6	8.5
Apparel	154.6	21.8
Furniture	59.2	4.3
Drugs	30.3	7.4
Misc. Manufacturing	50.0	14.4
Plastics and Rubber Products	76.9	0.4
Metal Products	152.5	-2.4
Special Industry Machinery	21.8	10.9
Other Non High Tech Mach.	192.8	8.1
Aircraft/Space/Defense	255.4	-226.7
Aircraft	87.4	-74.9
Shipbuilding	11.1	-1.5
Missiles/Space	25.2	-50.5
Search & Navigation Equipment	57.3	-42.0
Federal Civilian Defense	73.5	-57.1
Resource Based	474.8	0.9
Agriculture	384.4	20.8
Pres. Fruits & Vegetables	46.9	-6.0
Transp.–Wholesale Trade	643.9	27.4
Air Transportation	133.8	13.6
Wholesale Trade – Durables	473.8	15.1
Professional Services	817.5	182.2
Computer Services	250.0	137.0
Legal Services	119.3	-10.4
Engr. & Mgmnt. Services	448.2	55.6
Tourism & Entertainment	532.1	99.0
Hotels	183.8	-4.9
Motion Picture Production	148.1	58.9
Amusements	197.0	45.0
Total Economic Base	4,143.7	194.4
Total Jobs	15,503.5	1,310.8

Source: CCSCE estimates based on January through October EDD data. See Appendix Chart A-1 for a list of state basic industries.

CCSCE combines the 80 basic industries into seven major groups to explain major trends in California's economic base. These seven groups and their 1998 job totals are shown on the accompanying table.

The growth in population and population serving jobs (three out of four jobs in the state) is determined by how successful the state is in attracting basic industry production and jobs.

Why California's Economic Base Will Grow Faster Than the Nation's

California's economic base has been changing and adjusting to world market forces for more than 30 years. In the 1950s and 1960s and again briefly in the 1980s defense spending was a growth force in California's economic base. In the 1970s growth in high technology manufacturing and diversified manufacturing industries offset declines in the defense related sectors.

In the 1980s four sectors emerged to propel California's economic base forward. These sectors — foreign trade, high tech manufacturing, professional services, and tourism and entertainment — have been the principal determinants of growth in the California economy.

Each of these four sectors shares two characteristics:

- Each sector has above average growth prospects in national and world markets.

- In each sector California has a high and rising share of U.S. jobs and output.

The projected growth in these sectors will push long term growth in total jobs well above the national growth rate to 2005. Each sector is examined in detail below starting with foreign trade.

Foreign Trade

Foreign trade is an important part of California's economic base. Foreign trade meets the two criteria set forth above for making a significant contribution to California's future economic growth:

- Above average growth prospects in world and national markets

- Continuing strength in California's competitive position

Short term foreign trade trends in 1998 and the impact of world economic turmoil on California in 1999 are discussed in Section 3. The paragraphs below analyze the long term trends which CCSCE expects to continue in the decade ahead.

A Fast Growing Market — The volume of foreign trade has increased faster than Gross Domestic Product (GDP) in the national economy. Total trade volume including both goods and services rose from $821.3 billion in 1987 to $1,945.5 billion in 1997 — a nine year gain of 9.0% per year. During the same period GDP increased by 5.6% annually as shown on the table below.

United States Foreign Trade vs. Gross Domestic Product ($Billions)				
	1987	**1996**	**1997**	**Average Annual Growth Rate 1987-97**
Exports	$339.9	$847.0	$926.8	10.6%
Imports	481.4	932.8	1,018.6	7.8%
Total Trade	821.3	1,779.8	1,945.5	9.0%
Gross Domestic Product	$4,692.3	$7,661.6	$8,110.9	5.6%

Source: U.S. Department of Commerce; includes goods and services

U.S. exports led the growth in trade volume. Export volume reached $925 billion in 1997 – an annual growth rate of 10.6% since 1997. Import volume increased by 7.8% annually but imports were still higher than export volume in 1997.

Services are an important, and often overlooked, category of foreign trade. Between 1987 and 1997 service exports grew by 10.6% per year — roughly the same as the rate for goods exports. Service exports totaled $239.2 billion in 1997 — roughly one-third the size of goods exports.

United States Exports of Goods and Services ($Billions)			
	1987	**1997**	**Average Annual Growth Rate**
Goods Exports	$252.9	$687.6	10.5%
Services Exports	87.0	239.2	10.6%
Transp. & Travel	48.1	119.1	9.5%
Royalties, Licenses	10.2	33.7	12.7%
Education	3.8	8.3	8.1%
Financial Services	3.7	11.1	11.6%
Bus., Prof. Services	4.3	21.3	17.4%
Other	16.8	45.7	10.5%
Gross Domestic Product	$4,692.3	$8,110.9	5.6%

Source: U.S. Department of Commerce

The largest component of service exports is travel and transportation — $119.1 billion in 1997. The fastest growing category was business and professional services — increasing by 17.4% per year since 1987. This market area presents substantial opportunities for California — particularly with Pacific Rim countries.

Recent international trade negotiations began the process of opening Asian markets to U.S. financial and other services. United States firms are world leaders in providing efficient financial and retail services. The opening of foreign markets should accelerate the growth of exports in banking, insurance, securities, retail, and consulting services with California firms having a strong position to compete for Asian markets.

Foreign trade will continue to be a strong growth market as shown below. Long term projections prepared by the Bureau of Labor Statistics show a gain of more than 100% in U.S. exports between 1996 and 2006. The projected growth is 7.4% per year (in constant dollars) — far outpacing CCSCE's projected GDP growth of 2.6% per year.

Foreign Trade in the California Economy — Two sets of data are regularly collected about foreign trade in California. Data are collected on the volume of foreign trade (imports and exports combined) that pass through the three California customs districts — Los Angeles, San Francisco, and San Diego.

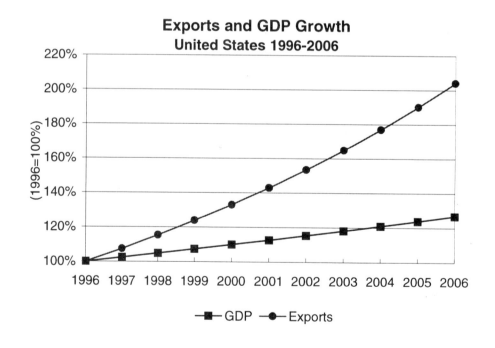

The customs district data have two distinct uses. First they are the only source of data on imports — amount, type and country of origin. Second, the customs district data provide a measure of total trade volume — not just exports produced in California. Some jobs in wholesale trade, finance, and the goods movement industries are related to total trade volume whether or not the goods and services are produced or consumed in the state.

The California World Trade Commission compiles U.S. Department of Commerce data on exports produced in California. The International Trade Administration now publishes data on exports produced in metropolitan areas. These data allow analysis of the amount and kinds of goods made in California for export.

Customs District Data — The customs district data for California confirm two findings:

- Foreign trade has been a fast growing sector in California.

- California's share of national activity is growing.

Between 1987 and 1997 the volume of trade (excluding services) handled by California customs districts grew by an annual average gain of 10.3% in dollar volume. The volume of U.S. trade grew by 8.9% per year during the same period.

California Foreign Trade Value of Exports and Imports 1987-1997 ($Billions)			
	Exports	**Imports**	**Total**
1987	$39.6	$78.3	$118.0
1990	$68.6	$97.1	$165.7
1997	$131.1	$184.7	$315.8
Average Annual Growth Rate 1987—1997			
California	12.7%	9.0%	10.3%
United States	10.5%	7.8%	8.9%

Source: U.S. Department of Commerce

California's share of total U.S. foreign trade increased steadily between 1979 and 1995 (page 1-8). California's ports handled 11.6% of U.S. volume in 1979. By 1995 the state's customs districts had increased the state's share to 21.3%.

Between 1996 and 1998 California's trade share declined to near 20% as Asian market growth slowed.

The Los Angeles Customs District handled $185.9 billion in trade volume in 1997. The Los Angeles District had a gain of 27.2% between 1994 and 1997 — slightly below the national average. Los Angeles has passed New York as the nation's largest customs district in terms of dollar volume. Trade volume growth through the ports of Long Beach and Los Angeles declined by 2.1% the first nine months of 1998.

Foreign Trade by Customs District
($Billions)

	1994	1996	1997	% Change 1997 vs. 1994
Los Angeles	$146.1	$168.8	$185.8	27.2%
San Francisco	80.5	105.4	107.0	32.9%
San Diego	13.0	18.4	23.0	76.3%
California	239.6	292.6	315.8	31.8%
United States	$1,170.3	$1,413.3	$1,550.0	32.4%

Source: U.S. Department of Commerce

The San Francisco Customs District had substantial trade growth in 1995 — followed by a slowdown in 1996 and 1997. Trade volume in the Bay Area is now heavily influenced by the region's fast growing technology exports. Bay Area trade growth led by Silicon Valley kept pace with the national average from 1994 through 1997.

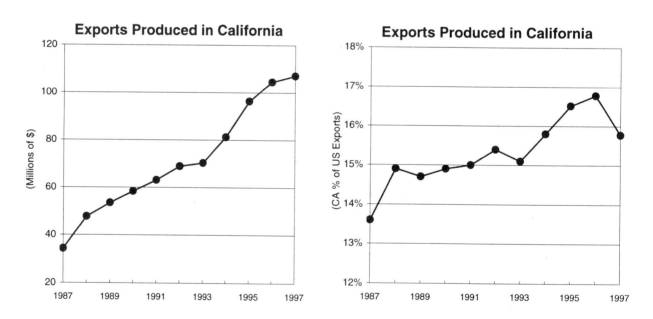

San Diego trade grew by more than 20% in 1996 and 1997 as Mexico's economy recovered. For the 1994-1997 period San Diego trade growth was more than twice the national average.

Exports Produced in California — In 1997 California firms produced $109.5 billion in goods for export. Exports produced in California more than tripled in the past nine years — growing from $34.3 billion in 1987.

California Export of Goods Produced in California 1987-1997 ($Billions)			
	1987	**1996**	**1997**
California	$34.3	$103.3	$109.5
United States	252.9	626.8	687.6
California as % of U.S.	13.6%	16.6%	15.9%

Source: U.S. Department of Commerce, California World Trade Commission.

Goods produced in California for export grew as a share of the U.S. total between 1987 and 1996 when the state's share hit a record 16.6% before declining in 1997 and 1998 as a result of the Asian export slowdown.

It is easy to understand why California has outperformed the national average in export growth in recent years despite the fall in aircraft markets and the recessions in Japan and Mexico:

- California's major trading partners have above average economic growth.

- California's exports are concentrated in high growth industries.

The top five California export partners border the Pacific Rim. Japan is the largest export market even though export volume has fallen recently.

Trade with Japan reached nearly $19 billion in 1996 before declining to $17.5 billion in 1997. (See Section 3 for the latest 1998 trends). California exports to Japan were near $4 billion in both electronics and computer equipment, and more than $2.5 billion in transportation equipment industries in 1997.

California Top Export Markets 1990-1997 ($Billions)			
	1990	**1997**	**% Change 1990-1997**
Japan	$10.3	$17.5	70%
Mexico	4.7	12.1	157%
Canada	5.8	11.4	97%
South Korea	3.8	7.0	84%
Taiwan	3.2	7.0	119%
Singapore	2.6	5.7	119%
U.K.	3.4	5.4	59%
Hong Kong	1.7	4.2	147%
Germany	3.7	4.1	11%
Netherlands	1.8	3.4	89%
Total Exports	**$58.4**	**$109.5**	**88%**

Source: California World Trade Commission

California's export markets are diversified. Japan accounted for 16% of the state's exports in 1997. Other Pacific Rim markets have grown rapidly in recent years. The fastest growing large export markets since 1990 have been Mexico, Hong Kong, Taiwan and Singapore.

Mexico is the second largest California export market after Japan. Exports to Mexico reached $12.1 billion in 1997 — a gain of 157% since 1990 despite the mid 1990s recession in the country.

Export growth to Mexico grew by 22% in 1996 and by 33% in 1997 as the economy began to recover. Mexico imported $4.0 billion in electronics and $2.1 billion in industrial machinery (mainly computers) from California firms in 1997. Exports to Mexico are up again in 1998.

Canada is the third largest export market for California firms with more than $11 billion in purchases in 1997. South Korea, Taiwan and Singapore all have posted declines in 1997 and 1998 trade volume but remain large customers. Three Western European countries round out the top ten with the Netherlands posting a large gain in 1997.

Computers, electronics, and aircraft are California's largest export industries. All have strong future growth prospects.

California Top Exports Industries 1990-1997 ($Billions)			
	1990	**1997**	**% Change 1990-1997**
Electrical Equipment	$11.8	$30.4	158%
Computers, Ind. Equipment	13.5	28.5	111%
Transportation Equipment	7.9	11.2	42%
Instruments	4.4	9.1	107%
Food Products	3.8	5.5	45%
Chemicals	2.7	4.5	67%
Crops	2.4	3.2	33%
Other	11.9	17.1	44%
Total Exports	**$58.4**	**$109.5**	**88%**

Source: California World Trade Commission

Electrical equipment exports increased to $30.4 billion in 1997. Industrial machinery (including computers) was a $28 billion export industry in 1997. Transportation equipment exports were over $11 billion. Instruments posted another gain to the $9 billion level in California exports.

Total Exports — Total exports of goods and services produced in California exceeded $150 billion in 1997. Manufacturing and mining exports were $99.9 billion and accounted for two-thirds of total exports.

Service exports, estimated at $47.8 billion, are probably the fastest growing export sector in California. Annual state estimates of service exports are not published yet by the Department of Commerce. CCSCE, in a 1987 study for the California World Trade Commission, estimated that California accounted for 20% of the nation's service exports. If the 20% share has remained constant since 1987, (it probably increased) California would account for $47.8 of the nation's $239.2 billion in 1997 service exports.

Agricultural exports in 1997 are estimated at $6.7 billion counting just unprocessed products and at $12.2 including processed food products.

California Total Value of Exports 1997 ($Billions)	
Manufacturing and Mining	$99.9
Services	47.8
Agricultural Products	6.7 - 12.2
Total Exports	**$154.4 - $159.9**

Source: California World Trade Commission; California Department of Agriculture; CCSCE.

High Technology

California's high technology sector meets CCSCE's criteria for being a major contributor to the state's future economic growth:[1]

- Above average growth in world markets

- A strong competitive position for the California industry

The graphs on 5-15 and 5-18 confirm these conclusions. The rest of this section fills in the details.

High technology industries have accounted for most of the gains in the nation's manufacturing production in recent years and this trend should continue in the decade ahead. Between 1979 and 1996 the nation's high tech output quadrupled to $473 billion (in 1992$) — an annual real increase of 8.8%. In contrast the rest of manufacturing posted just a 1.3% annual gain in production.

High tech production is expected to grow by 9.4% annually in the nation adjusted for inflation. This is more than four times as fast as the anticipated 2.% annual increase in real GDP and more than five times as fast as the expected growth in other manufacturing industries.

---

[1] CCSCE's definition of high tech includes computers (SIC 357), communications equipment (SIC 366), electronic components (SIC 367), and instruments except for search and navigation equipment (SIC 38 minus SIC 381).

United States
Output in High Tech and Other Manufacturing
(Billions of 1992$)

	1979	1996	2005	Average Annual Growth Rate 1979-1996	1996-2005
High Tech	$112.7	$473.1	$1,064.7	8.8%	9.4%
Other Manufacturing	2,398.2	3,001.5	3,454.5	1.3%	1.6%
Total Manufacturing	**$2,510.9**	**$3,474.6**	**$4,519.2**	**1.9%**	**3.0%**

Source: U.S. Bureau of Labor Statistics

California's Competitive Advantage is Increasing

California's share of high tech jobs and output is increasing. Innovation, entrepreneurship, and a booming export market have overcome four years of recession and the loss of some defense markets.

California is setting record levels in the state's share of high tech jobs, output, productivity, and exports. As shown on the graph below, in 1998 California's share of U.S. high tech jobs has reached a record high of 20.7%.

Sales data (only available through 1996) show a picture of sector by sector strength. Between 1992 and 1996 high tech production in California increased from $64.8 billion to $103.9 billion — a gain of 65%. CCSCE estimates that 1998 data, when published, will reveal that the state's high tech manufacturing firms shipped nearly $125 billion in sales to markets at home and abroad.

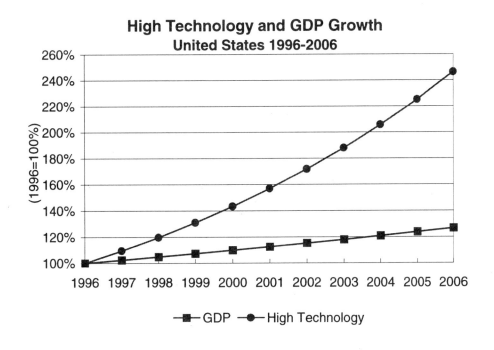

High Technology and GDP Growth
United States 1996-2006

Computer shipments in 1996 reached $32.5 billion — a doubling since 1987. California's share of domestic production was 31.5% — up from 1997 but below the 1992 record level. The state's competitive position showed steady share gains throughout the late 1980s and early 1990s.

Communications equipment is another sector where California firms are getting a larger share of a fast growing pie. Shipments rose to $16.0 billion in 1996 — a 309% gain over 1987 levels. California's share of the U.S. industry rose to 24.0% in 1996 from 15.5% just nine years earlier.

California
High Tech Manufacturing Shipments
1987-1996

	$ Billion 1987	$ Billion 1992	$ Billion 1996	% of U.S. 1987	% of U.S. 1992	% of U.S. 1996
Computers	$16.3	$23.3	$32.5	26.9%	34.9%	31.5%
Communication Equip.	5.3	7.5	16.4	15.5%	17.6%	24.0%
Elec. Components	13.6	18.2	32.4	27.1%	24.7%	25.3%
Meas. & Control Instr.	5.2	7.1	11.4	20.1%	20.6%	24.4%
Medical Instruments	4.1	7.5	9.7	17.7%	19.0%	20.4%
Other Instruments	0.8	1.2	1.6	5.0%	4.4%	5.6%
Total High Tech	**$45.1**	**$64.8**	**$103.9**	**21.0%**	**22.9%**	**24.7%**

Source: 1987, 1992 Census of Manufactures; 1996 Annual Survey of Manufactures

In electronic components California has a high and stable share of a fast growing pie. With $32.4 billion in 1996 shipments electronic components are the state's second largest high tech sector. California has 25.3% of 1996 sales down slightly from 27.1% in 1987 while actual sales more than doubled. The state's share probably remained high in 1997 and 1998 based on California's high share of industry jobs.

California firms accounted for nearly one-quarter (24.7%) of U.S. high tech sales in 1996 — an increase over the 1987 and 1992 shares.

California firms represent the high value added segment of the high technology industry. This means that California high tech workers are more productive, generally, than the national average.

California had 21.4% of high technology jobs as measured by the 1996 Annual Survey of Manufactures. However, California has a higher share of output

(24.7%) and an equally large share of high tech value added (24.5%) which represents wages and profits.

In most high tech industries California workers had high value added per worker. Value added in the California computer industry ($211,500 per worker in 1996) was more than 33% above the national average. In other high tech industries California's advantage was between 10% and 30% except for electronic components.

California's overall value added advantage was maintained between 1992 and 1996. In 1996 high tech value added per worker in California was 13% above the national average as shown below.

Industry	California Value Added in High Technology 1992 and 1996			
	Value Added per Worker 1992	Value Added per Worker 1996	California Relative to U.S. Average 1992	California Relative to U.S. Average 1996
Computers	$160,900	$211,500	137.9%	133.2%
Communications Equipment	127,400	191,500	114.5%	127.9%
Electronic Components	93,500	137,700	111.9%	96.3%
Meas. Control Instruments	84,700	129,800	107.7%	121.7%
Medical Instruments	107,700	147,200	109.1%	127.2%
Total High Tech	**$111,700**	**$156,600**	**113.2%**	**113.1%**

Source: 1992 Census of Manufactures; 1996 Annual Survey of Manufactures

Recent Trends Confirm California's Competitive Strengths

There is plenty of good news above California's high tech opportunities in 1997.

- Venture capital funding topped $1.2 billion in Silicon Valley in the third quarter of 1998. In the third quarter 207 firms received an average of $6.1 million in new funding. Silicon Valley has hit a new funding record each year in the 1990s.

- The number of high tech jobs reached a record level in 1998. More than 30,000 jobs have been added in the past two years. California's share of U.S. high tech jobs also reached a record — 20.6% in 1998.

High Technology

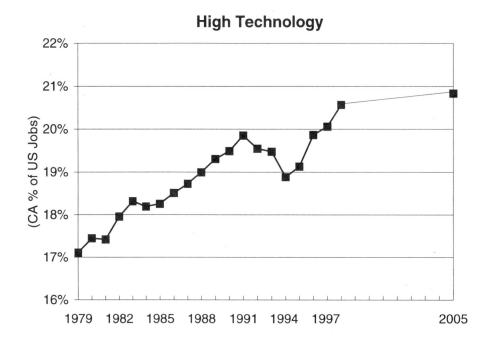

- Sales of the 150 largest companies in Silicon Valley hit a record $185.3 billion in 1997 — up 32% from 1995. Profits reached $15.4 billion — more than triple the 1993 total profits.

- Silicon Valley tied with New York as the largest exporting area in the United States in 1997 ($29.1 billion) — primarily on the basis of growth in high tech exports.

- The 1998 Fortune Magazine list of the 100 fastest growing companies in the nation includes 23 from California. Thirteen of the 23 companies involve high tech products or services. California firms lead the Fortune list. The top states are:

California	23
Texas	21
Florida	9
Massachusetts, New York	5

California is establishing a leadership role in technology markets of the future like multimedia, advanced telecommunications, and the use of the Internet.

Multimedia combines two California specialties — technology and entertainment. The technological genius of Silicon Valley and the creative genius of Hollywood are a world class combination that should bring job and wage growth to both regions.

One example of how combining talents can work is the joint venture of Silicon Graphics in the Bay Area with Dreamworks in Hollywood. Together the companies are developing the first all digital motion picture studio.

Advanced telecommunications is another future growth market. The use of wireless communications like cellular phones is opening up new possibilities for individuals and businesses.

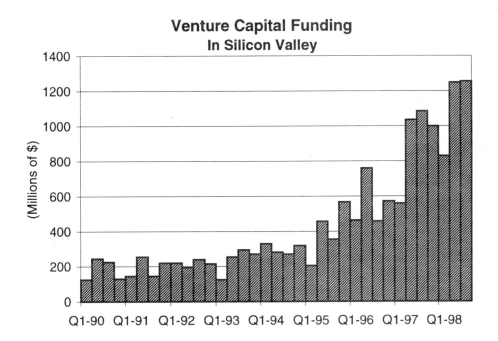

California firms are participating in these markets. Qualcomm in San Diego was selected to provide the technological standard in wireless communications by the regional Bell operating companies. Qualcomm has also developed a technology used throughout the trucking industry and is pursuing a joint venture with Microsoft for wireless transmission of e-mail and Internet services.

The Bay Area is the headquarters of the new industry emerging to help companies use the Internet as a business tool. The Internet represents the fastest growing niche in the "Information Age" economy because the amount of information available is increasing so fast.

Business needs tools to organize this information and provide access to managers in a user friendly environment. Firms like Yahoo, Netscape, Collabra, and Netcom are establishing a leadership position for California in these fast growing Internet markets.

California Firms on Fortune List
100 Fastest Growing Companies

Rank	Company	City	Sales $Mill	Business
4	Vitesse Semiconductor	Camarillo	$151.9	Gallium arsenide chips
5	Central Garden & Pet	Lafayette	$1,181.3	Lawn and pet products
8	Pairgain Technologies	Tustin	$291.2	Telecommunications
10	Sanmina	San Jose	$642.6	Electronics
13	Fidelity National Financial	Irvine	$935.2	Residential title insurance
20	CKE Restaurants	Anaheim	$1,442.5	Fast food
22	DSP Communications	Cupertino	$106.1	Digital cellular chips
23	Modtech	Perris	$151.0	Modular school rooms
29	Wet Seal	Foothill Ranch	$440.5	Clothing stores
34	Imperial Credit Industries	Torrance	$297.3	Commercial lending
37	Pacific Sunwear	Anaheim	$249.4	Clothing stores
51	Ascend Communications	Alameda	$1,195.4	Switches
54	Remedy	Mountain View	$143.1	Software
61	Peoplesoft	Pleasanton	$1,075.8	Software
66	Varco International	Orange	$661.3	Oil drilling equipment
67	National RV Holdings	Perris	$329.3	RV construction
74	Qualcomm	San Diego	$3,023.3	Telecommunications
76	Semtech	Newbury Park	$109.2	Analog chips
79	Asyst Technologies	Fremont	$161.9	Semiconductor equipment
81	Airtouch Communications	San Francisco	$4,163.0	Telecommunications
83	Datum	Irvine	$103.9	High tech clocks
94	Ducommon	Long Beach	$171.6	Airplane parts
98	Altera	San Jose	$636.9	Programmable circuits

Source: Fortune Magazine, September 28, 1998

How Many Jobs Could These Markets Provide?

It is very difficult to project trends in the number of high technology jobs. Two strong trends point in different directions:

- Output growth will be substantial. California should meet or exceed the national industry growth.

- On the other hand, productivity in high tech has been increasing even faster than sales.

The output gains point to higher job levels. The productivity gains point to the reduced need for workers.

California High Technology Jobs (Thousands)					
	1979	1984	1990	1998 Est.	2005
Computers	87.5	108.3	100.8	95.8	89.5
Communic. Equipment	24.3	28.5	30.5	37.8	41.9
Electronic Components	111.3	155.7	138.9	159.0	161.2
Meas. & Control Instruments	53.3	57.3	69.5	71.0	70.9
Medical Instruments	27.6	32.7	38.0	44.8	49.3
Other Instruments	12.7	11.7	13.1	10.1	8.8
Total High Tech	**316.7**	**394.2**	**390.8**	**418.5**	**421.6**
Share of U.S. Industry	17.1%	18.2%	19.5%	20.6%	20.9%

Source: EDD, CCSCE – 1997 based on January through October EDD data and 2005.

In the past two decades substantial production gains have not led to increased employment. This is the paradox of high technology manufacturing — rising output and falling job levels. The graph on page 5-22 shows a vivid picture of these trends.

Between 1979 and 1996 high tech shipments quadrupled in the United States yet job levels barely reached 1979 totals in 1996. The California performance has been better — but only slightly.

What about the future? CCSCE projects rising output but relatively steady job levels in high tech manufacturing. We acknowledge that these job projections may be off by a substantial margin in either direction.

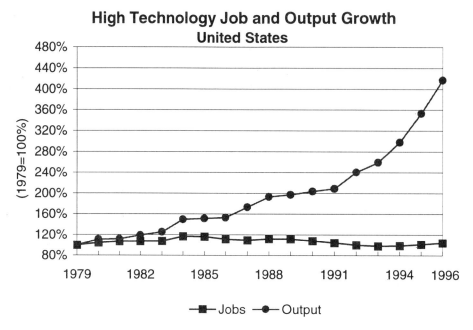

High Technology Job and Output Growth
United States

There are three sources of variation.

1. The U.S. industry may grow more slowly or rapidly than projected in terms of output. Previous projections of a slowdown in the growth of new products and total sales have not materialized. Current output growth projections remain high but not high enough to produce job increases. Even higher sales gains are possible which would require more workers.

2. A given level of output may require fewer or more workers than projected. Worker productivity has increased at very high rates in high tech. For example, the nation produces far more computing power than a few years ago with 100,000 fewer computer manufacturing jobs. If productivity growth is slower there will be many more high tech jobs and vice versa.

3. California's share of the national industry segments may vary from CCSCE's projections. Past industry share and CCSCE's projections are shown in the accompanying graphs on page 5-23.

   As shown on the graphs, California's share of the U.S. jobs does vary — but within a relatively narrow range.

High tech makes a valuable contribution to the California economy even if few direct jobs are created in high tech industries.

- High productivity has been accompanied by high wages and profits. Income gains have led to the creation of more and higher paying population serving jobs in areas with large high tech manufacturing bases.

Computers & Office Products

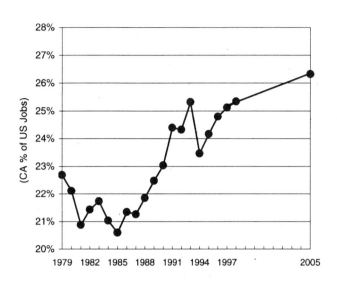

Communications Equipment

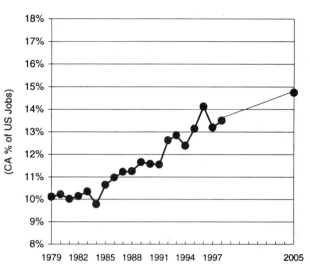

Medical Instruments

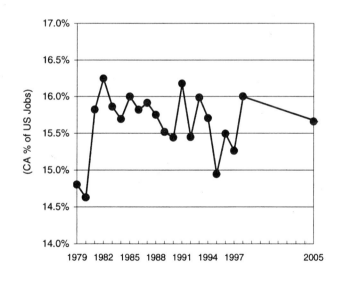

Electronic Components

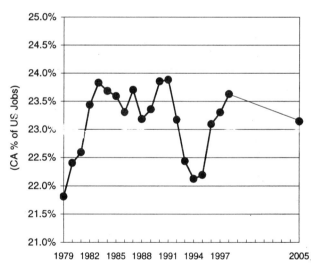

- High tech production does create jobs. Jobs are created indirectly in industries that supply high tech firms like computer services, engineering and design services, and wholesale trade.

One of the reasons why high tech manufacturing jobs haven't risen is that firms have contracted out some functions that used to be provided within the firm. Some high tech jobs simply moved from one industry to another. For example, contract manufacturing is classified in Engineering and Management Services not manufacturing and is therefore not in high tech.

Professional Services

Professional services have an increasing role in California's economic base. The three industries in CCSCE's professional services sector — computer services, engineering and management services, and legal services — will continue to be a fast growing source of high wage jobs.

Professional services does meet the criteria outlined at the beginning of this section for making a significant contribution to California's economic growth — 1) substantial future growth and 2) a strong competitive position for California firms.

First, the U.S. industry has and will continue to experience substantial job growth. Professional services jobs in the nation are projected to increase by more than 50% between 1996 and 2006. By comparison, total jobs in the nation will increase by just 14%.

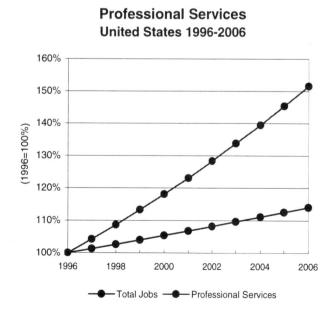

Professional Services
United States 1996-2006

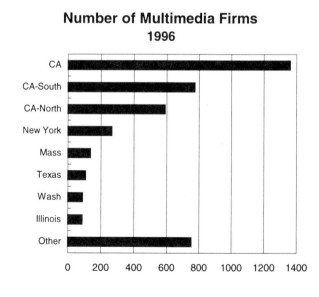

Number of Multimedia Firms
1996

Professional services jobs will lead the growth in the nation's economic base between 1997 and 2005. Computer services jobs are projected to grow by 1 million jobs to reach 2.3 million by 2005. Engineering and management services jobs will grow from 3.0 million jobs in 1997 to 3.8 million in 2005 — an increase of over 25%. Professional services jobs in the nation will increase by 2.3 million between 1997 and 2005.

Professional service firms in California sell to many markets. California's software and multimedia services are sold to consumers and businesses in state, national and worldwide markets.

Computer services (SIC 737) has added over 100,000 jobs in the past five years and job gains have recently averaged over 25,000 per year. Computer programmers work with others to develop new multimedia products like games, educational software, Internet pages, and graphics packages. Many firms also provide services to California's high tech manufacturing companies.

The largest concentration of computer service professionals is in Silicon Valley (58,900 in the first quarter of 1998). However, the Los Angeles, San Francisco, Orange County, Oakland, and San Diego metro areas also have substantial industry representation. Silicon Valley has led the recent job gains but all areas are participating.

By way of comparison it should be noted that Utah, well known for its state's software sector, reported 18,500 jobs in the first quarter of 1998.

California and Metro Areas Growth in Computer Service Jobs (Thousands)			
Metro Areas	**July 1993**	**1st Q 1998**	**Percent Change**
California	125.1	230.6	84%
San Jose	27.3	58.9	116%
Los Angeles	25.9	39.6	53%
San Francisco	18.0	36.7	104%
Orange County	12.0	22.8	90%
Oakland	11.3	22.0	95%
San Diego	8.9	14.9	67%
Sacramento	4.5	8.6	91%

Source: EDD

The California software industry is probably much larger in terms of jobs as many self employed workers do contract programming. The average salary in SIC 737 in early 1998 in California was $71,200.

The multimedia industry is getting a lot of attention in current discussions of California's economic base. There is no SIC industry definition for multimedia firms so it is both 1) hard to distinguish multimedia from other sectors like SIC 737 (Computer Services) and SIC 781 (Motion Picture Production) and 2) hard to get an accurate count of the industry's size in sales and jobs. It is likely that many "multimedia" firms are classified in the computer services sector since computer programming is a major component of multimedia products.

Multimedia involves a wide range of products and services and sales growth is clearly tied to the increasing use of the computer and the Internet in business and personal life around the world. Multimedia directories show agreement on the following major applications of multimedia: training or product promotion; education; games; graphics including animation; information kiosks; interactive TV; and an exploding variety of Internet uses.

California firms command a clear leadership position in the multimedia industry as shown on the graph above taken from data in The Multimedia Directory (1996) compiled by the Carronade Group. CCSCE has not made independent projections of industry growth but instead, accounts for industry in the computer services and entertainment sectors.

Engineering and management services (SIC 87) are the largest component of CCSCE's professional services sector. One growth area has been contract manufacturing. Some of Silicon Valley's high tech job growth shows up in SIC 87 (in services) and is not counted in manufacturing jobs.

California firms sell engineering and design services worldwide and international firms have regional centers in California. In the 1980s the sector added nearly 200,000 jobs.

California firms provide environmental cleanup services to superfund sites and provide auto design services to all major worldwide auto makers. California firms sell accounting, financial management and consulting services in state, national, and international markets.

As noted earlier, trade in business and professional services is a fast growing component of California's foreign trade. The United States has been working actively to open up Pacific Markets for construction, financial, and consulting services — all markets in which California firms will play a large role.

Computer Services

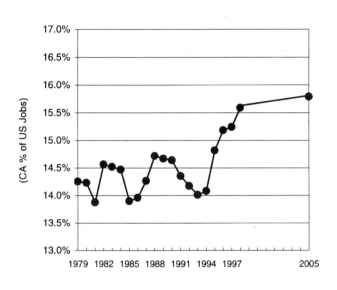

Engineering & Management Services

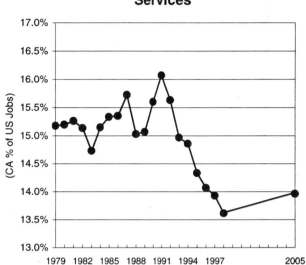

Legal Services

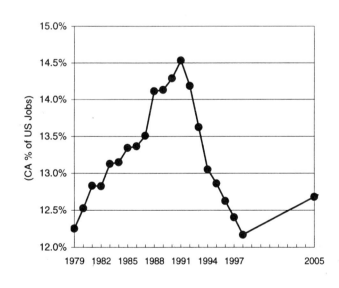

Professional Services

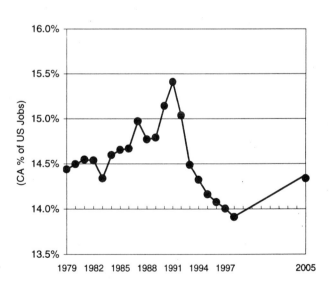

California has approximately 14% of the nation's professional services jobs in 1998. The state's share of computer service jobs has increased in the past four years after being relatively constant since 1979. On the other hand, California's share of legal, engineering and management services jobs has continued to decline since 1994 which is surprising given the strong statewide economic growth.

Using a conservative set of share assumptions, CCSCE projects that California will have 375,000 computer service jobs and nearly 540,000 engineering and management service jobs by 2005. The average salary in California's professional services sector was over $60,000 in 1998.

California Jobs in Professional Services (Thousands)				
	1979	**1990**	**1998 Est.**	**2005**
Computer Services	38.6	113.0	250.0	374.5
Legal Services	56.4	129.7	119.3	146.9
Engr. & Management Services	217.0	392.6	448.2	536.7
Total Professional Services	**312.0**	**635.3**	**817.5**	**1,058.2**

Source: EDD, CCSCE–1998 based on January through October EDD data and 2005.

Tourism and Entertainment

CCSCE includes hotels, motion picture production, and amusements in the tourism and entertainment industry of California's economic base. Tourism and entertainment serve international, U.S., and California consumers. California is a major destination for worldwide vacation travel and possesses some of the world's finest recreational attractions.

World travel is, in turn, a strong growth industry driven by rising incomes throughout the world and, especially, in Pacific Rim nations. While Asian tourism has declined recently, the long term growth potential remains very strong, especially the prospects of rising income and more travel freedom in China.

The explosive growth of motion picture and television exports continues despite recent international financial turmoil. Film and tape rental exports rose more than 300% in just six years — to $6.2 billion in 1997 from $1.9 billion in 1991. These figures demonstrate the strong international demand for U.S. entertainment products.

United States Film Exports

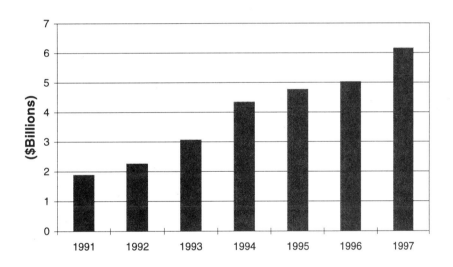

California also provides tourism and entertainment services to domestic consumers. The state is a major market for domestic business and vacation travel for the same reasons that attract foreign visitors.

Californians also travel within the state and use California's world class amusement and recreational facilities. For this reason tourism and entertainment, like professional services, has a local household serving component as well as an export component. As a result, tourism spending and employment did respond to the long California recession.

Tourism and entertainment meets CCSCE's criteria of 1) above average growth in U.S. and world markets and 2) a high and/or rising California share of the national industry. Supported by rising discretionary income in U.S. and world markets, BLS projects that tourism and entertainment jobs will grow more than twice as fast as total jobs in the nation between 1996 and 2006.

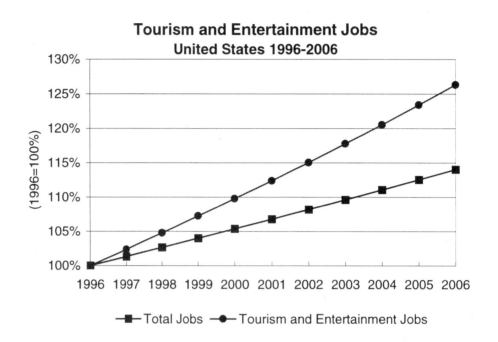

California has an above average share of jobs in hotels and amusements as shown on the accompanying graphs and a very high (50%+) share of motion picture production. While the state's share in each industry fluctuates and was constrained by the recession, the long term trend remains up.

Recent Events — Approximately 110,000 jobs have been added in the tourism and entertainment sector (+26%) since 1993 when the statewide recovery began.

- Motion picture production added 50,000 wage and salary jobs (probably over 75,000 total jobs including self employed workers) driven by record levels of film starts and exports. In 1998 the growth in production days and employment levels slowed significantly after 1997's record levels.

- The hotel sector had a strong year with occupancy levels above the breakeven point and sustained increases in average room rates. Southern California markets joined the hotel recovery in 1997 and 1998 posting a 9% gain in average room rates to over $105 despite the Asian slowdown.

- Amusement sector employment is flat in 1998 after strong increases in 1996 and 1997. Nearly 35,000 jobs have been added since 1993. New expansions are underway at Disneyland, Moscone Center, and the Orange County

Convention Center and new sports facilities are underway or planned in San Francisco and San Diego where a new baseball stadium was approved on the November 1998 ballot.

California had 13.9% of the national sector in 1979, 15.1% in 1990, and 14.3% in 1998.

Long Term Trends — CCSCE projects that California's tourism and entertainment jobs will increase by more than 20% between 1998 and 2005. The sector will add over 150,000 jobs with a gain from 532,100 jobs in 1998 to 694,500 jobs in 2005. The largest gain, as shown below, is in the motion picture industry.

CCSCE projects an increase in California's share of the national industry to a record 16.4% — driven by a rapid projected increase in motion picture/multimedia jobs in the nation. These projections could easily be exceeded if national and foreign demand continues to grow at the recent very rapid pace.

California Tourism and Entertainment Jobs (Thousands)				
	1979	**1990**	**1998 Est.**	**2005**
Hotels	109.9	191.9	187.0	210.5
Motion Picture Production	54.6	89.2	148.1	224.7
Amusements	100.9	152.0	197.0	259.3
Total Tourism & Entertainment	**265.4**	**433.1**	**532.1**	**694.5**

Source: EDD, CCSCE – 1998 based on January through October EDD data and 2005

California Tourism Statistics — The Division of Tourism in the California Trade and Commerce Agency compiles and publishes data related to California's tourism industry. The following section is drawn from their data. In 1997 travel spending in California totaled $61.3 billion. This includes spending by California and out of state travelers.

The leading categories of spending in 1997 were retail shopping ($14.3 billion), ground transportation ($10.3 billion), air transportation ($8.4 billion), restaurants ($8.8 billion), and lodging ($8.7 billion). Travel spending increased from $33.7 billion in 1987 to $61.3 billion in 1997. This is a gain of more than 80% in actual dollars and represents a more than 50% inflation adjusted increase in tourism spending.

California Travel Spending in 1997 ($ Billions)	
Retail Shopping	$14.3
Ground Transportation	10.3
Restaurants	8.8
Air Transportation	8.4
Lodging	8.7
Recreation	6.6
Food Stores	3.8
Travel Services	.4
Total	**$61.3**

Source: Division of Tourism in the California Trade and Commerce Agency

Travel spending supported 673,000 jobs in 1996. The major employers were restaurants (208,000), lodging (137,000), retail sales (91,000), and recreation (98,000). Travel related jobs rose from 505,000 in 1987 to 673,000 in 1997. The job impacts represent only the travel related portion of each industry.

Economic Impact of Travel in California				
	1987	**1996**	**1997**	**Percent Change 1987-1997**
Spending	$33.7 billion	$58.3 billion	$61.3 billion	81.8%
Jobs	505,000	684,000	673,000	33.3%

Source: California Division of Tourism

Job growth in the amusement sector has slowed in the 1990s. California is the leading destination for foreign visitors with 26.6% of the foreign travel dollar. These markets have had to cope with two negative events in the 1990s — first, the urban disturbances in Southern California in 1992 and, more recently, the declines in Asian economic growth and rising foreign exchange rates.

Domestically, California captures 10% of the tourism market. This represents a slight decline from 1990 and state travel (among Californians) is just now recovering from the long recession of the early 90s.

As a result California's share of U.S. amusement jobs dropped from over 14% in 1991 to 13% in 1993 and 12.2% in 1998. CCSCE projects a modest rebound in

Hotels

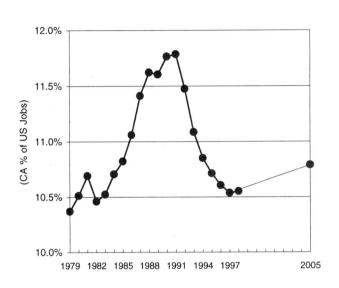

Motion Picture Production

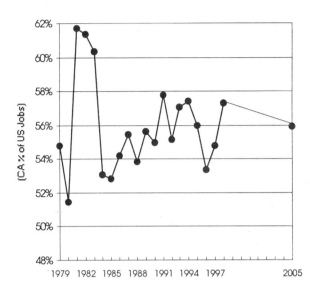

Amusements

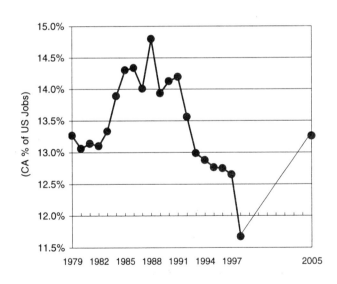

Tourism & Entertainment

share to 13.4% in 2005 based on strong disposable income growth in California and a recovery in Asian tourism.

Motion Picture Production

Motion picture production along with computer services have been the fastest growing high wage industries in California and the nation since 1990. Moreover, motion picture production and computer services are expected to be the fastest growing basic industries in the decade ahead.

Motion picture production jobs in California paid an average of $64,900 in 1997. This compares with the average for all industries of $34,185.

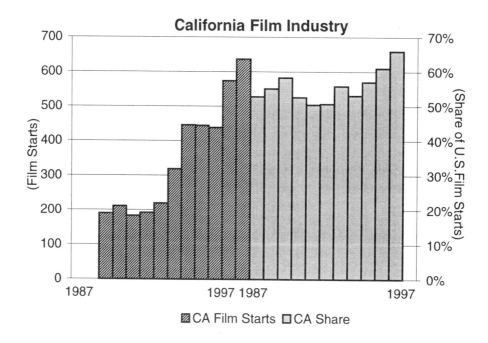

There are now more than 148,000 wage and salary jobs in motion picture production — a gain of 59,000 jobs from 1990. There are more than 50 self employed jobs for every 100 wage and salary jobs. As a result, total employment in the industry was estimated to be 226,000 in 1996 by a recent Motion Picture Association of America study.

The number of feature film production starts has risen rapidly since 1990 with the explosion in cable and video markets along with steady growth in movie box office receipts. There were roughly 200 film starts a year in the late 1980s which grew to 823 in 1997.

Motion picture production certainly meets the two CCSCE criteria set out at the beginning of this section:

- Rapid industry growth

- Strong California competitive position

Efforts are underway in Southern California to strengthen the region's competitive position. Initiatives involve expanding local specialized training facilities and instituting "one stop" permitting throughout the region.

California retains a dominant position in motion picture production as shown on the previous page. The state's share of major film starts has actually increased in recent years and California sites had a part in 66% of feature film starts in 1997 including those with locations in Canada and Australia.

Diversified Manufacturing

Diversified manufacturing is one of the strongest sectors in California's economic recovery. These industries have added more than 100,000 jobs since 1995 to reach a 1998 total of more than 1 million jobs – California's largest basic industry sector.

Diversified manufacturing industries are also the largest industry sector in terms of dollar volume with 1996 sales of nearly $140 billion – still more than high tech sales volume.

California Value of Shipments ($Billions)				
	1987	1992	1996	Average Annual Growth Rate 1987-1996
Diversified Manufacturing	$88.4	$109.3	$138.5	5.1%
High Technology	$45.1	$64.8	$103.9	9.7%

Source: 1987, 1992 Census of Manufactures; 1996 Annual Survey of Manufactures.

Diversified manufacturing is also California's strongest basic industry sector in terms of share gains – posting record high shares of U.S. jobs in 1996, 1997 and 1998. California firms are taking a leadership role in carving out growth niches in traditional manufacturing industries like textiles, apparel, furniture and toys.

Moreover, diversified manufacturing industries in California posted a 5.1% annual sales gain between 1987 and 1996 — despite 1990-1994 being in the midst of the

California recession. It is likely that diversified manufacturing sales increased another 15% between 1996 and 1998. Thus in 1998 diversified manufacturing is nearly a $160 billion sector in California.

California Diversified Manufacturing Shipments ($Billions)				
	1987	**1992**	**1996**	**Average Annual Growth Rate 1987-1995**
Beverages	$7.7	$9.7	$11.1	4.2%
Apparel	8.3	11.2	13.9	5.9%
Drugs	2.8	6.1	7.9	12.4%
Publishing	3.7	5.4	6.5	6.5%
Chemicals & Plastics	13.5	16.3	17.5	2.9%
Metal Products	15.5	16.4	21.5	3.8%
Special Ind. Machinery	1.6	2.7	7.4	18.6%
Other Machinery	16.8	18.9	24.0	4.0%
Furniture & Wood Products	8.4	8.2	9.6	1.6%
Misc. Manufacturing	3.2	4.0	5.8	7.1%
Other	10.2	14.3	19.0	7.1%
Total Diversified Manuf.	**$88.4**	**$109.3**	**$138.5**	**5.1%**

Source: 1987, 1992 Census of Manufacturers; 1996 Annual Survey of Manufactures.

Diversified manufacturing covers a wide range of industries. One way the sector can be disaggregated is into "light" industries such as apparel, textiles, beverages, toys (in miscellaneous manufacturing) drugs, and publishing, versus "heavy" industries such as steel, metal products, machinery, and chemicals.

California has done well in the "light" diversified manufacturing industries which do not involve intense production processes or significant pollution.

Apparel now employs more Californians than computers or aircraft. The apparel industry in California has added 45,000 jobs since 1979 while the national industry lost more than 500,000 jobs. In 1998 apparel accounts for 156,000 manufacturing jobs in the state.

The California apparel industry has prospered based on the state's talent in fashion and design. In women's apparel (SIC 233) California is now home to more than 32% of the national industry in terms of sales and production.

Apparel was a $13.9 billion industry in 1996 based on Annual Survey of Manufacturers data. Nearly $7.5 billion was accounted for by the women's fashion niche.

Apparel and textiles have made steady gains in share of national production and jobs. California has 19.9% of national apparel jobs in 1998 — up from 8% in 1979. Additional discussion of the textile and apparel industries is included in the Los Angeles Basin section.

Apparel Jobs
California vs United States

The drug industry has posted steady production and job gains in California driven by the state's strong position in biotech R&D. Drug industry sales rose by 12.4% per year between 1987 and 1996 resulting in $7.9 billion in 1996 shipments. The industry added 13,000 jobs between 1979 and 1998.

California has a leadership position in biotech R&D. Of the 317 public biotech companies in 1997 over one-third (108 firms) are located in the Bay Area, San Diego, and Los Angeles region.

Public Biotechnology Industry in 1997 Number of Firms	
San Francisco Bay Area	61
New England	54
San Diego	33
New Jersey	22
New York	20
Los Angeles—Orange County	14

Source: Ernst & Young

It remains difficult to assess how fast the industry will grow. Exciting opportunities in agriculture, health care, and environmental cleanup have produced continuing growth in R&D, sales, and employment. As yet, there has been no explosion of growth as in the early days of the computer and semiconductor industries.

California's niche is in R&D driven by existing companies and university-based research efforts. Major regional public-private partnership initiatives are underway in the Bay Area and San Diego to strengthen California's competitive position as an R&D leader.

More detail is included in the regional economy sections.

Special industry machinery (SIC 355) is California's hottest new growth industry. Special industry machinery includes the semiconductor equipment industry — those firms which manufacture the equipment to make semiconductors. The semiconductor equipment industry is included in SIC 3559 where employment has nearly doubled since 1994.

Industry employment rose by 7,500 between 1994 and 1998. The job growth was largest in Silicon Valley (Santa Clara County) where industry leader, Applied Materials, is located. However, other metro areas like Oakland and Orange County also posted substantial increases.

Output data is only available through 1996. Sales of special industry machinery surged from $1.6 billion in 1987 to $7.4 billion in 1996 resulting in an 18.6% annual growth rate – **the largest in the diversified manufacturing sector**. It is likely that most of these gains represented growth in semiconductor equipment manufacturing. Continued growth in 1997 and 1998 probably resulted in pushing industry sales above $8 billion.

Publishing is another growth area for the state in diversified manufacturing. Sales since 1987 grew by 75% to $6.5 billion in 1996. Job levels doubled between 1979 and 1998 to reach 32,600. California's share of the U.S. publishing industry grew from 7% in 1979 to over 9% in the 1990s.

Future prospects for continued share gains are bright. The publishing industry is becoming the information industry. Information will be "published" and distributed in many different media (e.g., electronically as well as on paper). California has a strong competitive position in information age technology and distribution.

Beverages (bottling plants) represent another growth segment. Sales rose by 4.2% per year between 1987 and 1996 to reach $11.1 billion. Jobs have increased slowly but steadily since 1979. The industry added more than 7,000 jobs in California since 1990 and California has a large (18.9%) and growing share of national jobs and output.

Chemicals and plastics are a big diversified manufacturing sector in California. The 1996 sales of $17.5 billion represent a moderate 2.9% annual gain over 1987. Job levels increased slightly between 1979 and 1998, though job levels are still below the 1990 peak. California has participated in the national industry growth averaging between 6.4% and 7% of industry employment during the 1980s and 1990s.

The furniture and wood products industry is now recovering from California's long construction decline. Job levels fell from 125,000 in 1990 to 92,300 in 1993 and sales growth was restrained by the sharp decline in California building which offset gains in other markets. California's industry share fell from 9.8% in 1990 to 7.1% in 1993. During the 1980s California captured between 9% and 10% of industry jobs.

Construction markets have been expanding since 1994 and job levels in furniture and wood products rose also. In 1998 industry job levels are up to 116,800 from 92,300 in 1993. California's share of the national industry has rebounded to 8.8% from 7.1% in 1993.

The furniture and wood products industry will certainly benefit from the projected rebound in construction activity in the decade ahead. CCSCE projects a continued increase in job levels and job shares back towards the peak mid 1980s state performance.

Furniture design and manufacture also is one of Southern California's craft industries where a concerted regionwide effort could bring the California industry to a new level of international competitiveness. This possibility (not included in CCSCE's job projections) is discussed further in the *Los Angeles Basin Section*.

Metal products and machinery job levels have rebounded in the last three years.

Heavy industry sectors saw substantial job losses in California and the nation between 1979 and 1994. Modest gains in production have been more than offset by efficiency gains leading to a loss of jobs. Moreover, the state's defense job losses had some spill-over effect to job losses in metal products.

The metal products industry (most of SIC 33 and 34 – primary and fabricated metal products) shed 70,000 between 1979 and 1993 – falling from 200,000 jobs to near 130,000 jobs in 1993. Half of these losses were directly related to defense cutbacks and the early 90s recession.

Job levels have rebounded since 1993 to exceed 150,000 in 1998 and the state's share of national jobs and output is also rising. Sales increased from $16.4 billion in 1992 to $21.5 billion in 1996 – the latest year for which data is available. CCSCE projects growing sales levels, a slight decline in jobs and a continued increase in California's share of this large manufacturing sector.

The industrial and electrical machinery industries (excluding high tech) are California's largest diversified manufacturing sector measured by jobs and sales. Machinery accounted for $24.0 billion in 1996 sales and more than 190,000 jobs in 1998.

Machinery sectors have added nearly 40,000 jobs since 1993 – making a strong recovery in both job levels and shares. California has recovered nearly all of the early 1990s share losses with the state's 8.0% share of U.S. jobs in 1998 up from 6.9% in 1993 and 8.1% in 1990 before the recession.

Summary: Past Performance, Future Prospects

In the 1970s California's diversified manufacturing sector solidly outperformed the nation. Job levels increased by 235,000 between 1972 and 1979 — a 30% gain. California began the 1970s with 5.8% of the national sector and ended with 7.0%. Import substitution was a factor in the 1970s with firms moving some production to California to replace goods previously imported from the Midwest and East.

During the early 1980s diversified manufacturing jobs declined in the state and nation. Between 1979 and 1983 125,000 jobs were lost in California and nearly 2.5 million in the nation. In 1983 diversified manufacturing job levels in California were 15% above decade earlier levels. During the same period diversified manufacturing jobs in the nation fell by 11%.

Diversified manufacturing jobs have rebounded strongly since 1993. **The 1998 job level (1,001,500) represents a record high in California**.

The data show clearly that California has not lost competitive advantage in this large sector. After rebounding from the early 90s recession, California firms captured 8.4% of the national sector in 1998 — **the highest share ever**. Moreover, as shown on the graph below, California's job gains over the past 25 years have come while national employment totals remain will below record levels.

The diversified manufacturing sector remains important for California's economic base. Even though the national industry will not have job growth in the years ahead, production will increase. BLS projects that output in the sector will increase by 20% between 1996 and 2006.

Apparel

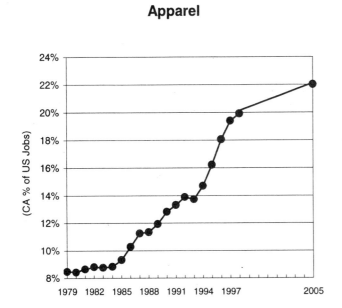

Beverages

Special Industrial Machinery

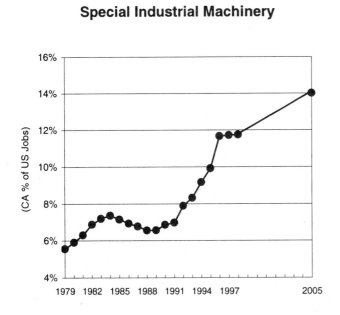

Drugs

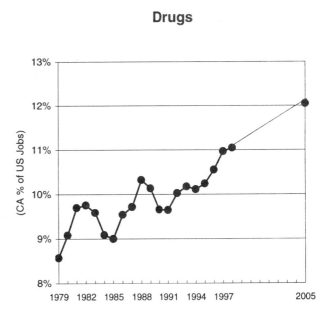

California
Diversified Manufacturing Jobs
1979-2005
(Thousands)

	1979	1990	1998 Est.	2005
Beverages	23.8	27.0	35.0	34.2
Textiles	16.0	16.1	24.6	31.5
Apparel	110.6	132.8	154.6	158.9
Publishing	15.8	29.6	32.6	32.0
Drugs	16.5	22.9	30.3	40.1
Special Industry Machinery	10.7	10.9	21.8	24.7
Other Non High Tech Machinery	216.8	184.7	189.2	198.6
Chemicals and Plastics	113.0	117.0	116.4	126.3
Furniture & Wood Products	125.6	121.1	116.8	123.5
Metal Products	199.8	156.5	152.5	148.7
Miscellaneous Manufacturing	42.1	35.6	50.0	57.3
Other Divers. Manuf.	85.5	63.3	77.7	82.6
Total Diversified Manufacturing	**976.2**	**917.5**	**1,001.5**	**1,058.4**
Share of U.S. Industry	7.0%	7.8%	8.4%	9.1%

Source: EDD, CCSCE – 1998 based on January through October EDD data and 2005

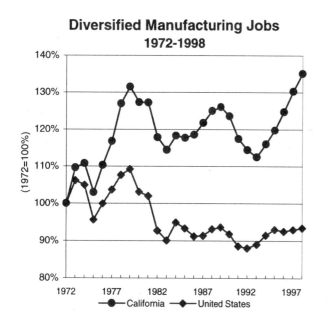

Diversified Manufacturing Jobs
1972-1998

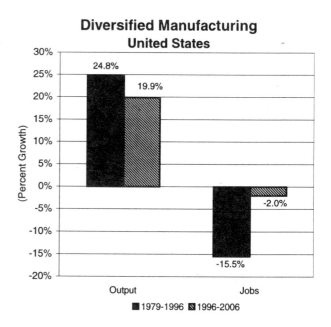

Diversified Manufacturing
United States

The growth in output will be enough to slow the job losses in diversified manufacturing. Nevertheless, like high tech, diversified manufacturing faces the paradox of rising sales with few new jobs. Productivity growth will lead to gains in real wages, and job gains in industries supplying goods and services to diversified manufacturing firms.

CCSCE's projections assume that the era of large share gains for most diversified manufacturing industries in California has ended. The projections assume that in most industries the state's share of U.S. jobs and output recovers to near 1990 levels but does not increase thereafter.

However, share gains are expected to continue in a few industries, and these will push the state's share of the sector higher. Share gains in industries like apparel, textiles, beverages, drugs, special industry machinery, and miscellaneous manufacturing (toys) will raise California's share of the national diversified manufacturing sector from 8.4% in 1998 to 9.1% by 2005.

Total jobs in the sector are expected to increase from 1,001,500 in 1998 to 1,058,400 in 2005 — which will be a record job total for diversified manufacturing in California.

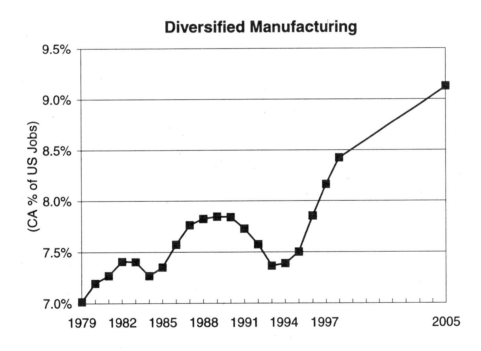

Diversified Manufacturing

The future of diversified manufacturing in the state and nation is tied to:

- The ability of the U.S. industry to adopt "high tech" production approaches like in the German textile industry where Germany expanded production with wage costs higher than in the U.S

- The ability of small and medium sized firms to expand

- The development of regional industry clusters where

— Private firms collaborate in supplier-producer-customer partnerships

— The public and private sector collaborate on public investment and rules and regulation uses

Textiles and miscellaneous manufacturing are examples of diversified manufacturing industries where California has added jobs **and** substantially increased the state's share of the national industry in the 1990s.

The California textile industry is relatively small with 25,600 jobs in 1998 and sales of $2.1 billion in 1996. However, the same trends seen in apparel are now occurring in textiles. California has added nearly 10,000 jobs since 1979 while the national industry lost more than 250,000 jobs. As a result, California's share of national jobs more than doubled to 4.3% in 1998.

The application of technology, regional industry collaboration, and the development of specialized textile niches of expertise in Southern California can lead to further gains in the California industry despite the fact that textile employment will fall nationwide. CCSCE projects that California will gain both jobs and industry share at least through 2005.

California has 50,000 miscellaneous manufacturing jobs in 1998 with $5.8 billion in 1996 industry sales. The industry is primarily located in Southern California with a strong position in the toy industry. Immigrant entrepreneurs have propelled the state's share up to 13.1% of the national industry in 1998. Further job and share gains are expected by 2005.

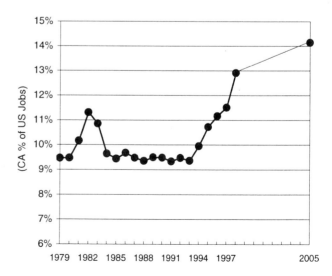

Textile Mill Products

Miscellaneous Manufacturing

Furniture & Wood Products

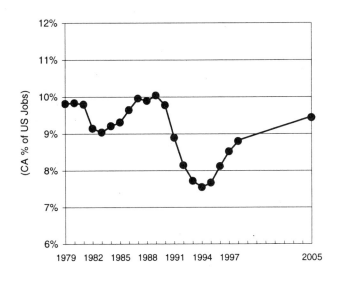

Chemicals & Plastics

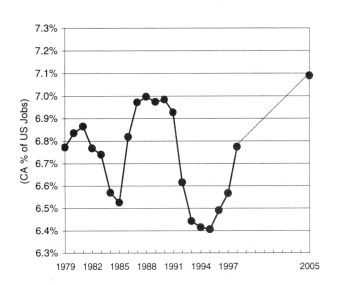

Metal Products

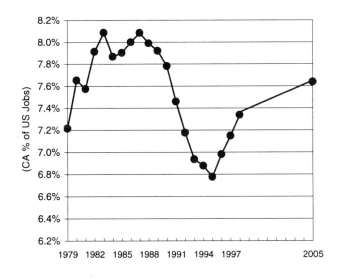

Non High Tech Machinery

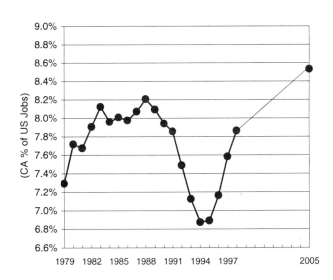

Aircraft, Space and Defense

Four major trends summarize the outlook for California's aircraft, space, defense sector:

- Job levels are stabilizing after shrinking by more than 50%.

- Commercial markets (especially exports) are growing and have replaced defense as the main force driving the industry.

- The future for California firms is as a partner and supplier to the large aerospace mega-firms which have emerged and which have their main operations elsewhere.

- Most bases slated for closure have been closed. Base re-use remains an exciting opportunity for new economic activity in California though large scale activity is still years away.

California lost approximately 280,000 aircraft, space, defense jobs from the 1986 peak levels. More than 220,000 direct manufacturing jobs disappeared along with nearly 60,000 civilian DOD jobs. The sector represented 9% of California's manufacturing jobs in 1998 down from a peak of 26% in 1960.

The job declines are now over. Defense related manufacturing industry jobs have stabilized in 1997 and 1998 after several years of sharp declines. Most base closures are now finished and the remaining open bases have few jobs left.

California's job losses have been the result of two factors — 1) declining U.S. defense spending and 2) a loss in share.

- Between 1986 and 1996 the national industry lost more than 800,000 jobs as a result of falling real defense outlays.

- During the same period California's share of the sector fell from 21.9% to 16.0%. The share declines were especially sharp in aircraft and missiles/space where several firms relocated facilities outside the state. Approximately, 100,000 of the 280,000 lost jobs were the result of the state's loss in share.

- Between 1996 and 1998 national job levels recovered in aircraft (+65,000) and stabilized in missiles and defense electronics. California job levels rose slightly in the three industries. **As a result, California's share of sector jobs continued to fall — reaching 15.5% in 1998.**

Even after the recent industry declines, aircraft, space, and defense manufacturing is a large sector in California. Manufacturing sales totaled $28.0 billion in 1996 down from $38.5 billion in 1987. California's share of national manufacturing shipments fell from 26.6% in 1987 to 20.7% in 1996 — still a substantial share of the national industry.

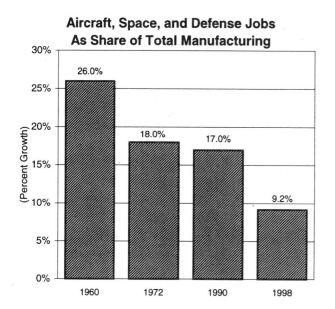

Aircraft, Space, and Defense Jobs As Share of Total Manufacturing

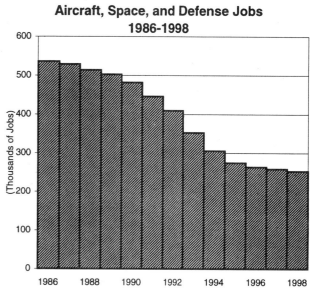

Aircraft, Space, and Defense Jobs 1986-1998

California Aircraft, Space, Defense Electronics Shipments 1987-1996 ($Billions)				
	1987	**% of U.S.**	**1996**	**% of U.S.**
Aircraft	$14.6	18.9%	$13.5	16.2%
Missiles, Space	14.1	53.7%	9.0	50.4%
Search & Navig. Equip.	9.8	27.1%	5.5	18.2%
Total Sector	**$38.5**	**26.6%**	**$28.0**	**20.7%**

Source: 1987 Census of Manufactures; 1996 Annual Survey of Manufactures

The national industry is expected to have renewed growth led by commercial aircraft and exports.

There has been a substantial shift from defense based production to civilian markets in recent years. These shifts, led by rapid domestic and export growth for commercial products, are expected to continue.

U.S. Aircraft and Space Sales ($Billions)		
	1988	**1998**
Total		
By Product Group	$95.5	$117.1
Civil Aircraft	19.0	49.4
Military	41.9	30.6
Missiles	10.3	7.5
Space	24.3	31.8
By Customer		
DOD & NASA	69.2	51.0
Other	26.2	66.1
Exports	26.9	59.0

Source: Aerospace Industries Association of America

- Total sales have risen in recent years though they are still below record levels adjusted for inflation. Industry profits reached a record $7 billion in 1998.

- Defense related sales have declined by 50% adjusted for inflation.

- Commercial sales and exports have doubled.

- Space related sales are up with commercial markets surging and defense related sales flat to down.

Major Southern California aerospace firms have become part of the industry's mega-merger giants. Rockwell's space and defense group and Douglas Aircraft in Long Beach are now part of Seattle based Boeing. Northrup Grumman is now part of the Lockheed-Martin Marietta group based in Bethesda, Maryland.

California production and job levels will increasingly depend on local firms' roles as partners in the operations of the mega-aerospace conglomerates. For example, Boeing will determine the fate of operations at Douglas Aircraft in Long Beach.

In the short term, commercial markets can be volatile as recent announcements of cutbacks at Boeing demonstrate. Boeing is now Southern California's largest private sector employer with 29,000 employees in mid 1998. Boeing's California workforce is expected to take a dip in 1999 and 2000 with layoffs of 6,000 workers associated with announced commercial aircraft cutbacks in Long Beach.

Aircraft & Parts

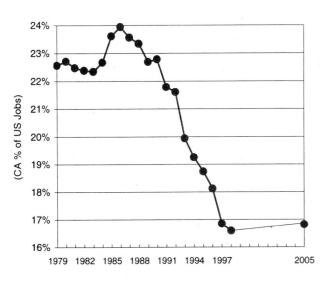

Missiles & Space

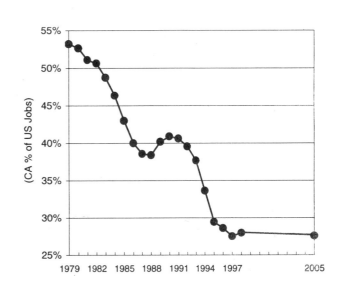

Search & Navigation Equipment

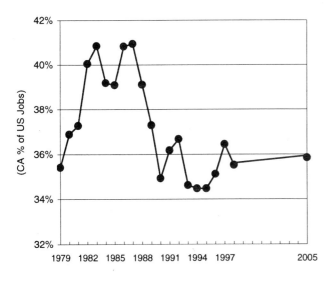

Defense Related

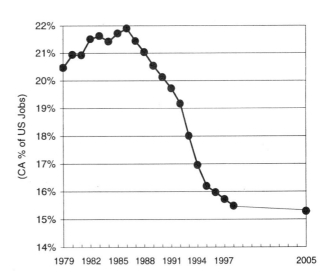

California Aircraft, Space, Defense Jobs 1979-2005 (Thousands)					
	1979	1986	1990	1998 Est.	2005
Ordnance	1.7	2.9	1.6	0.9	1.0
Aircraft	133.7	157.0	162.3	87.4	89.8
Shipbuilding	23.1	15.2	12.6	11.1	10.1
Missiles/Space	54.0	79.8	75.7	25.2	22.4
Search & Navig. Equip.	103.1	142.5	99.3	57.3	46.7
Defense Manufacturing	**315.6**	**397.4**	**351.5**	**170.9**	**169.8**
Federal Civilian DOD	128.7	138.8	130.6	73.5	69.3
Total Sector	**444.3**	**536.2**	**482.1**	**255.4**	**239.4**

Source: EDD–1979-1990, CCSCE–1998 based on January through October EDD data and 2005

CCSCE projects that aircraft, space, defense jobs will remain relatively constant in the decade ahead. Rising sales to the commercial sector will offset continuing job declines in the defense sector. Since the industry is in a major transition, CCSCE anticipates that unexpected events could make these job projections either too high or too low.

Base Closures and Re-Use

The list of major base closures scheduled or completed in California is shown on the accompanying table. In total about 125,000 direct jobs are affected in Rounds 1-4 of adopted base closure plans.

Most of the major base closings are completed. In this list are the largest base closing at Fort Ord as well as the Long Beach Naval Station, Norton and George AFB and Mather AFB and the Army Depot in Sacramento. Major base closing in Orange and Alameda counties are currently underway.

The remaining bases are mostly in large labor markets and their closures does not represent a threat to California's future economic growth. On the contrary, at this point, the bases represent an asset more than a liability.

Nearly all of the military bases closed in California represent valuable land now available in some of California's most strategic locations. In the long term these facilities will certainly add to the attractiveness of California as they are put to different private and public sector uses.

The establishment of a unique California State University Campus at Fort Ord and the rapid expansion of Packard Bell manufacturing operations at the Sacramento Army Depot site are examples of how valuable the former bases can be in alternative uses.

There are active plans for alternative uses at the Presidio, Treasure Island and Moffet Field and consideration of privatization of many activities at McClellan AFB. There are also several studies underway for the Alameda County bases.

Policies that speed the return of military bases into productive uses will benefit communities, firms, workers, and the overall economy.

Readers can keep up to date on base closing/re-use issues at the military base re-use site at www.cedar.ca.gov or from the Governor's Office of Planning and Research.

Base Closure Affecting
More Than 1,000 Direct Jobs

	County	Date	Jobs Military	Jobs Civilian
Round 1				
George AFB	San Bernardino	Closed	4,852	506
Mather AFB	Sacramento	Closed	1,988	1,012
Norton AFB	San Bernardino	Closed	4,520	2,133
Presidio	San Francisco	Transferred	2,140	3,150
Round 2				
Castle AFB	Merced	Closed	5,239	1,164
Fort Ord	Monterey	Closed	13,619	2,835
Long Beach Naval Station	Los Angeles	Closed	9,519	833
Tustin Marine Corp Station	Orange	By 7/99	4,105	348
Moffet Field	Santa Clara	Transferred	3,359	633
Army Depot	Sacramento	Closed	334	3,164
Round 3				
El Toro Air Station	Orange	By 7/99	5,689	979
March AFB	Riverside	Realignment	2,961	997
Mare Island Shipyard	Solano	Closed	1,963	7,567
Naval Air Station	Alameda	Closed	10,586	556
Naval Aviation Depot	Alameda	Closed	376	2,872
Naval Hospital	Alameda	Closed	1,472	809
Naval Public Works	Alameda	Closed	10	1,834
Naval Training Center	San Diego	Closed	5,186	402
Treasure Island	San Francisco	Closed	637	454
Round 4				
Long Beach Shipyard	Los Angeles	Closed	263	2,229
McClellan AFB	Sacramento	By 2001	2,757	8,828
Oakland Army Base	Alameda	1999-2001	52	1,811

Source: California Office of Planning and Research; Updates are available at
www.cedar.ca.gov

Agriculture

California's agriculture and related food products industries employed 592,900 workers in 1997 based on sales of $77.6 billion. California farmers and firms exported over $6 billion in agricultural products and another nearly $6 billion in processed food products in 1997.

California Agriculture and Food Products 1987-1997	Shipments ($Billions)		Jobs (Thousands)	
	1987	1997	1987	1997
Agriculture	$15.6	$26.8	345.0	413.3
Food Products	35.5	50.8	167.0	179.6
Total Sector	**$51.1**	**$77.6**	**512.0**	**592.9**

Source: EDD, California Department of Agriculture, Annual Survey of Manufactures, CCSCE

The leading farm products in 1997 were 1) milk and cream — $3.6 billion, 2) grapes — $2.8 billion, 3) nursery products — $1.8 billion, 4) cattle and calves — $1.3 billion, 5) lettuce — $1.2 billion and 6) almonds — $1 billion. The leading counties (1997 sales) were Fresno ($3.4 billion), Tulare ($2.9 billion), Monterey ($2.3 billion), Kern ($2.2 billion), Merced ($1.5 billion), and San Joaquin ($1.5 billion).

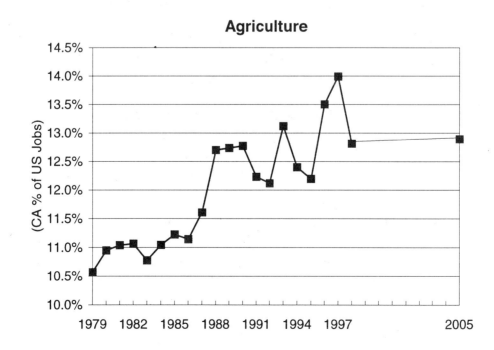

Agriculture

California's share of the nation's farm and processed food products has remained in the 10%-11% range for the past decade — roughly the same as the state's share of total jobs and income. However, agricultural employment in California has risen over the decade and risen as a share of the nation where farm jobs have continued to decline. For a number of reasons California farmers use more labor relative to output values than in the Midwest.

CCSCE expects that farm and food product sales will continue to grow along with the overall economy. Because expected sales growth is relatively modest, productivity increases will outrun production increases and lead to slight declines in total jobs in the sector.

Basic Jobs, Population Serving Jobs, and Total Jobs

Total Basic Jobs: The Growth Engine

California's economic base will expand more rapidly than the national average in the years ahead.

Total basic jobs will increase from 4.1 million in 1998 to 4.6 million in 2005. California's basic job growth rate is projected to be 1.5% per year in comparison to the nation's 0.7% annual growth.

The principal reason that California's economic base will expand faster than the national average is that California has a relatively high share of fast growing industries. The sectoral distribution of U.S. industry growth favors California. California has an above average share of the foreign trade, high tech manufacturing, basic professional services, and tourism and entertainment sectors — each of which is slated for above average growth in the years ahead.

California and United States Jobs in Economic Base 1979-2005 (Thousands)						
	1979	1990	1998	2005	Average Annual Growth Rate		
					1979-1990	1990-1998	1998-2005
California	3,257.5	3,949.3	4,143.7	4,607.8	1.8%	0.6%	1.5%
United States	31,263.0	32,381.6	34,962.3	36,628.4	0.3%	1.0%	0.7%
California Share of U.S.	10.4%	12.2%	11.9%	12.6%			

Source: BLS, EDD, CCSCE

California
Jobs by Major Basic Industry Group
1979-2005
(Thousand)

	1979	1990	1998	2005	Change 1979-1990	Change 1990-1998	Change 1998-2005
High Technology	316.7	390.8	418.5	421.6	74.1	27.7	3.1
Diversified Manufacturing	976.2	917.5	1,001.5	1,058.4	-58.7	84.0	56.9
Aircraft, Space, Defense	444.3	482.1	255.4	239.4	37.8	-226.7	-16.0
Resource Based	463.4	473.9	474.8	429.6	10.5	0.9	-45.2
Transp. & Whsle. Trade	479.5	616.6	643.9	706.2	137.1	27.4	62.3
Tourism & Entertainment	265.4	433.1	532.1	694.5	167.7	99.0	162.4
Professional Services	312.0	635.3	817.5	1,058.2	323.3	182.2	240.7
Total Basic Jobs	**3,257.5**	**3,949.3**	**4,143.7**	**4,607.8**	**691.8**	**194.4**	**464.0**

Source: EDD, CCSCE; 2005—CCSCE

United States
Jobs by Major Basic Industry Group
1979-2005
(Thousand)

	1979	1990	1998	2005	Change 1979-1990	Change 1990-1998	Change 1998-2005
High Technology	1,851.3	2,005.0	2,034.7	2,023.0	153.7	29.7	-11.7
Diversified Manufacturing	13,914.0	11,697.8	11,906.5	11,640.9	-2,216.2	208.7	-265.6
Aircraft/Space/Defense	2,170.7	2,395.1	1,649.5	1,566.5	224.4	-745.6	-83.0
Resource Based	4,808.8	4,161.8	4,109.1	3,670.8	-647.0	-24.5	-438.4
Transp. & Whsle. Trade	4,437.6	5,056.5	5,667.4	6,044.0	618.9	612.2	376.6
Tourism & Entertainment	1,919.8	2,869.4	3,718.2	4,308.3	949.6	848.8	590.1
Professional Services	2,160.8	4,196.0	5,876.8	7,374.8	2,035.2	1,680.8	1,498.0
Total Basic Jobs	**31,263.0**	**32,381.6**	**34,962.3**	**36,628.4**	**1,118.6**	**2,609.7**	**1,666.1**

Source: BLS, CCSCE – 1997 based on January through September BLS data and 2005 based on BLS projections.

As a result, California's share of total U.S. basic jobs will increase. In 1979 California had 10.4% of total basic jobs. By 1990 the state's share had risen to 12.2%. During the recession California's share fell to 11.3% and by 1998 had recovered to 11.9%. CCSCE projects that California will have 12.6% of U.S. basic jobs in 2005.

The largest job gains in California's economic base will come in professional services, tourism & entertainment and transportation & wholesale trade. High tech manufacturing output will expand in the decade ahead, but job gains will be limited in that sector. All key sectors will benefit from the expansion in California exports to fast growing Pacific Rim economies .

Basic jobs in California fell between 1990 and 1994 and also declined as a share of the nation. Most of the basic job losses were associated with declines in the aircraft, space, defense sector. Total basic jobs fell by 300,000 between 1990 and 1994 — more than half were lost in the state's aircraft, space, defense industries.

The speed of decline in California's economy between 1990 and 1994 surprised most economists including CCSCE. The defense downsizing and construction decline went farther and faster than expected in economic forecasts made early in the 1990s.

California has now regained all the basic jobs lost in the early 1990s. New sectors in technology, trade, and high wage service industry jobs have emerged to lead the state's economy.

The decline of older industries and emergence of new industries means that the economic recovery was also a transition. The jobs in aircraft will not fully come back. Many workers will not get their former jobs back. However, the difficulties of transition do not negate the finding that California will, once again, outpace the nation in job gains.

Total Basic Jobs

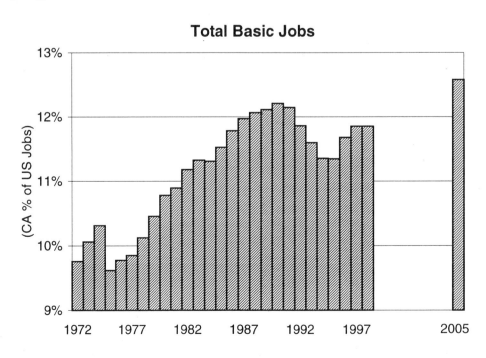

Any surprises in the decade ahead are likely to be on the upside as evidenced by the job surges in 1997and 1998. There are a number of industries with the potential for very rapid growth and in which California has a strong competitive position. In addition, California can gain market share in older industries based on merging design and craft skills with modern technology — industries like textiles, furniture, apparel and toys.

A range of alternative job projections is discussed below on page 5-61.

Projection of Non Basic Jobs

The impact of basic job growth depends on the associated growth in non basic or "population serving" jobs. The ratio of population serving jobs to basic jobs (i.e., the number of population serving jobs supported by each 1,000 basic jobs) is quite similar in California and the U.S. — varying by no more than 2.5% from the national average between 1979 and 1997 as shown on the graph.

However, non basic job growth in California has been steadily lower than the national average since 1979. In the 1970s California had 2% more population serving jobs per 1,000 basic jobs than the nation. This was consistent with California's higher average household income.

After 1982 the California ratio had dropped below the national average — despite faster growth in California household income. The resulting declines from 1979 to 1995 held back the rate of total job growth in California.

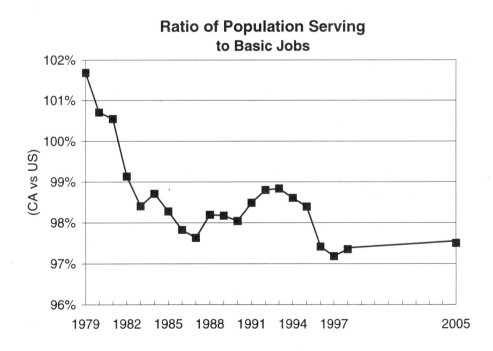

Ratio of Population Serving
to Basic Jobs

CCSCE assumes that California's population serving/basic job ratio between 1997 and 2005 will be at the relatively low levels experienced in the 1980s when California's economic base was growing rapidly. The projection of total jobs in California in 2005 could easily be 500,000 to one million higher in the event that the ratio of population serving to basic jobs in California moves back toward the national average.

Total Jobs

Total jobs in California are projected to increase to 17.8 million in 2005 as a result of the growth in California's economic base. Job growth in California will outpace the national average because jobs in the state's economic base will grow faster than the nation. California will have 11.8% of U.S. jobs in 2005 — up from 11.2% in 1997 and 10.8% in 1979.

California jobs will grow by 2.0% per year after growing by 2.4% per year in the 1980s and 1.1% between 1990 and 1998. Jobs in the nation are projected to increase by 1.1% per year during the 1998-2005 period — lower than the 1.6% annual rate between 1990 and 1998 as a result of slowing labor force growth.

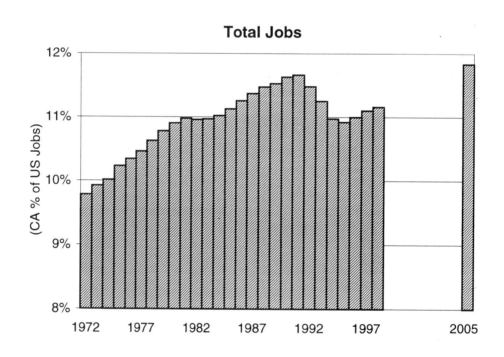

California and United States Total Jobs 1979-2005 (Thousands)						
					Average Annual Growth Rate	
	1979	**1990**	**1998**	**2005**	**1979- 1990**	**1990- 1998**	**1998- 2005**
California	10,932.0	14,192.7	15,503.5	17,766.8	2.4%	1.1%	2.0%
United States	101,405.4	122,116.8	138,896.1	150,113.8	1.7%	1.6%	1.1%
California Share of U.S.	10.8%	11.6%	11.2%	11.8%			

Source: BLS, EDD, CCSCE

Job Growth by Major Industry Group — Job growth in each of California's major industry sectors is shown below. Services will provide the largest number of new jobs (1.3 million) followed by Trade at more than 400,000. Services and Trade also provided the most new jobs in the 1980s.

Manufacturing jobs will account for a very small proportion of new jobs in California just as in the nation. CCSCE projections indicate a gain of just 51,900 manufacturing jobs by 2005. On the other hand manufacturing jobs are expected to decline nationwide.

Manufacturing remains an important sector in California's economy. Expected growth in production and sales will create jobs in supporting industries. Manufacturing job projections are somewhat uncertain in the sense that changes in the rate of productivity growth will affect how sales gains are translated into direct job growth.

Even if CCSCE's projected manufacturing job gains are doubled or tripled, the fact remains that most of California' new jobs **and** new high paying jobs will be created in nonmanufacturing industries.

Government jobs are projected to grow by 188,000 to 2005. California's population, especially school age population, will grow substantially. CCSCE assumes that government jobs will grow more slowly relative to population growth. Even so, the amount of population growth suggests continued increases in state and local government and education jobs over the long term.

Construction jobs should rebound from current recession levels. Growth in jobs, households, and population will support increased levels of construction activity.

California
Jobs By Major Industry Group
1990-2005
(Thousands)

	1990	1994	1998	2005	Change 1990-1994	1994-1998	1998-2005
Agriculture	363.6	379.7	384.4	343.0	16.1	4.7	-41.4
Mining	37.7	31.9	29.3	27.2	-5.8	-2.6	-2.1
Construction	561.8	464.3	600.3	629.9	-97.5	136.0	29.6
Manufacturing	2,068.8	1,777.3	1,970.6	2,022.5	-291.5	193.3	51.9
Transp., Pub. Utilities	612.2	619.0	696.0	799.3	6.8	77.0	103.3
Trade	2,992.7	2,845.1	3,106.3	3,540.2	-147.6	261.2	433.9
Fin., Ins., & Real Estate	808.8	770.6	794.2	906.1	-38.2	23.6	111.8
Services	3,343.1	3,558.2	4,208.5	5,458.8	215.1	650.3	1,250.3
Government	2,074.8	2,093.2	2,218.9	2,406.9	18.4	125.7	188.0
Self Employed	1,329.2	1,415.0	1,495.0	1,633.1	85.8	80.0	138.1
Total Jobs	**14,192.7**	**13,954.2**	**15,503.5**	**17,766.8**	**-238.5**	**1,549.3**	**2,263.3**

Source: 1990 and 1994—EDD with CCSCE estimate of self employed; 1998—CCSCE based on January-October EDD data; 2005—CCSCE

Comparison of CCSCE's Recent Job Projections

CCSCE has held a consistent view of California's long term growth outlook through the recession and recovery. The 1999 projections are similar in terms of total jobs to last year's long term outlook.

- CCSCE's projected California share of U.S. jobs (11.8%) is consistent with our recent projections.

- Annual job growth at 323,300 is also consistent with our recent projections.

- As a result 17.8 million jobs are projected for 2005 — close to the CCSCE projections prepared before the long recession.

In 1994 when California was still near the bottom of the prolonged recession, these projections found considerable skepticism. Now, most economists agree on these overall dimensions of California's future growth. The four sectors identified by CCSCE in 1993 — high tech manufacturing, foreign trade, entertainment and tourism, and professional services — are now generally acknowledged as industries in which California has and will continue to exercise a world leadership position.

	1995 Base Year	1996 Base Year	1997 Base Year	1998 Base Year	2005	Average Annual Growth
California **Comparison of 1995, 1996, 1997 and 1998 Total Job Projections** **(Thousands)**						
Total Jobs						
1999 Projections				15,503.5	17,766.8	323.3
1998 Projections			15,007.9		17,806.5	349.8
1997 Projections		14,584.2			17,406.7	313.6
1995 Projections	14,180.6				14,242.2	306.2
1994 Projections					17,401.3	310.0
Share of United States						
1999 Projections				11.2%	11.8%	
1998 Projections			11.1%		12.0%	
1997 Projections					11.9%	
1995 Projections	11.0%				11.8%	
1994 Projections					12.1%	

A Range of Growth Alternatives

CCSCE prepared a range of alternative projections of jobs by industry in California. The alternatives were built around different assumptions for two key projection factors:

- The share of U.S. basic industry jobs locating in California

- The number of population serving jobs associated with a given level of basic industry jobs

The assumptions for the CCSCE "most likely" alternative are described above in this section.

Alternative California/U.S. share assumptions were determined as follows:

Low — The low share assumption was generally that there would be no increase from the state's 1998 job shares.

High — For some industries (particularly fast growing industries) a share assumption higher than the "most likely" share was selected from the 1983-1991 period. For other industries the high share assumption was the same as in the baseline alternative.

Alternative assumptions about the ratio of population serving to basic jobs were determined as follows:

Steady — The baseline alternative assumed that California would have fewer population serving jobs per 1,000 basic jobs as compared to the nation as shown on page 5-57. The baseline ratio was used in the "steady" alternative.

Rebound — CCSCE examined the implication of an alternative assumption where the California ratio of population serving to basic jobs moved back towards the national average. This assumption has the effect of raising the projection of total jobs for a given level of basic industry job growth.

Quantitative Results

The number of jobs in California in 2005 is projected to range from 16.9 million to 18.9 million. This means that the state will gain between 1.9 and 3.9 million jobs in the next eight years.

CCSCE's baseline projections — the "most likely" set — result in a gain by 2005 of 2.3 million jobs for a total of 17.8 million jobs. In this alternative California will experience a job gain of 14.6% versus the national increase of 8.1% between 1998 and 2005.

Between 1970 and 1990 California jobs grew by 81.5% versus a 50.4% increase in the U.S. economy.

In the lowest alternative (where low California share of basic jobs and no increase in the relative ratio of population serving/basic jobs is assumed), total jobs grow by slightly less than 2 million between 1998 and 2005. California will still slightly outpace the nation because the composition of U.S. job growth favors California.

The highest alternative (ALT 6) results in a projected gain of 3.9 million jobs between 1998 and 2005. The state would see a 23.3% job gain compared to 8.1% in the nation. The high alternative results in California capturing a slightly higher share of U.S. growth than in the 1970-1990 period.

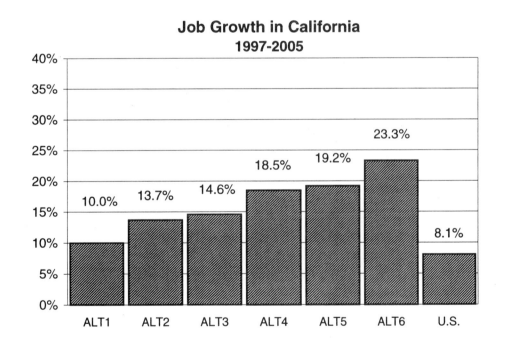

California
Range of Total Jobs in 2005
(Thousands)

Assumption for Calif vs. U.S.

	Share of Basic Jobs	Ratio of Pop Serving to Basic Jobs	Total Jobs	Difference from Base Case
1	Low	Steady	17,056.1	-4.1%
2	Low	Rising	17,636.0	-0.8%
3	Medium	Steady	17,766.8	Base Case
4	Medium	Rising	18,381.7	3.4%
5	Rising	Steady	18,495.2	4.0%
6	Rising	Rising	19,124.0	7.6%
1998			15,503.5	

Source: CCSCE

Job Growth in California
1997-2005

ALT1	ALT2	ALT3	ALT4	ALT5	ALT6	U.S.
10.0%	13.7%	14.6%	18.5%	19.2%	23.3%	8.1%

Total Population

1997 marked the turnaround in population growth in California. The state added 574,000 residents from July 1996 to July 1997. CCSCE expects that final estimates will show that California's population growth will be similar in 1998 as strong job gains continued.

Why did California's population growth slow so dramatically between 1992 and 1996 and why does CCSCE expect future population growth to exceed 600,000 per year? The answer lies primarily in the relationship between job growth and domestic migration.

Domestic migration slowed after the state's large job losses and has rebounded with the strength of California's economic recovery.

	Natural Increase	Foreign Immigration	Undocumented Immigration	Domestic Migration	Population Growth
Components of Population Growth (Thousands)					
1997-1998 Est.	310	131	99	20	560
1996-1997	317	137	99	21	574
1995-1996	319	102	99	-200	320
1994-1995	337	145	99	-308	273
1993-1994	356	189	99	-371	273
1992-1993	372	187	99	-329	329
1991-1992	397	149	125	-47	623
1990-1991	397	94	125	5	621

The Components of Population Growth

The state's population growth has four main sources.

- Natural Increase — Births minus deaths

- Legal Foreign Immigration — Including an estimate of emigration (people leaving California to reside in foreign countries)

- Undocumented Immigration — Estimated by the Immigration and Naturalization Service (INS) and California Department of Finance

- Domestic Migration — The movement of people between California and other states

Natural Increase

Natural increase (births minus deaths) accounted for less than half of California's population growth in the 1980s. Since 1990 natural increase has accounted for most of the state's growth and natural increase was larger than the state's population growth in the 1992-1995 period when total migration was negative.

The amount of natural increase in California has been declining since 1990 from near 400,000 per year to below 320,000 during each of the past three years. The number of births in California rose during the 1980s to above 600,000 in 1990 and then declined steadily to below 550,000 in 1997 and 1998. The number of deaths is rising slowly each year.

Foreign Immigration

INS reports that between 150,000 and 250,000 people have applied for legal immigration status in California each year since 1990. The net increase in foreign immigration is lower because each year some people leave California to live in foreign countries. The net annual contribution to population growth from legal immigration has been between 100,000 and 190,000 in recent years.

Undocumented immigration is estimated to have averaged 125,000 per year between 1988 and 1992. Recent INS estimates put undocumented immigration at near 100,000 per year into California between 1992 and 1996.

Legal and undocumented foreign immigration have been relatively steady contributors to California's population growth so far in the 1990s.

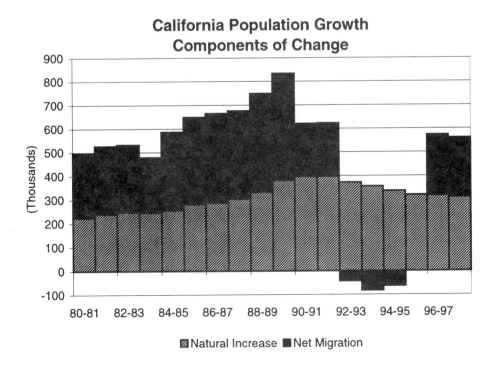

California Population Growth
Components of Change

Domestic Migration

Domestic migration **responded sharply** to the recession. It is the change in the direction and amount of interstate migration flows that has caused the recent decline in California's population growth.

Trends in domestic migration captured a great deal of attention in the news prior to the 1996 economic recovery. As the graph indicates, net domestic migration into California had moved from a significant plus in the late 1980s to an estimate out-migration of near 300,000 per year in the 1992-1996 period.

Migration trends **do** respond to short term fluctuations in job growth. The principal reason for long distance migration (in contrast to moves **within** a metropolitan area) is for job opportunities. Workers (and their families) migrate to regions with good job prospects.

Net domestic migration turned sharply negative after the recession began. In the late 1980s net domestic migration averaged nearly 200,000 per year **into** California. Between 1990 and 1992 net domestic migration was near zero. Between 1992 and 1996 net domestic migration was negative as many more people left California for other areas than relocated to the state.

The changes in domestic migration trends **followed** changes in job growth rates. The upsurge in the late 1980s followed record job growth in 1983 and 1994. The recent drop in domestic migration came **after** the recession started and **after** California unemployment rates soared in comparison to national unemployment as shown on the graph below.

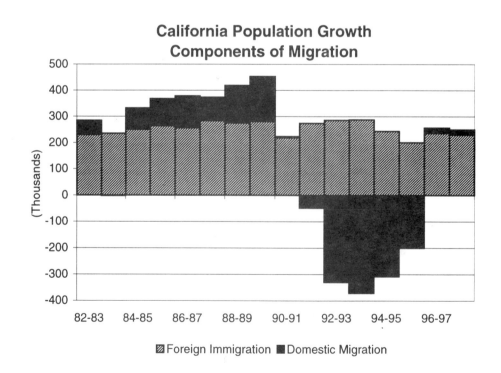

Four consecutive years of strong job growth have finally led to a reversal of domestic migration flows. CCSCE expects that domestic migration was positive in 1998 and that total population growth was between 550,000 and 600,000.

However, the reliability of the domestic migration data is still not solid as many states do not fully report drivers' license address changes for California.

Unemployment Rate Difference
California less United States

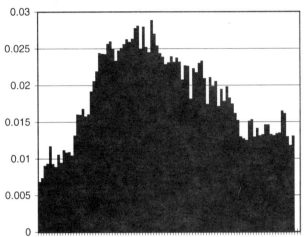

Job Growth vs Migration
California

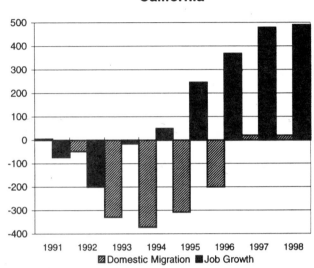

Future Population Growth

Based on anticipated job growth in the state, CCSCE projects that California will add 4.2 million resident between 1998 and 2005. By 2005 California will have 37.8 million residents.

The state will continue to grow faster than the nation. California's population will increase by 12.7% while the national growth rate is projected to be 5.9% or less than half as large.

California and United States Population Growth 1998-2005 (Resident Population in Thousands)				
	1998	**2005**	**Growth**	**Percent Growth**
California	33,550.0	37,800.0	4,250.0	12.7%
United States	270,029.0	285,892.0	15,863.0	5.9%
California as % of U.S.	12.4%	13.2%	26.7%	

Source: U.S.—Census Bureau; California—CCSCE.

Population growth in California will be at a faster pace than the 1990-1998 growth estimates discussed above. Between 1998 and 2005 growth will average 607,000 per year — compared with 474,000 annual population increases since 1990. Nevertheless projected growth will be far less on a percentage basis than gains in the 1970s and 1980s.

In the decade ahead California's population will increase by 1.7% per year. Since 1990 growth has averaged 1.4% per year and in the 1980s the state population grew by 2.3% annually.

California will capture a large share of the nation's population growth. The state will get 26.7% of U.S. growth in the decade ahead compared to 27.4% of national population growth in the 1980s.

By 2005 California will account for 13.2% of U.S. population — up from 12.4% in 1998 and 10.5% in 1980.

Total Households

California added 767,700 households between April 1, 1990 (Census) and January 1, 1998. Household gains averaged approximately 100,000 per year — well under the 200,000+ gains in the mid 1980s.

There are some good reasons why household growth was relatively small between 1990 and 1998.

- Population growth slowed as the recession caused a net outflow of workers and their families.

- The recession restrained home buying as households faced uncertainty about job and income prospects and saw steadily falling home prices. As a result some young adults moved in with their parents or set up multiple person living arrangements.

- A large share of California's population growth was from recent immigrants. These immigrants sometimes formed multiple family households for economic or cultural reasons.

Even taking reduced population growth into account, the number of new household was smaller than expected. If residents had formed households at the same rates as in 1990, another 185,000 households would have been formed between 1990 and 1998.

Household Trends 1990-1998 (Thousands)	
1990 Census	10,380.6
Household in 1998	11,127.6
Actual Increase	767.7
Household increase using 1990 household formation rates	952.7
Difference	185.0

What Will the Future Bring?

Many of the factors that restrained household growth since 1990 have disappeared.

- Job growth is expected to lead to higher population growth. Population gains between 1998 and 2005 will equal the annual growth of the 1980s.

- Affordability is rising

  — Real household incomes are growing to record levels.

  — Housing prices are still down from 1990 levels in many areas of the state and are much closer to prices in competing regions.

  — Mortgage rates are expected to remain below 7%.

- Fertility rates are slowly declining and a smaller share of future population growth will be children.

Another major plus factor for housing is the anticipated population growth in the under 25 population. One factor in the early 1990s housing slowdown was the nearly 1,000,000 decline in the 20-34 age group — the first time entrants into the housing market. The 20-34 age group will increase by more than 400,000 in the years ahead.

The largest population growth between 1998 and 2005 will be in the 45-54 and 55-65 age groups. The leading edge of the baby boom will turn 55 in 2005.

The major unknown in California housing markets is the future household forming behavior of minority and immigrant adults. California's Hispanic and Asian residents (native born and immigrants) will account for a majority of the projected gain in the 35-54 age group.

Historically the 35-54 age groups have been the peak family formation group. Minority residents in the under 35 age group have had sharp declines in their household formation behavior since 1980 — meaning that many young adults (ages 20-34) are living in other households.

The key question is whether these residents, as they reach age 35 and with an expanding economy, will move out and form separate households. A second key question is whether recent immigrants will respond to rising job and income levels by "unbundling" i.e., forming separate households.

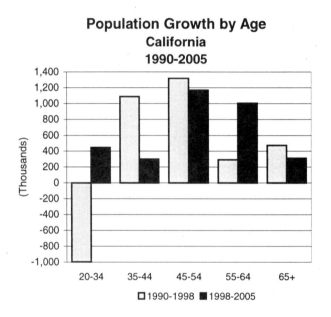

Population Growth by Age
California
1990-2005

CCSCE and others have anticipated a renewal of household growth since 1995. Clearly a strong rebound has not occurred yet.

CCSCE has prepared three sets of household projections based on different assumptions about household formation rates. The baseline projections (used in most report tables) assume that age and ethnic specific household formation rates remain at 1996 levels. This assumption means that none of the declines in household forming behavior experienced in the 1980s will be reversed — despite rising household incomes and substantial increases in affordability.

CCSCE also prepared a lower set of household growth projections. In the lower projections, CCSCE assumes that the decline in household formation rates in the early 1990s will be continued. This alternative is possible if 1) income gains do not materialize as expected or 2) the cultural patterns of multi-family households for immigrants remain stronger for recent immigrants than for previous generations despite rapid gains in income. Finally, CCSCE has a higher household growth alternative which assumes some reversal of recent declines in household formation rates.

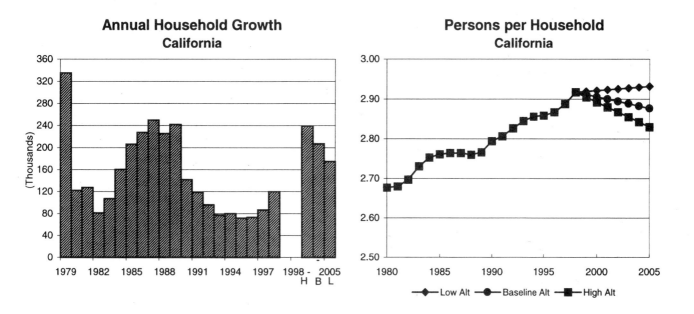

Annual Household Growth
California

Persons per Household
California

In the baseline assumptions the number of households will increase by 1.5 million to reach 12.7 million in 2005. This results in an average annual growth of 207,300 households per year — lower than the rate experienced between 1985 and 1989.

The lower assumptions result in 240,000 fewer households being formed in California by 2005. Household growth will equal 1.3 million or roughly 175,000 per year between 1998 and 2005. The high assumption will result in 12.9 households in 2005. Household growth would average nearly 240,000 per year between 1998 and 2005. **In all three cases household growth will recover from recent lows based on 1) strong population growth and 2) rising housing affordability.**

	California Alternative Household Projections 1990-2005 (Thousands)				
				Average Annual Growth	
	1990 Census	**Jan 1 1998**	**July 1 2005**	**1990-1998**	**1998-2005**
Households					
Baseline	10,380.9	11,127.6	12,682.6	96.4	207.3
Low			12,442.6		175.3
High			12,922.6		239.3

Income and Spending

This section describes the past and projected growth of income and spending in California. All data are expressed in 1998$.

Total, Per Capita and Average Household Income

California represents 12.7% of the national market in terms of income and spending. California is by far the largest state economy, having a total income more than 50% higher than New York the next highest state. In 1998 total income in California reached $905 billion. The state's income exceeds the GNP of all but six nations — the United States, Japan, Germany, France, the United Kingdom and Italy.

Comparison of California and U.S. Income Trends — In recent years per capita income in California has grown more slowly than in the nation. The explanation and implications of this trend are a subject of discussion and concern in California. In the section below CCSCE describes what is known about comparative income trends in the state and nation.

Even after the long state recession, Californians have income levels that are higher than the national average. In 1998 per capita income in California ($26,982) was 2.0% above the U.S. average. Annual wage levels in California ($34,000) were roughly 10% above national levels. Average household income ($81,350) was 15% above the national level.[2]

	California and United States Comparison of Income Measures 1998		
	California	United States	California as % of U.S.
Total Personal Income (Billions)	$985.2	$7,143.1	12.7%
Per Capita Income	$26,982	$26,453	102.0%
Average HH Income	$81,350	$70,445	115.5%
Average Wage (1997)	$34,000	$30,400	111.8%

Source: U.S. Department of Commerce, CCSCE

---

[2] CCSCE uses per capita and average household income series based on estimates of **total personal income** prepared by the U.S. Department of Commerce. Census estimates (based on the **money income** definition) are lower than the ones based on total personal income because the money income definition excludes non money income items like fringe benefits and there is underreporting in the money income surveys.

California Wages Remain High, Per Capita Income Falls Relative to the Nation

How are California residents doing in terms of income growth? The answer depends on whether one examines average wages, per capita income or average household income.

Average wage levels in California remained 10%-11% above the national average throughout the long California recession. Wage growth in California, adjusted for inflation kept pace with nationwide gains through 1996.

It is likely that California wages outpaced national gains in 1997 and 1998. Wage and salary income growth rose by 7.9% in 1997 and 9.0% in the first half of 1998 as shown below.

California Personal Income (Percent Change)		
	1997	**1st Half 1998**
Total Personal Income	6.0%	6.8%
Wages and Salaries	7.9%	9.0%
Other Labor Income (Benefits)	2.0%	9.3%
Proprietors Income	5.3%	10.1%
Property Income	4.9%	3.2%
Transfer Payments	2.8%	0.5%

Source: California Department of Finance

On the other hand, per capita incomes in California have declined sharply relative to the national average. By 1998 per capita income in California was only slightly above the national average after being 10%-20% higher in the 1960s and 1970s.

There are two explanations. One reason for the **long term** decline in relative per capita incomes in California is the higher proportion of children in the population. Per capita income is total income divided by population so increases in the proportion of children will dilute per capita income.

In the 1960s and 1970s California had fewer children as a share of total population than the nation. This trend has reversed in the 1990s. Now California has a higher proportion of children. This trends is expected to continue in the decade ahead.

The rapid growth in children in California's population relative to the national average has caused a decline in California's relative per capita income.

The second important trend is that average wages in California rose steadily in the 1980s compared to national wages and have grown at the same rate as the nation during the 1990s. In the 1980s the gain in relative wages offset the increase in California's proportion of children in the state's population. In the 1990s the recession combined with average growth of wages in California and the rise in the share of children in the state's population caused a sharp drop in relative per capita income.

Since 1994 California's per capita income has grown slightly faster than the national average. The long term outlook is for California to grow near the national average as long as the state continues to have a higher proportion of children.

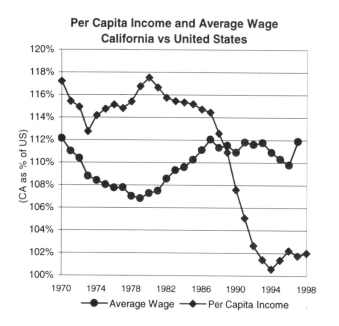

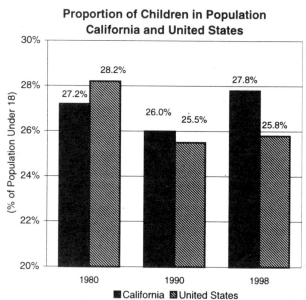

Average household incomes rose to 15% above the national average in 1998. One factor keeping average household incomes relatively high is the large household size in California. In addition to having more children, the state's households also have more adults. Thus California has an above average proportion of two earner households.

Projected Income Growth in California — Total personal income (in 1998$) is projected to grow at 3.5% annually in California between 1998 and 2005. Total income will rise from $905.2 billion in 1998 to over $1.1 trillion in 2005.

The California market will continue to grow faster than the nation. United States income growth is projected at 2.6% per year to 2005. California's projected 3.5% real (i.e., inflation adjusted) annual gain compares with the 3.3% annual growth between 1980 and 1990. Real wage gains will be higher in the coming decade and offset a decline in the rate of population growth.

Per capita income, adjusted for inflation, declined by more than 5% between 1990 and 1994. With the strong recent economic recovery, per capita income in 1998 reached $26,982 or 4% above the 1990 level.

California Income Levels and Growth 1990-2005 (1998$)	Per Capita Income	Average HH Income	Total Personal Income (Billions)
1990	$25,885	$74,666	$775.1
1994	$24,425	$71,794	$776.5
1998	$26,982	$81,350	$905.2
2005	$30,490	$90,875	$1,152.5
Low	$29,457	$86,287	$1,113.5
High	$31,989	$94,814	$1,209.2
Average Annual Growth Rates			
1990-1994	-1.4%	-1.0%	0.0%
1994-1998	2.5%	3.2%	3.9%
1998-2005	1.8%	1.6%	3.5%
Low	1.3%	1.2%	3.0%
High	2.5%	2.4%	4.2%
U.S.	1.8%	1.6%	2.6%

Source: 1990, 1994—U.S. Department of Commerce (deflated by CCSCE); 1998, 2005—CCSCE

Per capita income is projected to grow by 1.8% annually between 1998 and 2005 compared to 1.0% in the 1980-1990 period. Per capita income (in 1998$) will increase from $26,982 in 1998 to $30,490 in 2005.

Average household income in 1998 surpassed 1990 levels (measured in 1998$) by 9% after falling in the early 1990s. The rebound in average household income was created by job gains and the continuing increase in the number of workers per household.

Average household income will grow by 1.6% annually between 1998 and 2005 — the same rate as in the 1980-1990 period. Household incomes will grow more slowly than per capita incomes because household growth is expected to surge as rising income allows multi-family households to unbundle and create separate households. Average household income, adjusted for inflation, is projected to increase from $81,350 in 1998 to $90,875 in 2005.

There are several different measures of average household income. CCSCE uses a measure of total personal income per household which is estimated as $81,350 in 1998. The Census Bureau publishes measures of average household money income which excludes fringe benefits and other nonmonetary income. CCSCE's estimate of average household money income in 1998 is $60,500.

The Census Bureau also published an estimate of median household money income (half of all households have more than the median and half have less). CCSCE's estimate of 1998 median household income in California is $43,000. Average household income exceeds median income by more than 35% because a high share of income gains are received by high income households.

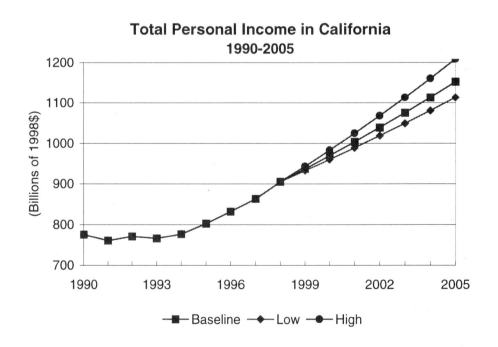

Total Personal Income in California
1990-2005

California Alternative Measure of Household Income 1998	
Average Household Personal Income	$81,350
Average Household Money Income	$60,500
Median Household Money Income	$44,000

The Basis for Projecting Income Gains — CCSCE projected the growth in total personal income in California by examining two trends:

- Growth in income per job and

- Growth in total jobs

CCSCE projects that income per job in California will grow by 1.7% per year above the rate of inflation. This will be an improvement over the 1980s performance which had increases of 0.9% per year. National productivity growth will increase driven by corporate investment and restructuring.

CCSCE expects that average wages will grow faster in California than the nation. California's competitive advantage in new high wage industries should offset the remaining defense related job losses.

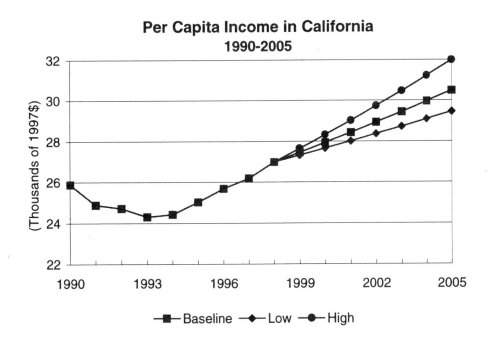

Per Capita Income in California
1990-2005

CCSCE Recommends Reviewing a Range of Income Projections. The answer to the question, "How much will prosperity increase in California?" depends on the rate of productivity growth and, therefore, the rate of real wage growth in the state and nation. Since there is uncertainty about whether and how much productivity growth will improve, CCSCE has prepared a range of income and spending projections.

Low income projections were based on the assumption of 1.1% annual growth in income per job. This was slightly (.2% per year) higher than the rate of productivity growth between 1979 and 1993. High income alternatives were developed assuming growth in income per job of 2.2% per year.

Total personal income in 2005 is projected to range between $1,114 billion and $1,209 billion. The projected growth rates range from 3.0% per year (low) to 4.2% (high) compared with the 3.5% baseline projection.

Growth in per capita income ranges from 1.3% per year (low) to 2.5% per year (high) compared with the 1.8% annual growth projected in the "most likely" alternative.

The difference between the low and high annual income growth rates for California is equal to $108 billion in 2005. Depending on how the nation meets the productivity challenge, average household incomes in California will increase by approximately $5,000 (6%), $9,500 (12%), or $13,500 (17%) between 1998 and 2005.

Taxable Sales

Taxable sales fell by 10%, adjusted for inflation, between 1990 and 1994. Spending fell faster than income as confidence declined and major expenditure items were postponed.

In 1998 real spending on taxable sales finally exceeded 1990 levels. CCSCE estimates that taxable sales reached $361.2 billion in 1998 – 6% ahead of the inflation adjusted $340.1 billion in 1990.

Real taxable sales have increased by 4.0% annually since 1994 with strong income gains **and** a low rate of inflation both acting to support higher spending levels.

California Taxable Sales 1990-2005 (Billions of 1998$)	
Year	**Taxable Sales**
1990	$340.1
1994	$308.6
1998	$361.6
2005	$455.2
Low	$435.7
High	$469.4
Average Annual Growth Rates	
1990-1994	-2.4%
1994-1998	4.0%
1998-2005	3.3%
Low	2.7%
High	3.8%
U.S.	2.4%

Source: 1990 and 1994 — California Board of Equalization (Taxable Sales) adjusted to 1998$ by CCSCE; 1998 and 2005 — CCSCE

The ratio of taxable sales to personal income fell steadily during the 1980s and early 1990s. The main reasons were 1) a higher share of income going to housing and services in the 1980s and 2) a drop in consumer confidence in the early 1990s.

The percent of personal income spent on taxable sales has stabilized at near 40% since 1993. CCSCE had expected an upturn in the ratio by this point in the economic recovery but it has not happened.

CCSCE expects that the ratio of taxable sales to personal income will decline in the future. Internet sales (many of which are not taxed) will increase as a share of consumer spending. In the long term the growth of electronic commerce will restrict the growth of the sales tax base unless e-commerce transactions can be captured in the tax base.

CCSCE projects that taxable sales in California will grow by 3.3% per year (in 1998 dollars) to reach $455.2 billion in 2005. This compares to a 2.4% annual gain nationally.

Progress in raising real wages (through productivity increases) will make a substantial difference in the size of the California market in the years ahead. Spending gains could average between 2.7% and 3.8% annually, resulting in a $35+ billion difference in the size of the California market in 2005.

Taxable Sales as a Percent of Income
California

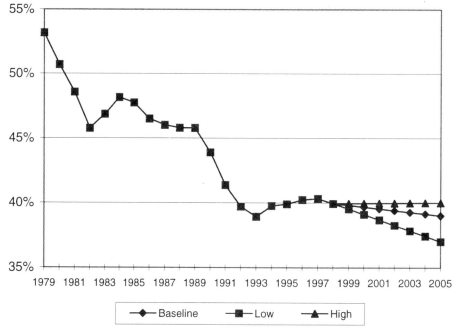

Construction Activity

Construction activity rose rapidly throughout California in 1997 and 1998. The value of new building increased by 40% with gains in both residential and nonresidential sectors. Continued job growth is expected to push construction volumes towards the mid 1980s record levels in the decade ahead.

The strongest markets were in industrial building where four consecutive years of strong job growth used up much of the available vacant space and pushed lease rates up throughout the state. Southern California and San Diego markets are leading the current growth as Bay Area activity takes a pause after leading the construction recovery in 1995, 96 and 97.

Residential building picked up but remains low in comparison to mid 1980s building activity. In mid year resale housing prices began to set records in many regional markets for the first time since the recession began in 1990. The tightening of resale markets is leading to an increase in new home building.

The longer term fundamentals point to rising levels of construction activity in California. Job, population, and household growth will return to 1980s levels and should bring continuing increases in both residential and nonresidential markets.

Construction: A Large and Cyclical Industry — The value of new building construction activity (excluding public works) in California averaged $31.3 billion per year between 1970 and 1998 measured in 1998 prices. At the peak in 1988 and 1989 the new construction market reached $50 billion or 8% of California's total output. However, construction levels then dropped to near $25 billion until the 1997-98 rebound.

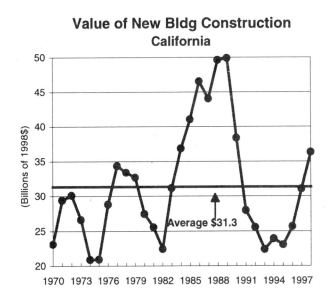

Value of New Bldg Construction
California

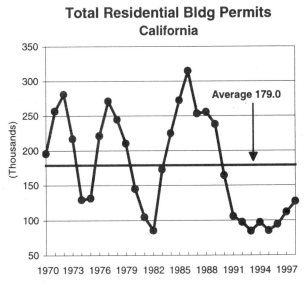

Total Residential Bldg Permits
California

An average of just under 180,000 new homes have been built each year since 1970. The peak year for units was 1986 when a surge in multi-family units pushed total construction to a record 314,600 units. The peak year for residential valuation ($34 billion in 1998$) was in 1989. Residential permit levels and dollar volumes staged a modest recovery in 1997 and 1998.

Construction related jobs reached record levels in 1998 with 766,000 jobs representing 5% of all jobs in the state. The more than 160,000 jobs lost during the recession have been fully recovered and construction related employment should set new records in 1999 and beyond.

Construction cycles are normal in California. The state's construction cycles have coincided with periods of recession in the state and national economy. Each residential cycle had high years of 270,000 units or more and low years near 100,000 units. The current cycle is different mainly because low residential building levels persisted so long beyond the end of California's recession.

California Construction Related Jobs (Thousands)			
	1989	**1993**	**1998**
Construction	560.0	445.5	600.5
Lumber, Wood Products	69.6	46.0	57.6
Furniture	59.0	44.9	59.2
Stone, Clay, Glass	55.2	45.0	48.7
Total Construction Related Jobs	743.8	581.4	766.0

Source: EDD; 1997—CCSCE based on January through October EDD data.

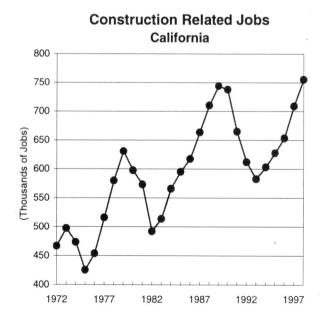

Construction Related Jobs
California

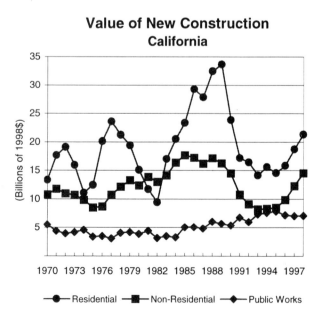

Value of New Construction
California

Recent Trends in California Construction Markets — There was a sharp decline in California construction activity after 1989. The construction downturn in California was much more severe than the nationwide cycle.

Total new building construction at $36.3 billion in 1998 was still 27% below the 1989 peak of $49.9 billion — all measured in 1998 prices. The sharpest decline was in the Los Angeles Basin (-45%) but the San Diego and Sacramento and San Joaquin Valley markets also remained substantially below pre-recession peaks. The Bay Area surpassed pre-recession construction volumes in 1997 and added a small gain in 1998.

The housing decline was felt throughout the state and persisted into 1998 when residential building was still nearly 50% below 1989 levels. The greatest gap was in the Los Angeles Basin (-62%) but no region has yet generated a strong residential building recovery.

California Construction Trends (Billions of 1998$)					
	New Building Construction			**Residential Permits (Thousands)**		
	1989	**1993**	**1998**	**1989**	**1993**	**1998**
Los Angeles Basin	$26.4	$9.1	$14.2	116.4	28.8	43.1
San Francisco Bay Area	8.7	5.3	10.0	35.6	15.1	23.5
San Diego	4.5	1.7	3.5	18.7	5.6	12.5
Sacramento	3.6	1.8	3.0	20.8	8.8	15.1
San Joaquin Valley	3.6	2.5	2.8	27.3	16.4	15.9
Other	3.2	2.0	2.8	18.8	9.9	12.0
California	**$49.9**	**$22.4**	**$36.3**	**237.7**	**84.6**	**124.7**

Source: Construction Industry Research Board; 1998 estimates by CCSCE based on Jan-Oct CIRB data.

Residential Building Trends: Analysis and Outlook — The residential market in California was due for a correction in 1989 — well before the national and state recession began.

Between 1987 and 1989 median resale housing prices in California rose 38% from $141,700 to $195,640. Affordability fell sharply. In 1987 over 32% of California households could afford the median priced home. By 1989 the share had fallen to 17%.

In addition to getting out of line with housing prices elsewhere in the nation, overall housing prices in California got out of balance with income growth in 1988 and 1989. After a long period during which income growth kept pace with housing prices, the sharp 1988 and 1989 price increases pushed housing costs out of the buying range for many households.

It was time for a correction in California's housing market.

Two sets of factors will lead residential building levels higher throughout California — 1) renewed job and population growth and 2) higher levels of affordability and housing prices more in line with competing markets.

Resale housing prices in California are now 60% above the national average — back to levels seen in the late 1970s and early 1980s. Resale housing prices in the state are, once again, near record levels but now, in many areas of California, are competitive with prices in other western metro areas.

Housing affordability has rebounded from the low of 17% (of California households who could afford the median priced house) to near 40%. The 40% level is higher than during the mid 1980s when more than 250,000 new units were constructed each year.

There are three main determinants of affordability 1) income; 2) housing prices and 3) interest rates. Trends in household income and interest rates continue to push affordability higher. Between 1990 and 1998 average household income in California increased by 32.1% in current dollars (inflation was near 25% for the period) while median home prices rose by just 4.5%.

Median Housing Prices
California and United States

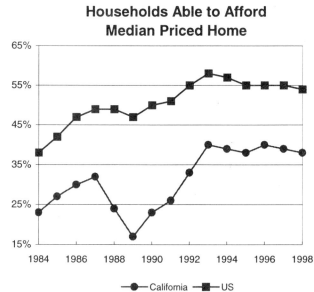

Households Able to Afford
Median Priced Home

It is likely that **median** household incomes increased by less than **average household incomes** but the household income/price ratio certainly rose during the past eight years. Household income gains are continuing and, there is some evidence, spreading to middle income households.

Resale prices have turned up sharply in 1998 in most regions of the state. Most forecasters expect median prices to rise more in line with incomes in 1999 and beyond.

Mortgage rates fell during the last half of 1998 and offset some of the rebound in median prices. The short and long term outlook for inflation is good in the United States and mortgage rates should stay near the current 7% subject to the normal cyclical fluctuations. The interest rate component of affordability is the best in twenty years.

There is one more positive note for future California home building. Prices in many regions of the state are now close to or below prices in competing markets.

Median resale prices in three large markets 1) the Central Valley, 2) Riverside-San Bernardino and 3) Sacramento are now well below median prices in other western markets.

- Median prices in the Central Valley are near $117,000 — still below earlier levels. In Sacramento median prices are near $125,000 — down from the $140,000 range and in the Riverside-San Bernardino area median prices are also near $125,000 and down from the $140,000 range.

- Meanwhile, median prices in Denver rose from $86,400 in 1990 to $149,000 in 1998; in Las Vegas from $93,000 to $130,000; in Portland from $79,500 to $160,600; and in Salt Lake City from $69,400 to $133,300.

- As a result, prices in more expensive markets like Los Angeles and San Diego are now much closer to prices in competitive markets.

Demographic trends also point to higher household formation as discussed above in the *Population and Households* sections. Household growth in California is expected to average near 207,000 per year between 1998 and 2005. This year's surge in resale housing makes it easier to understand how the demographic and affordability trends point to a strong residential market in California in the years ahead.

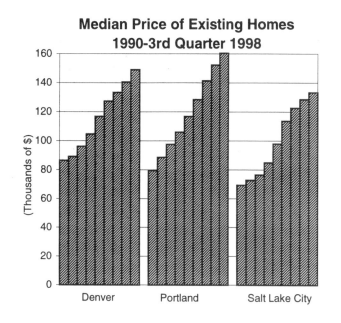

**Median Price of Existing Homes
1990-3rd Quarter 1998**

(Thousands of $)

Denver   Portland   Salt Lake City

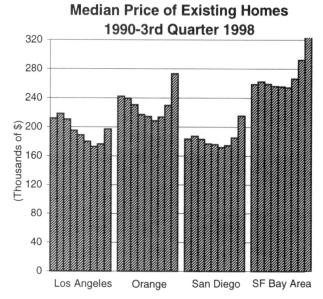

**Median Price of Existing Homes
1990-3rd Quarter 1998**

(Thousands of $)

Los Angeles   Orange   San Diego   SF Bay Area

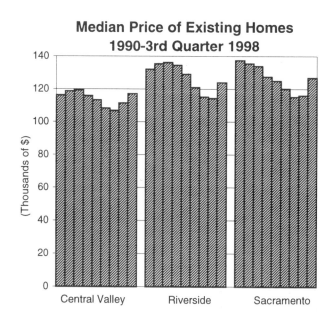

**Median Price of Existing Homes
1990-3rd Quarter 1998**

(Thousands of $)

Central Valley   Riverside   Sacramento

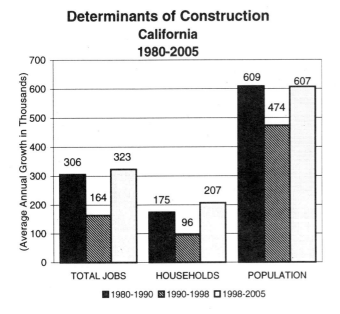

Determinants of Construction
California
1980-2005

(Average Annual Growth in Thousands)

TOTAL JOBS — 306, 164, 323
HOUSEHOLDS — 175, 96, 207
POPULATION — 609, 474, 607

■1980-1990 ⊠1990-1998 ☐1998-2005

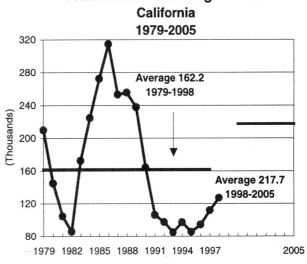

Total Residential Bldg Permits
California
1979-2005

(Thousands)

Average 162.2
1979-1998

Average 217.7
1998-2005

1979 1982 1985 1988 1991 1994 1997 2005

Nonresidential Construction: Analysis and Outlook

Total nonresidential new construction (excluding public works) in California peaked in the mid 1980s at near $18 billion measured in 1998 prices. By the end of 1998 total nonresidential valuation remained 20% below these levels at $14.5 billion — even with a strong 1997 and 1998 recovery.

It is helpful to disaggregate the nonresidential market in order to understand what has happened in the current downturn and to assess the prospects for recovery. The decline in commercial and industrial construction is well known to anyone who follows the California economy.

Commercial construction includes office buildings, retail stores, and hotels as well as parking garages, recreation facilities, and service stations. After averaging $7.5 billion per year in new construction in the 1980s, over building and recession combined to reduce new commercial valuation to $2.3 billion in 1993. Industrial building also declined sharply reflecting the job losses since 1989.

1998 brought the highest level of commercial construction (near $5 billion) since 1990. The surge was led by office construction which more than doubled in 1997 and by hotels and amusement facilities in 1998. Job growth led to declining vacancy rates and rising lease rates which is creating the demand for new building.

Industrial building continued a five year upward trend. Industrial building valuation doubled between 1996 and 1998 to reach $2.4 billion — very near the record levels of the mid 1980s.

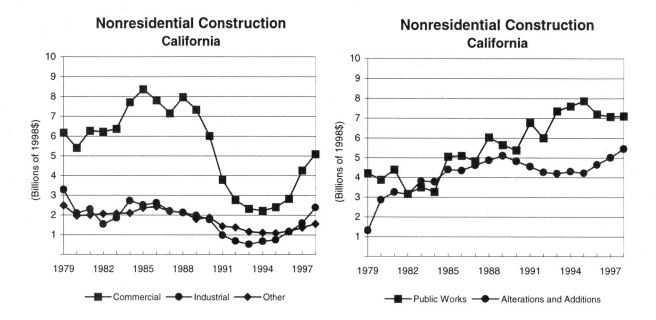

Two categories of nonresidential construction gained significantly between 1979 and 1997. The value of alterations and additions grew steadily to 1989 and remained between $4 billion and $5 billion until 1998. It was the second largest category of nonresidential building in 1997 and then reached a new record of $5.3 billion in 1998. Alterations and additions are related to upgrading the existing stock of buildings. The size of the existing stock of buildings has always grown in California even when new construction slows down.

California Nonresidential Construction (Billions of 1998$)			
	1989	**1993**	**1998**
Commercial	$7.3	$2.3	$5.1
Industrial	2.0	0.5	2.4
Other Nonresidential	1.8	1.2	1.6
Alterations-Additions	5.1	4.2	5.3
Heavy Construction	5.7	7.4	7.1
Total Building Construction	16.2	8.2	14.5
Total (Incl. Heavy)	**$21.9**	**$15.6**	**$21.6**

Source: Construction Industry Research Board; 1998 estimates by CCSCE based on Jan-Oct CIRB data

Heavy construction ("public works") has grown. It is the largest category of nonresidential building in California — over $7 billion throughout the 1990s. Heavy construction includes streets, bridges, sewage and waste systems, electric power and water facilities, and port and airport construction. In 1997 and 1998 public works construction continued at a $7 billion annual volume.

Outlook for Future Growth

Nonresidential building has turned the corner in California. Four years of strong job growth have produced a boom in nonresidential construction.

Total nonresidential construction should continue to grow in 1999 and beyond. CCSCE projects that the fundamental determinants of construction activity — job and household growth — will show sustained increases in the decade ahead. Job growth will increase to over 300,000 per year after five years of no growth at all.

Infrastructure in particular shows solid growth potential.

- Infrastructure spending should surge. There is a large backlog of port, airport, transportation and environmental projects required to support the state's economic growth and quality of life. Infrastructure funding has strong business support as evidenced by the recent California Business Roundtable report and the continuing work of the California Council for Economic and Environmental Balance (CCEEB).

- School and prison construction should also expand to meet a surge in school enrollment and prison population.

- Infrastructure funding received a boost from passage of expanded federal transportation funding in 1998 and the passage of many state and local bond issues and transportation taxes in California led by November's $9.2 billion state school bond initiative.

Office and industrial building should expand as job gains and low vacancy rates combine to make new facilities profitable. As Southern California reached new job records in 1998, all regions now have fully recovered from the long recession and are in the midst of long term growth at levels which outpace the national economy.

California Growth After 2005

California's population will continue to increase after 2005 adding another 7 million residents by the year 2020. Population growth will be driven by the 2.3 million new jobs added between 2005 and 2020. More than 2.4 million households will be added in California during these years.

California and United States 2005-2020				
	2005	2020	Change	Percent Change
Jobs				
California	17,766.9	20,177.8	2,410.9	13.6%
United States	150,113.8	166,035.3	15,921.5	10.6%
Population				
California	37,800.0	44,963.6	7,163.6	19.0%
United States	285,982.0	322,742.0	36,760.0	12.9%
Households				
California	12,682.6	15,103.7	2,421.1	19.1%
United States	109,000.0	123,002.3	14,002.3	12.8%

Source: CCSCE except U.S. Population – Census Bureau.

Job growth will slow after 2005 as the baby boom generation starts to retire. For the first time in recent U.S. history, population will grow faster than jobs as labor force growth slows sharply.

California is expected to continue growing faster than the nation between 2005 and 2020. However, California will grow somewhat closer to the national growth rate during these years.

CCSCE prepared a range of growth projections for 2020 as shown below:

California Range of Growth Projections 2005-2020				
	2005	**Low**	**2020 Baseline**	**High**
Jobs	17,766.9	18,764.4	20,177.8	21,780.9
Population	37,800.0	41,416.1	44,963.6	49,084.2
Households	12,682.6	13,819.9	15,103.7	16,378.6

Source: CCSCE

- Job growth will range from 1 million to 4 million depending on 1) U.S. labor force growth, particularly the retirement decisions of baby boomers and 2) California's share of future U.S. job gains.

- Population will increase from 3.6 million to 11.2 million based on 1) California's job growth and 2) California's fertility, particularly fertility trends in California's Hispanic population.

- Household growth will range from 1.1 million to 3.7 million depending on 1) California's job and population trends and 2) household formation rate trends, particularly for recent immigrants.

There is broad agreement that California will experience continued growth. CCSCE and the California Department of Finance projections are similar for 2005 and 2020 and the UCLA Business Forecasting Project projections are slightly higher.

Comparison of California Population Projections (Millions)		
	2005	**2020**
CCSCE	37.8	45.0
Department of Finance	37.4	45.4
UCLA	38.6	49.4

Source: DOF (Dec. 1998); UCLA (Sept. 1998)

KEY ISSUES FACING CALIFORNIA

KEY ISSUES FACING CALIFORNIA

The California economy is in a period of strong economic growth. The 400,000+ jobs added in 1998 cap four consecutive years of robust job and income growth.

The findings in Section 5 suggest that California firms and workers are well placed to participate in the leading sectors of the 21st century economy. California should regain its traditional role as a growth leader in the U.S. economy in the coming years.

The economic trends of the past four years have erased two concerns that were voiced often in the early 1990s.

- **California remains an attractive location for growth industries.** California is a center of innovation and leadership in many highly competitive world growth sectors like motion pictures, multimedia, Internet tools, semiconductor equipment manufacturing, and many other sectors that draw on the technological, design, and creative talents of California firms and workers.

- **California can prosper without high defense procurement spending.** California's economy has absorbed substantial cuts in defense related manufacturing and has re-emerged as a manufacturing job leader.

Each year CCSCE reminds readers that abundant opportunities do not mean guaranteed success. In this section each year CCSCE discusses some of the major public policy challenges facing California in securing prosperity for the state's workers and their families.

Three challenges will be directly addressed by business, community, and public policy leaders in 1999.

1) **Californians will continue to push for development of a long term economic strategy.** More budgetary resources will bring more options for investing in California's future. Yet there is still no basic agreement on the most appropriate or effective public policy role in creating the foundations for private sector economic growth.

2) **The impacts of growth are a major policy issue for 1999.** Job growth has led to increased congestion and escalating housing costs in many areas of California. As job growth continues and spreads, more communities will feel some negative impacts from economic growth. On the other hand a high quality of life is one of California's major attractions for new firms and industries.

In 1998 CCSCE prepared a major report on land use and the California economy. The report, sponsored by business and community foundations, discusses the connections between land use choices, a high quality of life and economic prosperity in California.

3) **Californians know that economic growth by itself is not enough to meet the income and health needs of all residents**. Four years of strong economic growth is raising incomes for most residents including, finally in 1997 and 1998, for lower wage workers. Overall economic growth remains the most powerful weapon against poverty and poor health.

   At the same time Californians recognize that there are limits to what economic growth alone can achieve. Moreover, economic growth by itself does not provide the tools for all residents to fully participate in the economy – including welfare recipients and working poor families hoping to move up or middle class workers aspiring to fill some of California's high skilled job shortages.

   CCSCE's affiliate organization – the Institute of Regional and Urban Studies – has been working with The California Wellness Foundation to examine the connections between the health of Californians and these issues of work and income. We report below on the growing recognition that work and health are profoundly connected.

CCSCE's discussion of these issues in Section 6 has two purposes: ① to show how the California economy is related to each issue and ② to discuss how information and, particularly, information about the economy is helpful in making public policy choices.

Challenge One: Developing a Long Term Economic Strategy for California

Abundant opportunity does not equal guaranteed success. California will need to work hard to convert opportunities into gains in real wages, income, and profits.

California does start with an advantage. The state's economic base is already well positioned in future growth sectors. California's challenge is not to create a new economic base but, rather, to nurture and expand the state's leadership position in key industries.

The actions of California's firms and workers will be the primary determinant of the pace of economic growth. Private sector investment and management decision will be critical for converting opportunity into prosperity.

Public policy has a significant role to play in creating a positive environment for private investment. Public policy affects the economy in many ways as shown on the accompanying chart. The new administration will have a chance to develop a new set of priorities for the state's role in supporting economic growth.

Themes for A California Economic Strategy

Some themes in California now are gaining momentum because they simultaneously address business and residents' perspectives:

- The economy depends on California's education system

- A strategic infrastructure plan is needed for the economy and for quality of life

- A high quality of life is a competitive asset for California businesses

Education and Training

The new California Business Roundtable Business Climate Survey confirmed the growing consensus that education is the number one public policy priority in a California economic strategy.

> "This emphasis on K-12 education receives a strong endorsement from California Voters and Business Leaders alike. Both groups concur that quality education is essential for the state's future economic growth."
>
> 1998 California Business Climate Survey

In December another business coalition – California Business for Education Excellence – was formed with members such as the American Electronics Association, the California Business Roundtable, IBM, Hewlett-Packard and Boeing. The groups' priority is to make sure that high academic standards are implemented in California.

1999 will bring opportunities for reorganizing California's public sector training programs. Federal workforce program reforms were adopted last year which give flexibility to state agencies in program design.

Moreover, a year long planning effort of four key groups – the Superintendent of Schools, Secretaries of Trade and Commerce and Health and Welfare, and Chancellor's Office of the California Community Colleges has produced a draft California Integrated Workforce Development Plan. The draft Plan will be discussed in early 1999 and, hopefully, brought to the Legislature for policy development this year.

Attracting Private Investment Requires Public Investment

A Diverse Economy Requires A Diverse Economic Strategy

Business Costs & Regulatory Environment
Workers' Compensation
Taxes and Fees
Housing Prices
Tort Reform
Capital Access
Streamlined Permitting
Market Based Environmental Regulations

Education and Training
K-12
Higher Education
School to Work Transitions
Reform of Public Sector Training Programs

Infrastructure
Highways & Public Transportation
Ports
Airports
Water Systems & Solid Waste Disposal

Quality of Life
Good Schools
Low Crime
Air Quality
World Class Amenities

Helping Industries Organize for Success
Reducing Trade Barriers
Increased R&D and Technology Support
Fostering Industry Networks and Collaboration
Linking Industry with Government and Schools
Regional Economic Initiatives

The draft Plan includes principles which CCSCE has stressed for many years:

1. A workforce preparation strategy should be **universal**, applying to all segments of California's labor force, and **lifetime oriented** by helping residents pursue upward mobility over time in response to new changing needs and the changing needs of the California economy.

2. The workforce strategy should be based on information about where the economy is headed in terms of occupations and skills.

3. Any public workforce strategy should incorporate the expertise of the private sector both in terms of what is needed and how training can be done effectively.

Business Costs and Regulatory Environment

These issues were the lead concern of California's business community in the early 1990s. While education, infrastructure and quality of life now lead the business agenda according to the recent California Business Roundtable Business Climate Survey, regulatory issues are still important.

Regulatory reforms are currently being discussed in several areas related to the California economy: toxic cleanup and base reuse, land recycling, school construction, more development permit streamlining and air and water quality. Moreover, there are ongoing challenges of making government more efficient both in terms of costs and customer service.

High housing costs are an area of significant concern to California businesses as well as to residents seeking new housing. Assuring that housing is available for California workers has become a priority issue for future economic growth. California had 11 of the 25 least affordable metro areas for housing in 1998.

Housing Affordability		
	Share of Homes Affordable for Median Income	National Rank of 193 Metro Areas
San Francisco	21.6%	193
Santa Cruz	28.5%	192
Salinas	35.3%	189
San Jose	35.8%	188
Santa Rosa	37.6%	185
San Luis Obispo	42.0%	182
San Diego	42.5%	181
Santa Barbara	44.7%	180
Los Angeles	45.6%	179
Oakland	45.8%	178
Orange County	50.9%	171
United States	64.3%	

Source: National Association of Home Builders

Infrastructure

The pressure is growing for development of a long term infrastructure strategy and related policies for California. The California Business Roundtable added another report last year in support of the need for infrastructure spending and policies and their latest business climate survey reports. "California Business Leaders and Voters also agree that increased investment in improving streets and highways, schools and colleges and other public facilities are extremely important for California's future."

The California Council for Environmental and Economic Balance (CCEEB) has a set of infrastructure principles and priorities (www.cceebweb.org/cpr). In December, 1998 the Legislative Analyst's Office (www.lao.ca.gov) issued a set of recommendations for "Overhauling the State's Infrastructure Planning and Financing Process." The Local Governance Consensus Project and the newly created Assembly Budget Commission will also wrestle with infrastructure issues in 1999.

There are four principle challenges in developing an infrastructure strategy:

- Identifying and prioritizing infrastructure needs
- Identifying the best approach to expand the state's infrastructure capacity (e.g., new building versus more efficient use of existing capacity)

- Developing agreement on funding sources and strategies
- Developing an integrated long term planning process

An ongoing challenge is to find a balance between **reform** and **resources**. Both are desired as current education dialogues show clearly.

For example, meeting California's infrastructure challenges will require a mix of reform and resources. Increasing infrastructure **capacity** doesn't always mean more building although plenty of new construction will be required. For example, conservation has been an important tool in providing "new" water and electricity for residents and businesses.

School and transportation construction will pose challenges to our creativity in expanding capacity to meet the requirements of growth. Reforms in construction practices and how schools and roads are used can be important tools in making the large upcoming public investments effective in terms of outcomes and cost.

There is hope that 1999 will bring the development of a long term capital planning strategy in California as more and more groups are realizing its importance to both economic growth and quality of life.

Infrastructure issues are also discussed later in this section related to land use decisions and the California economy.

Quality of Life

The importance of quality of life to the California economy is discussed later in Section 6 in the excerpt from CCSCE's report **Land Use and the California Economy: Principles for Prosperity and Quality of Life**.

Helping Industries Organize for Success

One of the major developments in this area has been the explosion of collaborations between business and government, business and schools and business and the community. All of these efforts, patterned after the path-breaking collaboration in Silicon Valley – Joint Venture: Silicon Valley Network, emphasize the importance of regional economies and regional connections. In many ways the California economy is a collection of regional economies and many public policy challenges like air quality, transportation, land use and education are regional in scope.

The state has a role in supporting these regional efforts through the development of statewide policies, e.g., on education, workforce, and infrastructure, that meet the need of California's regional economies. One part of developing an economic strategy for California in 1999 is deciding the best way for the Legislature and Governor to work with regions and regional groups.

Challenge Two — Combining Economic Growth with a High Quality of Life: The Need to Improve Land Use Decisions

In 1998 CCSCE was asked by Californians and the Land to examine the connections between land use decisions, quality of life and the California economy. This section contains an excerpt from the final report **Land Use and the California Economy: Principles for Prosperity and Quality of Life**. A copy of the full length report is available at no charge from Californians and the Land (415) 281-0415.

Introduction

For many years California's rapid growth has created tensions between the goals of economic prosperity and quality of life. These tensions have often focused on land use decisions – from battles over individual development proposals to statewide initiatives to protect the coast and preserve open space for all present and future residents. Many groups have searched for comprehensive solutions that combine economic and environmental goals and values but so far Californians have not found agreement on how to plan for the future.

This report was commissioned from the Center for Continuing Study of the California Economy (CCSCE) by "Californians and the Land," a group of leaders from California's business, government and environmental sectors. Californians and the Land, convened by the William and Flora Hewlett, James Irvine, Environment Now and David and Lucile Packard Foundations and the Bank of America, works to foster public discussion and to develop public and private sector actions that will improve the alignment of Californians' common desire for continued economic growth and for protection and improvement of our quality of life.

Summary

Californians must be prepared for a resumption of high levels of job, population and household growth. The strength of California's leading industries should push California growth rates above the national average for at least the next twenty years.

There is a compelling business case for improving land use decision making in California – to attract the entrepreneurs and workers who will lead California's knowledge-based industries. There is also a compelling community case for improving land use decision making in California – to maintain a high quality of life for ourselves and future generations.

Californians should be prepared for 3 million more jobs, 6 million more residents, and 2 million more households in the next ten years. This growth will give California a slowly increasing share of the nation's jobs, people, and households – consistent with the state's strong economic growth prospects.

After ten years California's growth will slow but only modestly. By 2020, based on conservative CCSCE projections, California will add approximately 5.1 million jobs, 12.4 million people, and should need 4.3 million more housing units.

A strong economy is raising incomes for most Californians and providing an increase in living standards for the first time in the 1990s. A continuing strong economy provides opportunities to include more and more residents in the state's prosperity.

This growing prosperity attracts even more new residents to California and increases pressures on land, the environment and quality of life. More jobs attract more people and most new residents want to live in California's existing urban regions. Taking bold actions to preserve California's quality of life and environment in the face of a strong economy will make California even more attractive to workers and entrepreneurs. **This is the paradox of a strong economy**. Yet it is the only realistic chance for Californians to have both economic prosperity and a great place to live.

Residents have many choices about where growth will occur and what the impacts will be. **This report is about those choices**. The place to begin is by recognizing the importance of a high quality of life to business and to general economic prosperity.

A high quality of life is, increasingly, a critical determinant in attracting entrepreneurs and workers in global industries. Firms and employees in these industries have choices about where to locate. They can and do demand good schools, clean air and water, efficient transportation, excellent public services and great recreational and cultural amenities – in short, a high quality of life.

> "Silicon Valley remains a center of innovation and entrepreneurship because of its people. If we lose the talent that distinguishes us – whether to congestion, poor schools, inadequate housing, or environmental degradation – we lose the **essential** element of our success."
>
> Becky Morgan
> President & CEO
> Joint Venture:Silicon Valley Network

Land use decisions play a critical role in determining the quality of life in California and, therefore, in how many high wage, high growth firms can locate and actually choose to locate in California's regions. These locational choices have a direct impact on the opportunities available to California workers to earn a rising standard of living for their families. Failure to protect the natural attractiveness of California can, therefore, hurt the state's future prosperity.

CCSCE has identified five principles for improving California's land use decision making – principles for simultaneously achieving economic growth, environmental and quality of life goals.

Principle One: Regional Perspectives are Required

Regions are the critical geographic area for organizing land use decisions in California. The blunt fact is that residents and business leaders cannot assess the impact of local land use decisions without a regional perspective.

Planning for adequate land for housing, jobs, preservation of unique land resources **and** open space requires a regional perspective. However, Californians remain in conflict about bringing a regional focus to land use decision making. Local communities control most land use decisions in California today. Local funding mechanisms make it impossible for local communities to assess and act on regional impacts, even if local residents are willing.

Developing a regional perspective should be based on analyzing existing information and developing new information where appropriate. Figuring out how local land use plans fit together to meet regional needs requires more than agreement on goals and values. **Developing a regional perspective requires the simultaneous and active analysis of information about regional jobs, population, households, infrastructure, and land resources**.

CCSCE suggests that a first step is to take existing regional growth projections along with data on land use, zoning and environmental needs and see whether and how the growth can be accommodated. Can the projected jobs and households be located while conserving unique land resources and providing open space? What are the choices that emerge when you see "how to fit the growth on the land"?

Principle Two: Land Must Be Used More Efficiently

There are four reasons why higher densities must be a key element of the solution to California's growth: ① higher densities are the only way to accommodate expected growth in California's major urban regions; ② there is a direct trade-off between higher density, the options for open space and the pressures for unplanned growth patterns; ③ if California's existing urban regions cannot accommodate the anticipated growth, then the pressure for growth to spillout into California's agricultural, coastal, and mountain regions will intensify; and ④ enormous investments have been made in existing cities which are available to serve future growth.

It will not be possible to accommodate expected growth in most California regions unless large cities like Los Angeles, San Diego, San Jose, San

Francisco, Oakland and Fresno are part of the solution. Cities have the largest potential for increasing densities, for re-using abandoned and underutilized land, and for integrating job, housing and shopping sites to reduce travel demands.

> "Sprawl negatively affects the quality of life for employees. Silicon Valley has to grow up – not out"
>
> Carl Guardino, President
> Silicon Valley Manufacturing Group

The requirements for making the major cities in California vital and attractive places to live and work are broad and challenging. They include affordable and attractive housing, good schools, a tax base and fiscal rules that support high quality public services, jobs and programs that provide opportunities and raise incomes for low skilled workers, and safe neighborhoods for all residents **and** businesses. In addition these cities need to remain centers for culture, dining, and shopping – places where Californians want to work, live and visit.

> "Land use decisions determine whether we have a livable, tolerant community in Southern California. Economic development and environmental needs must be connected. Inner cities must be attractive, vital and safe or residents will want to leave"
>
> Denise Fairchild, President
> Community Development Technologies
> Center, Los Angeles

One approach to increasing densities and making cities more attractive at the same time is **urban land recycling**. California's older cities have abandoned or deteriorated manufacturing plants, dry cleaning facilities, closed gas stations and stores and homes which have seen better days. Some sites are in neighborhoods that need better policing and transportation. Some sites have toxic contamination from past uses.

There are numerous problems to be worked out from funding toxic cleanup to providing public services in neighborhoods to land use and tax policies that promote redevelopment. The payoff, however, is substantial in terms of the potential to redirect growth to areas that want growth and have a basic foundation of existing infrastructure and public services.

> "Land recycling is a vital tool for making California a more livable place. Land recycling can form the centerpiece of a more sensible, and sustainable approach to land use and development.
>
> By using our land in a way that increases the average density in existing urban areas to an average of only 3 housing units per acre, all new

residents could be housed without developing a single additional acre of open space."

George B. Brewster, Executive Director, California Center for Land Recycling

Principle Three: Public Investment is Required

Public facilities are over crowded throughout most of California. Roads are over capacity at peak hours. Schools were short of classroom space even before class size reductions created more demand. Airports and ports are operating near peak capacity.

This is **before** the coming surge of growth.

A conservative estimate of ten year infrastructure requirements totals well over $100 billion. Even though these infrastructure projects could help attract high wage growth industries and, simultaneously, improve the quality of life for Californians, serious obstacles have left a large funding gap.

Economic prosperity and quality of life goals will also require long term funding for open space, air quality, habitat protection, and preserving California's unique land resources – in short, funding to maintain and improve California's environmental infrastructure.

One obstacle is that money is not the only way to increase infrastructure capacity and Californians have been skeptical to write large checks until they are comfortable that other options have been considered **and** that there are mechanisms to assure accountability. Peak hour (congestion) pricing, sharing facilities among communities, and the use of technology in some teaching settings are all ways to increase capacity without more building. The bottom line is that one part of an infrastructure strategy for California must address issues of accountability and non building approaches to capacity expansion.

Another obstacle is that Californians are not in agreement on who should pay for new infrastructure. Californians are particularly divided on the question of whether new residents and businesses should be entirely responsible to pay for new infrastructure – "growth should pay for itself." While this slogan is initially attractive to some people, there are two reasons to take a different view.

- While some infrastructure directly serves new residents and businesses (e.g., new schools and roads in an undeveloped area), much of the new infrastructure either modernizes existing facilities or also serves existing residents and businesses.

- There is broad agreement that California's last wave of infrastructure spending ended in the 1960s. Since then residents and businesses have not paid to keep pace with growth and serious infrastructure shortages have developed.

For these reasons, placing the burden of funding infrastructure solely on new residents and businesses will lead to inadequate funding relative to the state's economy **and** create an equity imbalance between new and existing residents and businesses.

Principle Four: Fiscal Reform is Essential

Meeting economic prosperity goals requires fiscal reform. Funding infrastructure for economic **and** quality of life goals requires fiscal reform. Creating land use planning incentives for sustainable regions requires fiscal reform.

1) Current fiscal rules give the wrong land use planning incentives. Cities compete against each other for retail activity while housing, and even manufacturing, projects don't pay fiscally. High development fees are imposed because other revenue sources are inadequate but the fees raise the price of housing and encourage sprawl.

"Today, however, land use planning no longer creates a healthy balance in California's communities. All too often, communities are forced to make land use planning decisions based entirely on budget decisions. The question of how to create healthy, balanced communities has become secondary to the immediate need to balance the budget."

Restoring the Balance: Managing Fiscal Issues and Land – Use Planning Decisions in California; California Planning Roundtable

High development fees are a feature of California's post - Proposition 13 local government finance system. These fees, designed to help revenue - starved communities finance infrastructure and public services, add substantially to the cost of new housing.

"Our analysis shows that the fees imposed on new construction are significant, typically falling in the range of $20,000 to $30,000 per development. In one community, the fees and assessments totaled 19 percent of the mean sales price."

Who Pays for Development Fees and Exactions, Marla Dresch and Steen M. Sheffrin, Public Policy Institute of California.

2) Current fiscal rules make infrastructure funding difficult. There is no requirement for a long term infrastructure strategy even though ten

year funding requirements exceed $100 billion. In addition, the two-thirds vote requirement for the state budget and local bond issues means that California's future infrastructure is controlled by just one-third of the Legislature and the voting public.

"The tax structure should enhance the state's economic competitiveness, taking into consideration the level and quality of public services the tax system finances. Particular concern should be paid to the capability of the tax system to support investment in planned infrastructure critical to the state's economic competitiveness and to accommodating the state's rapid population growth. In particular a simple majority of local voters should be able to approve general obligation bonds for infrastructure projects if the projects are included in a local capital improvement plan. The tax system should not include fiscal disincentives to sustainable development and should have minimal influence on local land use decisions."

Concepts for State and Local Tax Structure Reforms, California Prosperity Through Reform Project, California Council for Environmental and Economic Balance

3) Fiscal reform must include mechanisms that allow local government revenues to keep pace with economic growth. The sales and property tax base that local communities depend on is not growing as fast as the California economy. Fiscal reform must simultaneously improve land use planning incentives **and** provide a revenue base that keeps pace with demands of job and population growth.

Since 1990 total personal income in California has grown by 35.5% – slightly outpacing the rate of population growth and inflation (30.9%). Personal income tax revenues – the **state government's** major tax base – have grown even faster.

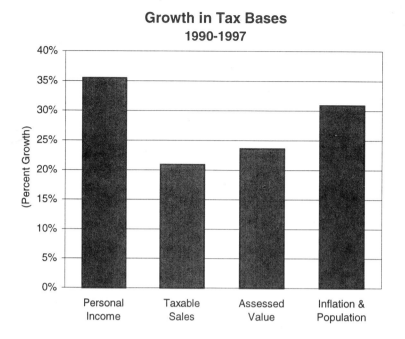

Growth in Tax Bases
1990-1997

(Percent Growth) — categories: Personal Income, Taxable Sales, Assessed Value, Inflation & Population

The sales tax base has grown by just 20.9% during the same seven years while assessed value has grown by 23.6%. Sales tax revenues are likely to continue falling behind income growth as consumers spend an even greater fraction of their income on non-taxable items such as many Internet transactions.

While the property tax base has grown rapidly in some years and some communities, the overall property tax base will always be limited by the 2% annual cap on assessed value increases of specific property. The sales tax and property tax bases that currently finance local governments in California are not keeping pace with economic growth. Even one time adjustments, such as giving local governments a higher share of the sales tax, do not solve the long term challenge of providing local governments with a revenue base that keeps pace with economic growth and provides positive incentives for smart land use decisions.

If local communities do not have enough revenues to adequately fund public services, one clear impact of growth will be a decrease in the level of public services for existing residents.

Principle Five: Equity Considerations Must Be Included

Complicated, and usually unintended, equity impacts can result from land use planning and decisions. For example, policies that restrict housing have relatively more impact on young and newly arriving households. Policies that limit job growth can block opportunities for upward mobility. On the other hand, policies that make California's cities more vital and attractive will also especially help California's poorer and minority residents.

"Addressing urban poverty will require the political and moral commitment of significant numbers of people who are not poor. Some have sought to appeal for such support by raising fears that urban problems will "spill over" to outlying areas, an approach which predisposes suburbanites to view urban areas as places to be avoided and contained. Others have evoked the power of conscience and compassion, motives which are unfortunately less present when a broad range of people feel economically insecure.

We suggest a third approach which emphasizes common ground: The fates of our region and its low-income communities are inextricably intertwined, which means that attempts to address poverty and neighborhood decline help all residents of the region. We are, after all, in the same boat – and if one end springs a leak, the whole vessel will eventually go down."

> **Growing Together: Linking Regional and Community Development In A Changing Economy, Summary Report – April 1997**; Manuel Pastor, Jr.; Peter Dreier; J. Eugene Grigsby III; Marta López-Garza

Equity considerations must be part of the public discussion about developing strategies to deal with future growth in California. A discussion about equity is especially important in California where ethnic minorities will soon be a majority of the state's population and where immigrants come everyday seeking the American dream.

Breaking the Logjam on Land Use Decisions – Finding Comprehensive Solutions

Californians have many good ideas for encouraging economic growth and many good ideas for strengthening our quality of life. Separate groups are working for more housing, greenbelts and agricultural preservation, environmental justice, fiscal reform, streamlining regulatory processes, and revitalizing urban neighborhoods.

None of these ideas **alone** is a solution to combining economic growth and a high quality of life. Greenbelts are not the solution. More housing is not the solution. Fiscal reform, regulatory reform and attractive cities are not the solutions. These ideas are **parts** of the solution.

Real agreement, real compromise, and real solutions will only come when residents and business, agriculture, community and environmental groups, and local and state political leaders reach beyond their individual narrow agendas to embrace part of someone else's agenda. Solutions must combine housing **and** open space – both in adequate amounts to meet projected growth. Solutions must combine fiscal **and** regulatory reform **and** accountability.

California's economy has been through wrenching changes so far in the 1990s. Industries have had to develop new products and markets in a fast-paced global economy. Workers have had to adjust to new skill requirements and new ways of working. Yet, Californians are adapting to the new economy. Californians will enter the 21st century with a stronger economic base, higher incomes, and more opportunities than were present ten years earlier.

The question today is whether Californians can show the same resilience and innovation in meeting the unprecedented challenges of land use planning to sustain our economy, environment and quality of life as we did in responding to defense downsizing and the global economy.

Challenge Three: Economic Growth Alone Does Not Address All the Work and Health Needs of Californians

Four years of economic growth **have** made a difference to many Californians. Average wages and income are up strongly reaching record levels and far outpacing consumer price increases. Moreover, in 1997 and 1998 low income Californians finally shared in the wage growth.
A strong economy had substantial impact on reducing unemployment and raising incomes. Economic growth remains the most important tool for raising incomes and reducing poverty.

Other policies are also important. The increase in California's minimum wage contributed to the strong wage gains for low income workers. The federal Earned Income Tax Credit has a substantial impact on reducing poverty for working families. Many working Californians are facing difficulties in obtaining and paying for health insurance.

For several years CCSCE has discussed the need for comprehensive workforce policies in California. Such policies help prepare residents to fully participate in the state's economic growth. Welfare recipients, residents working at poverty level wages, and middle class workers facing stagnant wages and obsolete skills can all benefit from skill building policies.

Moreover, California's economy requires more skilled workers. The most important economic challenge facing California firms is finding qualified workers.

The Connection Between Work and Health

There are strong connections between the work and health status of Californians. Income, job satisfaction, and related issues like work schedules and job security all show strong theoretical and statistical connections to measured and reported health status.

CCSCE's affiliate organization, the Institute of Regional and Urban Studies, is working with The California Wellness Foundation on a multi-year program (The Future of Work and Health) examining the connections between work and health and the implications of these connections for public policy in California.

One reason to emphasize the connections between work and health in **California Economic Growth** is that they offer the possibility of broadening the discussion of California's workforce preparation policies to include constituencies who are primarily focused on improving the health of Californians.

The strong connections between jobs, income and health are symbolized by the motto of the Future of Work and Health Program – "a good job is one of California's best health promotion policies".

Income Affects Health

The following summary is from a presentation by George Kaplan, Professor and Chair of the School of Public Health at the University of Michigan at a conference on April 23, 1998 sponsored by the Future of Work and Health Program of the California Wellness Foundation.

There really is substantial reason to believe that there is a strong, intimate, and important connection between people's economic and physical well-being and health. There is also an important connection between the economic well-being of communities and the health of those communities. So, both at an individual and population level, economic forces may be considered some of the fundamental causes of health and disease.[1]

It is not just that poor people have worse health than rich people. There is a steady gradient relating increasing income and wealth to better health status. Kaplan followed 7,000 adults in Alameda County from 1965 on and compared their household income and death rates. Even from the start, those who had inadequate family incomes did worse, those who had very adequate did best, and those in the other two groups did intermediate in an ordered way. That ordering remains constant over 19 years.

The areas in which people live and the economic health of the areas in which people live are also strongly associated with their mortality. Initially, Kaplan and colleagues collected data on the health status of those people who lived in impoverished Oakland communities and those who lived in more affluent Oakland communities. Nine years later, when the health outcomes of those two

---

[1] A full transcript of Kaplan's remarks and charts in available at www.tcw.orgwhi_conference.htm. All 25 presentation charts are accessible in color at the website.

groups was compared, researchers found that people who lived in the impoverished areas actually died at a faster rate than those who did not. This finding couldn't be explained away. People weren't dying at a faster rate because they were smoking, drinking, and staying out late at night, had lower incomes or education, or were without health insurance or jobs. There seemed to be something about the areas in which they lived.

Different research shows similar findings on rates of disability and a variety of other health outcomes. At least two dozen studies indicate that socioenvironmental properties of residential areas seem to be strongly associated with the health and risk factor trajectories of the residents of those areas. Many of these characteristics are rooted in the socioeconomic structure of the areas. People who live in economically troubled areas are more likely to become less physically active over time and to die faster than people in areas with greater economic health. That finding seems to be independent of their individual characteristics. So, the economic level of areas seems to be important.

Even beyond that, there are now a whole series of studies which show the level of income inequality within a city or area seems to be important. So, the equity, or fairness, of income distribution is beginning to look like another fundamental structuring device for health.

In the United States, at the state level, there is a strong relationship between the proportion of total household income received by the least well-off 50% and age- and income-adjusted mortality. So, states with the most unequal distribution of income, like Louisiana, Mississippi, Alabama, Kentucky, and New York, have higher mortality rates than those with more equal distribution of income, like Hawaii, Utah, New Hampshire, Wisconsin, and Vermont.

The equality or inequality of the income distribution was not just related to mortality. It was also related to infant mortality, disability rates, violent crime rates, homicide rates, medical expenditures, unemployment rates, rates of incarceration, the percent of people on AFDC or food stamps, and the percent of people without insurance. So, the equity of the income distribution seems to capture a lot of what's happening in terms of health and social indicators at the state level.

1999 – An Opportunity to Develop a Workforce Preparation Strategy for California

Four current trends symbolize California's challenges in developing new workforce preparation strategies and programs:

- In 1997 California developed state rules and programs to move welfare recipients into the workforce. Despite recent caseload declines, there are more than 400,000 adult welfare recipients in California who must find jobs or eventually face reduced welfare support.

  The first step for most welfare recipients will be low paying entry level jobs – in competition with millions of Californians seeking similar jobs.

- There are approximately 1 million California workers who meet the strictest definition of "working poor". These workers are doing everything that the new laws require of welfare recipients yet they live in households with incomes below poverty level.

- California's business leaders are calling for increases in the number of highly skilled workers. **It is in the high skilled occupations that employers have difficulty filling available jobs**. Moreover, California's economy is anchored by industries that depend on technological leadership for competitive advantage.

- Most Californians work in jobs that require somewhere between entry level skills and highly technical training. Four years of strong income growth has brought some increases in living standards for these workers and their families. Yet, even in 1999 many "in the middle" have seen two decades of wage stagnation, increasing pressures and changes in their work life.

- Including the middle class in California's workforce preparation strategy is very important for several reasons:

  — The middle class target for welfare recipients. The major goal of welfare reform is to help recipients and their families move out of poverty **through work**.

  — If escaping poverty for workers and children is an accepted goal for welfare recipients, then the same goal must apply to people who are **already working but still poor**.

  — Many members of the middle class are also being left behind in terms of rising living standards.

— It is existing middle skilled workers who are the best candidates for getting additional training to fill existing high skilled job vacancies.

Seeing Labor Force Policy Connections

One of the criticisms of existing workforce preparation programs is that the nation has many separate programs but no overall policy or strategy. For example, there are programs for 1) unemployed workers, 2) workers displaced by trade policies, 3) welfare recipients, 4) disadvantaged youth, and 5) workers affected by defense conversion.

Moreover, the nation has a workforce policy for the most skilled workers in the forms of large programs of support for college students and students in specialized graduate training.

On the other hand there is no organized workforce strategy for existing workers. The working poor and middle level workers who want training to raise their living standards face a hit and miss system of both world class private sector training and a total vacuum of programs depending on what industry and size of firm they work in. For example, there is no workforce strategy designed to help the working poor escape poverty.

CCSCE believes that the best answer for meeting the needs of the California economy is a universal workforce strategy, i.e. a strategy that addresses the needs of all workers and firms simultaneously. With that goal in mind, a starting point is to understand the labor force connections between different groups of workers.

Connection 1: Welfare Recipients and the Working Poor

Developing workforce strategies to help working poor families will be the next step in welfare reform policy. It is already being discussed in many states and the National Governors' Conference has identified the working poor as a policy focus area in 1998.

Welfare recipients are interested in strategies to help the working poor escape poverty because that is where they will be soon. The working poor are interested in escaping from poverty and have the additional incentive that unless more upward paths out of poverty are established, their job markets will see substantial increased competition from former welfare recipients.

There will be a strong push to make the support programs designed for welfare recipients available to existing low wage workers. There are two reasons why this push will occur:

1) Many welfare recipients will not be able to retain jobs without some support, for example, with child care.

2) If support is given to former welfare recipients who are now working and poor, it will be difficult to justify withholding similar services from similarly situated residents who have been working all along.

Finally, it will then be clear to everyone that former welfare recipients and other working poor residents share a common hope – to get a better job and escape from poverty for themselves and their families.

Building Skills Will Get Increased Attention

As former welfare recipients and the working poor become one group trying to move up from poverty, public policy strategies to increase skill and training levels will become more important. While public policies to help welfare recipients get first jobs may emphasize job search and "good worker" attributes like effort and punctuality, the next step up will be based primarily on skills acquisition.

Since there is no organized public and private approach to helping low wage workers move up from poverty, developing an overall strategy will be a first necessary step. This will require the bipartisan commitment that public policies to help existing workers upgrade their skills is appropriate.

Connection 2: Middle Class Workers and Meeting California's High Skill Shortages

The labor force challenge that threatens California's lead industries is a shortage of skilled workers.

It is not realistic to expect that these shortages will be filled mainly by new entrants into the labor force or by people moving up from entry level jobs.

It is more realistic to expect that existing workers with experience and some skills already are the best candidates to move up in the near term. This is the strategy being used by companies who can afford to do in-house training.

Most companies cannot afford to do their own technical training. The Intel – San Jose City College model suggests a broader approach. Private companies working with community colleges and specialized post – secondary training institutions can develop programs that have a larger scale but retain direct industry input into the program design.

Policies that help existing workers move up to take higher skilled vacancies directly support the expansion of high wage jobs in California.

Connection 3: Connecting the Top, Middle and Entry Level Workforce

There is little disagreement that California needs a workforce strategy to help welfare recipients enter the job market and a workforce strategy to help California's lead industries find all the highly skilled workers they can hire. What is now being increasingly understood is the implication that California also needs a workforce strategy for the middle groups.

1) A middle class move up strategy helps middle class workers **and** directly addresses critical skills shortages.

2) A middle class move up strategy gives hope to the working poor (including former welfare recipients) that upward mobility into middle class jobs is a real possibility for escaping poverty.

3) **A middle class move up policy is a welfare to work policy.**

There is no great shortage of entry level workers in California. Helping existing entry level workers move up is critical to the transition of welfare recipients into entry level jobs. Otherwise California will have instituted a sort of "musical chairs" in the low skills job market where an increasing number of workers compete for a limited number of jobs.

Workforce Preparation: Developing a Universal Approach in California

A major effort is underway in California to reexamine the state's workforce preparation ideas and programs. Based on our ongoing work on the California economy, CCSCE offers some principles to guide the state's effort. We believe that California can be a model for the nation in developing information on future workforce trends and finding successful approaches.

- Workforce preparation should be viewed as a **universal challenge** – not as a set of programs for special groups. The different groups listed above share part of a **common challenge** – to prepare for the future world of work in California.

  Workforce preparation is for everybody and needs to be continually pursued. America's businesses are the leaders in workforce preparation. Many of the nation's best models for lifelong workforce preparation have been developed by private corporations where the value of highly skilled and motivated employees is well known.

- The primary focus of workforce preparation should be oriented to the **future** California economy. What skills, education, and specific training will be needed to be successful not just today but over time and into the 21st century economy?

Many current programs are oriented to putting people to work immediately. While this is a worthy goal, it forces attention on today's, not tomorrow's, jobs and skills.

By focusing on workforce preparation as a **universal** challenge oriented to **future** needs, California can be a leader in developing policy approaches that will help the state and nation.

REGIONAL ECONOMIC GROWTH

REGIONAL ECONOMIC GROWTH

This section presents a more detailed examination of the economic trends in four major economic regions in California. These regions, outlined on the map, are the six county Los Angeles Basin, nine county San Francisco Bay Area, San Diego Region (containing San Diego County), and the four county Sacramento Region. These regions represent labor market areas which means that most of the people who work in the region also live in the region although not always in the same county in which they work. While there is some inter-regional commuting even among these large regions, for the most part these are the regions within which job growth and housing growth must balance.

The section begins with a comparison of economic growth rates among the regions. Which regions led the state in the first half of the 1990s and where will the growth occur in the decade ahead?

Next each regional economy is examined. The analysis for each region includes:

- Examination of recent and current economic trends

- Description of the present and projected economic base

- Long term trends in job growth

- Long term trends in income and spending

- Analysis of construction activity — past, current, and projected

MAJOR ECONOMIC REGIONS
OF CALIFORNIA

1 LOS ANGELES BASIN

2 SAN FRANCISCO BAY AREA

3 SAN DIEGO REGION

4 SACRAMENTO REGION

5 REST OF STATE

Comparison of Economic Regions

Total Jobs

- California will add 2.3 million jobs between 1998 and 2005 — an average gain of nearly 325,000 jobs per year. California will have an overall job increase of 14.6% — outpacing the nation's projected 8.1% gain.

  The California economy began a strong economic recovery in 1994. Between 1990 and 1994 California lost an average of 59,600 jobs per year while the U.S. economy added over one million jobs annually.

  However, between 1994 and 1998 all regions of California have reached record job levels. The state averaged job growth of 387,300 per year as California maintained a leadership in most fast growing basic industries.

  The 1994-98 recovery was centered in the urban coastal regions. The recovery demonstrated the long term strength of the economic bases in the Los Angeles Basin, San Francisco Bay Area and San Diego. These regions reestablished their leadership position in the California economy and the state's major growth industries.

California and Economic Regions Total Jobs 1990-2005 (Thousands)					Average Annual Growth		
	1990	1994	1998	2005	1990-1994	1994-1998	1998-2005
Los Angeles Basin	6,944.3	6,552.4	7,175.9	8,222.0	-98.0	155.9	149.4
San Francisco Bay Area	3,224.9	3,193.6	3,617.4	4,142.6	-7.8	105.9	75.0
San Diego Region	1,089.6	1,085.3	1,222.1	1,473.4	-1.1	34.2	35.9
Sacramento Region	691.1	719.9	803.1	943.2	7.2	20.8	20.0
Rest of State Region	2,242.8	2,402.9	2,685.0	2,985.7	40.0	70.5	43.0
California	**14,192.7**	**13,954.2**	**15,503.5**	**17,766.9**	**-59.6**	**387.3**	**323.3**
United States	**122,035.4**	**127,138.6**	**138,896.1**	**150,113.8**	**1,275.8**	**2,939.4**	**1,602.5**

Source: 1990, 1994, and 1998—BLS, EDD, and CCSCE; 2005—United States: BLS; California and regions: CCSCE

- The Los Angeles Basin has participated in the state's strong job growth since 1996 and has added more than 600,000 jobs since 1994. By 1998 the Basin had recovered from the early 90s recession and had nearly 250,000 more jobs than in 1990. The Basin was the hardest hit region during the 1990-1994 recession. The basin accounted for most of the state's job losses, primarily as a result of aerospace and construction declines.

- The Basin is projected to add 1 million jobs by 2005. The average annual increase of 149,400 is similar to the gains experienced in the 1994-98 recovery. The Basin is expected to grow at near the state average.

  The Basin economy is benefiting from strong growth in foreign trade, motion pictures, apparel, and media/software. The aircraft/defense sector has stopped declining and the outlook for commercial aircraft is now positive. The region faces new opportunities in textiles, furniture, and toys — all older manufacturing sectors where the region's advantage in design can be combined with the introduction of new technology.

- The San Francisco Bay Area will add more than 500,000 jobs by the year 2005. While the Bay Area's growth rate is the lowest among California regions, the area will account for more than one in five new state jobs. The Los Angeles and San Francisco regions will gain a combined 1.5 million jobs between 1998 and 2005 — two-thirds of California's job increase.

  Foreign trade, computer services (e.g., multimedia, software, and Internet related services), and jobs related to serving the region's high tech manufacturing complex are leading the Bay Area economy which gained more than 100,000 jobs per year for the past four years. The Bay Area has had more than a 50% increase in technology exports since 1994 and future prospects remain strong despite the current Asia related slowdown.

- San Diego began a strong economic recovery in 1994 after four years of no growth. The region is expected to be the state's job growth leader in the decade ahead with a 20.6% job increase — nearly 36,000 added jobs per year.

  The San Diego region will participate in the state's foreign trade growth and will be aided by the region's proximity to Mexico. Exports to Mexico of California products are up 75% since 1995. Cross border manufacturing facilities in electronics, TV, and toys are boosting jobs in the region. Bio-tech and telecommunications manufacturing (led by international leader Qualcomm) bring long term growth opportunities.

- The Sacramento region will add approximately 20,000 jobs a year and grow by 17.4% to 2005. The region gained jobs during the 1990-94 statewide recession and job growth has continued since 1994.

The Sacramento region has grown as a competitive location for activities seeking a California alternative to the higher-cost coastal regions. High tech manufacturing jobs are still growing with Packard Bell, Apple, HP, Intel, and NEC having major operations in the region and Oracle (software) announcing plans to build facilities in the region. The region is also growing as a distribution center for I-80 goods movement into and from the state.

State government, a major sector in Sacramento's economic base, is expected to add jobs. Renewed revenue growth plus the move to have states administer programs like welfare and job training will push state employment higher. There has been substantial growth in legal and consulting services related to state capitol activity.

- The Rest of State region, led by the San Joaquin Valley, added jobs during the California recession. Agriculture expanded in production and exports. Households continued to locate in the region and commute to jobs in the Bay Area and Sacramento.

Growth has been closer to the state average since 1994 as the San Joaquin Valley grew more slowly than the urban coastal regions. Most leading growth sectors remain firmly centered in the Los Angeles, Bay Area and San Diego regions.

The older resource base (agriculture, mining, timber) will see job declines in the decade ahead. Regional growth will be driven by relocation of firms and workers from the big urban areas of California based on cost and quality of life considerations.

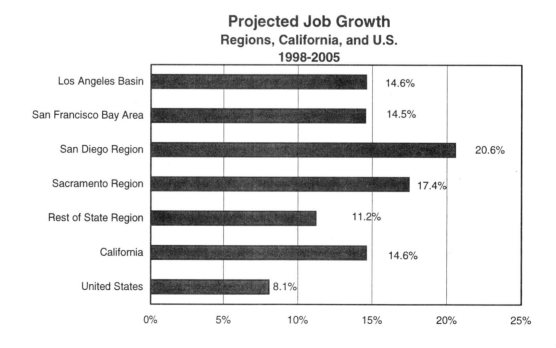

Projected Job Growth
Regions, California, and U.S.
1998-2005

Los Angeles Basin	14.6%
San Francisco Bay Area	14.5%
San Diego Region	20.6%
Sacramento Region	17.4%
Rest of State Region	11.2%
California	14.6%
United States	8.1%

Total Personal Income

- Total personal income (adjusted for inflation) is expected to grow by 3.5% annually between 1998 and 2005 — outpacing the 2.6% national growth rate. All regions of California will have income growth rates above the national average ranging from a 4.0% annual increase in Sacramento region to a 3.2% annual growth rate in the Bay Area.

- California regions experienced **very strong real income growth** during the past four years. Annual growth rates ranged from 4.2% in the Bay Area and San Diego to 3.5% in the Rest of State region.

- The Los Angeles Basin is the state's largest market and will represent a buying pool of nearly $540 billion in 1998$ by 2005. In 1998 the Los Angeles market was larger than all states except New York and Texas. The Bay Area market ($238.9 billion in 1998) exceeded the incomes of all but eight states.

- The Sacramento and San Diego regions will have the highest income growth rates in the state, but the Los Angeles and Bay Area markets will still account for 72% of the state's nearly $1.2 trillion income pool in 2005.

	1990	1994	1998	2005	1990-1994	1994-1998	1998-2005
Los Angeles Basin	$376.3	$364.1	$423.0	$538.6	-0.8%	3.8%	3.5%
San Francisco Bay Area	195.5	202.7	238.9	297.3	0.9%	4.2%	3.2%
San Diego Region	61.0	62.2	73.3	95.8	0.5%	4.2%	3.9%
Sacramento Region	38.0	39.6	46.2	60.7	1.0%	3.9%	4.0%
Rest of State Region	104.2	107.9	123.7	160.1	0.9%	3.5%	3.8%
California	**$775.1**	**$776.5**	**$905.2**	**$1,152.5**	**0.0%**	**3.9%**	**3.5%**
United States	**$5,999.9**	**$6,323.2**	**$7,143.1**	**$8,553.4**	**1.3%**	**3.1%**	**2.6%**

California and Economic Regions
Total Personal Income
1990-2005
(Billions of 1998$)

Average Annual Growth Rate

Source: 1990, 1994, and 1998—U.S. Department of Commerce; California Department of Finance, CCSCE; 2005—CCSCE

Per Capita Income

- Per capita income varies significantly among the economic regions in California. The San Francisco Bay Area has one of the highest per capita incomes in the nation. In 1998 Bay Area per capita incomes averaged $35,381 — 34% above the national average – while per capita incomes in other regions were close to or below the national average.

- Real per capita incomes (i.e., adjusted for inflation) are projected to grow by 1.8% per year between 1998 and 2005 throughout the regions of California. This is far faster than the 0.5% annual growth rate for the 1990-98 period.

- Real per capita income gains have been very strong since 1994 - averaging near 2.5% per year in most regions of California.

- Wages in California (adjusted for inflation) have kept pace with nationwide growth in the 1990s. The decline in relative per capita incomes in California outside the Bay Area is caused primarily by the high proportion of children and above average unemployment rates and not by below average wage growth.

California and Economic Regions Per Capita Personal Income 1990-2005 (1998$)					Average Annual Growth Rate		
	1990	1994	1998	2005	1990-1994	1994-1998	1998-2005
Los Angeles Basin	$25,546	$23,277	$25,783	$29,198	-2.3%	2.6%	1.8%
San Francisco Bay Area	32,304	31,849	35,381	40,067	-0.4%	2.7%	1.8%
San Diego Region	24,299	23,451	26,003	29,447	-0.9%	2.6%	1.8%
Sacramento Region	25,483	24,759	27,230	30,836	-0.7%	2.4%	1.8%
Rest of State Region	20,207	19,501	21,069	23,859	-0.9%	2.0%	1.8%
California	**$25,885**	**$24,425**	**$26,982**	**$30,490**	**-1.4%**	**2.5%**	**1.8%**
United States	**$24,057**	**$24,285**	**$26,466**	**$29,909**	**0.2%**	**2.2%**	**1.8%**

Source: 1990, 1994, and 1998—U.S. Department of Commerce; California Department of Finance, CCSCE; 2005—CCSCE

Average Household Income

- Average household incomes in California have remained well above the national average, even throughout the 1990-1994 recession. Real household incomes throughout California have rebounded since 1994 (+3.2% annually after inflation) as wages rose and unemployment rates fell.

  In 1998 California's average household income was $81,350 — 15.5% above the national average.

- The measure of average household income shown below is total personal income per household. The Census Bureau uses a **money** income measure which produces lower household income estimates and also reports median incomes which are considerably lower than average household income estimates.

- The Bay Area has the highest household incomes — $100,647 in 1998 or 40% above the national average. Average household income in the Los Angeles Basin was 15% above the national average.

- Real (i.e., inflation adjusted) household incomes will grow by 1.6% annually in California – the same as the annual gain nationally.

California and Economic Regions Average Household Income 1990-2005 (1998$)				Average Annual Growth Rate		
	1990	**1994**	**1998**	**2005**	**1990-1994**	**1994-1998**	**1998-2005**
Los Angeles Basin	$76,282	$71,297	$81,132	$91,136	-1.7%	3.3%	1.7%
San Francisco Bay Area	87,050	87,649	100,647	112,685	0.2%	3.5%	1.6%
San Diego Region	68,768	67,213	77,039	85,496	-0.6%	3.5%	1.5%
Sacramento Region	68,370	66,266	73,577	81,442	-0.8%	2.7%	1.5%
Rest of State Region	59,276	57,602	63,136	70,585	-0.7%	2.3%	1.6%
California	**$74,666**	**$71,794**	**$81,350**	**$90,875**	**-1.0%**	**3.2%**	**1.6%**
United States	**$65,257**	**$65,875**	**$70,445**	**$78,472**	**0.2%**	**1.7%**	**1.6%**

Source: 1990, 1994, and 1998—U.S. Department of Commerce; California Department of Finance, CCSCE; 2005—CCSCE

Total Taxable Sales

- Total taxable sales declined throughout California between 1990 and 1994 as a result of the economic downturn. The decline in spending exceeded the income loss as confidence declined and longer term purchases were postponed.

  Taxable sales have rebounded strongly since 1994 with average real (i.e., inflation adjusted) gains of 4.0% per year statewide. Growth has been especially strong in the Bay Area and San Diego (5.5%+ per year) and below average in the Rest of State region.

  Nevertheless, for the 1990-98 period taxable sales growth was modest ranging from near 0% in the Los Angeles Basin and Rest of State region to 2.0% per year in the Bay Area.

- Total taxable sales will grow rapidly in California in the decade ahead. Real spending (i.e., adjusted for inflation) will grow by between 3.0% and 3.9% per year among regions — and each region will have growth faster than the national average. The San Diego and Sacramento regions will have the highest growth rates while the Bay Area, as a result of relatively low population growth, will have the smallest annual gains in taxable sales.

- Spending in the Los Angeles and Bay Area markets will increase by a combined $65 billion in 1998$ between 1998 and 2005. These two regions will still account for 71% of the state's taxable sales by 2005.

California and Economic Regions Total Taxable Sales 1990-2005 (Billions of 1998$)					Average Annual Growth		
	1990	1994	1998	2005	1990-1994	1994-1998	1998-2005
Los Angeles Basin	$161.6	$142.6	$164.1	$206.2	-3.1%	3.6%	3.35
San Francisco Bay Area	81.1	76.7	95.0	116.7	-1.4%	5.5%	3.0%
San Diego Region	26.1	24.0	29.8	39.0	-2.0%	5.6%	3.9%
Sacramento Region	17.6	17.0	19.6	25.4	-0.9%	3.6%	3.8%
Rest of State Region	53.7	48.2	53.0	67.8	-2.7%	2.4%	3.6%
California	**$340.1**	**$308.6**	**$361.6**	**$455.2**	**-2.4%**	**4.0%**	**3.3%**

Source: 1990, 1994 and 1998—California Board of Equalization; CCSCE; 2005—CCSCE

Population

- California's population is projected to increase by over 4.2 million between 1998 and 2005, averaging just over 600,000 new residents a year. The state will account for 13.2% of the nation's population in 2005 — up from 12.4% in 1998.

- Population growth slowed sharply during the recession as domestic migration turned negative. CCSCE expects that the state added nearly 600,000 residents in both 1997 and 1998 as continuing job growth reversed domestic migration trends and, once again, drew people into California.

- The Los Angeles Basin will add 2.0 million new residents (291,500 annually) to reach a population of 18.5 million in 2005. The Basin then will be home to more people than any state except Texas and, possibly, New York.

- The San Francisco Bay Area's job growth will require a substantial increase in population. The Bay Area will add 675,000 residents by 2005. Other workers will choose to live in adjacent counties outside the region.

The Bay Area is the only region in California where annual population gains so far in the 1990s are running ahead of 1980s growth levels. There are many regional efforts directed at making future housing growth more accessible to major job sites.

California and Economic Regions Population 1980-2005 (Thousands)				Average Annual Growth		
	1980	**1990**	**1998**	**2005**	**1980-1990**	**1990-1998**	**1998-2005**
Los Angeles Basin	11,589.9	14,640.8	16,407.3	18,448.0	305.1	220.8	291.5
San Francisco Bay Area	5,179.8	6,020.1	6,753.6	7,420.1	84.0	91.7	95.2
San Diego Region	1,861.8	2,498.0	2,819.8	3,252.7	63.6	40.2	61.8
Sacramento Region	1,099.8	1,481.2	1,697.2	1,968.9	38.1	27.0	38.8
Rest of State Region	3,936.6	5,118.1	5,872.1	6,710.4	118.2	94.2	119.8
California	**23,667.9**	**29,758.2**	**33,550.0**	**37,800.0**	**609.0**	**474.0**	**607.1**
United States	**226,542.2**	**248,718.3**	**270,029.0**	**285,982.0**	**2,217.6**	**2,663.8**	**2,279.0**

Source: 1980 and 1990—U.S. Census Bureau; 1998 and 2005—CCSCE (for July 1)

- San Diego experienced a return of strong population growth in 1997 and 1998 – averaging more than 60,000 per year and reversing a pattern of low annual gains in the early 1990s. The strong economy will continue to attract residents and annual gains in the decade ahead should match 1980s levels.

  Growth will put pressure on cities and the county to re-evaluate some current land use decisions so that housing may be located closer to job sites.

- The Sacramento and Rest of State regions led the state in population growth in the early 1990s. Recent population growth has trailed other areas as job gains in the San Joaquin Valley slowed. These regions should be among the state's fastest growing regions in future years.

- Despite high growth rates in the Sacramento, San Diego and Rest of State regions, the overall pattern of population shares will remain quite stable. The Los Angeles and San Francisco regions contained 69% of the state's population as of 1998. By 2005 these regions will still house more than two of every three Californians (68.4%).

- Each region in California will grow faster than the nation in the period to 2005. Even the slowest growing Bay Area region will have population gains of 10% compared to the projected 6% national gain.

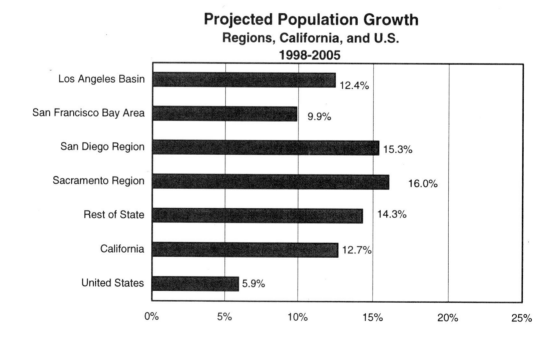

Projected Population Growth
Regions, California, and U.S.
1998-2005

Households

- California is projected to gain slightly more than 1.5 million households by the year 2005 — an increase of 207,300 per year. This growth is below record levels (e.g., 1985-1989) but is higher than the average growth in the 1980s and much higher than the household growth between 1990 and 1998.

- The Los Angeles Basin will add over 90,000 households per year leading all U.S. metropolitan markets. The Rest of State region will average 41,000 new households per year.

- California will account for 20% of the nation's new households between 1998 and 2005. CCSCE expects a surge in new household formation now that the economy is growing again. Moreover, household incomes are increasing significantly compared to housing prices for the 1990s.

- Household growth rates vary among regions in relationship to variations in job and population growth. The major other determinants of household growth are household formation rates which depend on:

  - Age and ethnic characteristics of the population

  - Trends in real household income

California and Economic Regions Households 1980-2005 (Thousands)							
					Average Annual Growth		
	1980	1990	1998	2005	1980-1990	1990-1998	1998-2005
Los Angeles Basin	4,169.5	4,933.6	5,214.1	5,910.3	76.4	36.2	92.8
San Francisco Bay Area	1,970.5	2,245.9	2,374.1	2,638.3	27.5	16.5	35.2
San Diego Region	670.1	887.4	951.8	1,120.3	21.7	8.3	22.5
Sacramento Region	416.3	556.5	628.1	745.5	14.0	9.2	15.6
Rest of State Region	1,403.6	1,757.6	1,959.5	2,268.2	35.4	26.1	41.2
California	**8,630.1**	**10,380.9**	**11,127.6**	12,682.6	175.1	96.4	**207.3**
United States	**80,390.0**	**91,947.0**	**101,400.0**	**109,000.0**	**1,155.3**	**1,220.3**	**1,013.3**

Source: 1990—U.S. Census Bureau; 1994 and 1998—U.S. Census Bureau, California Department of Finance (for Jan 1) and CCSCE; 2005—U.S. Census Bureau (U.S.) and CCSCE (for July 1)

Definition of Regional Economic Base

The classification of industries as basic and population serving changes as the analysis area moves from the state to the regional level. Once again seven categories of basic industries are used:

High technology   Diversified Manufacturing
Aircraft/Space/Defense   Resource Based
Transportation & Wholesale Trade   Professional Services
Tourism & Entertainment

However, the industries in each category are different in some cases at the regional level because the regional economic bases are broader in definition than the state economic base.

The regional economic bases include generally all industries classified as basic for California plus additional industries which are population serving at the state level but for which the regions compete for location. The best example is state government which is population serving at the state level of analysis, i.e., these jobs serve state residents. State government jobs are clearly basic (or open to competition) at the regional level as Sacramento's uniquely high share attests. Other examples of industries that are population serving at the state level and basic at the regional level are: stone, clay and glass; trucking; and hotels.

California Jobs By Major Basic Industry Group Regional Definition 1990-2005 (Thousands)						
					Change	
	1990	1994	1998	2005	1990-1994	1994-1998	1998-2005
High Tech Manufacturing	361.4	314.7	381.0	379.7	-46.7	66.3	-1.3
Diversified Manufacturing	1,285.1	1,196.6	1,348.8	1,414.3	-88.5	152.2	65.5
Aircraft, Space, Defense	480.5	304.3	254.5	238.4	-176.2	-49.8	-16.1
Resource Based	473.9	477.5	474.8	429.6	3.6	-2.7	-45.2
Transp. & Wholesale Trade	1,058.5	994.9	1,131.2	1,260.9	-63.6	136.6	129.7
Professional Services	1,248.8	1,261.4	1,442.3	1,740.1	12.6	180.9	297.8
Tourism & Entertainment	433.1	457.9	532.1	694.5	24.8	74.2	162.4
Total Basic Jobs	**5,341.3**	**5,007.3**	**5,564.7**	**6,157.4**	**-334.0**	**557.4**	**592.7**

Source: 1990, 1994, and 1998—EDD, CCSCE; 2005—CCSCE

The differences can be seen clearly by comparing Appendix Charts A-1 and A-2. The High Technology, Aircraft/Space/Defense, and Resource Based categories are nearly identical. The other groups are larger at the regional level. California's economic base using the regional definition is shown on the previous page.

The regional professional services category is changed in the 1999 edition. In previous editions the entire business services (SIC 73) industry was included in the regional definition of professional services. Beginning this year CCSCE has developed regional jobs estimates for jobs in computer services (SIC 737) which replaces business services in the professional services category and conforms to how SIC 73 and SIC 737 are categorized in the California/United States analysis.

The regional definition is used in the rest of the report and comparisons of each regional economic base to California should use the California economic base table on the previous page. Since the regional and state definitions of economic base do differ, it is necessary to use one California table when comparing to the U.S. and another when comparing to the regions.

The data in **California Economic Growth — 1999 Edition** are based on the 1987 SIC Code industry definitions. CCSCE extended some series back to 1979 where the 1987 SIC definitions were not comparable to the 1972 code and **EDD did not revise historical data**.

LOS ANGELES BASIN

LOS ANGELES BASIN

Summary

The Los Angeles Basin, home to 16.4 million residents and 5.2 million households, is the world's 12th largest economy. With a gross regional output in 1998 of $500 billion the Basin represents half of the large California market and accounts for over 5% of the nation's jobs and spending.

1994-1998: Recovery and Growth

The Los Angeles Basin is completing four consecutive years of economic recovery. Job growth from 1994 through 1998 outpaced the national average and in 1998 the region had 250,000 more jobs than in 1990 when the long recession began.

Los Angeles County remains below the pre-recession peak in jobs but just recently exceeded 4 million nonfarm wage and salary jobs – a level last reached in March 1991. All other metro areas in the region have now far surpassed the previous highs in jobs, income, and spending.

Construction markets joined the recovery in 1997. Housing prices rose strongly in 1998. Non residential construction is booming and vacancy rates are falling. Residential permit levels are finally rising as 1999 begins.

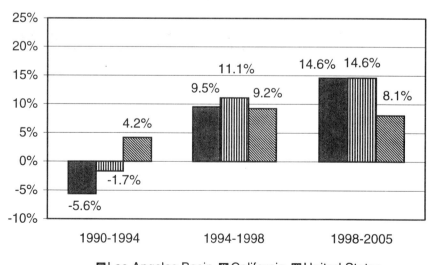

Past and Future Job Growth
Los Angeles Basin

■ Los Angeles Basin ⦀ California ⧄ United States

The Los Angeles recovery has been led by motion picture production, foreign trade, and gains in older manufacturing sectors like apparel, textiles, furniture, and toys where the region's creative talent has carved out growth niches. Moreover, aircraft job losses have ended and a modest turnaround is in sight based on rapid growth in commercial aircraft orders from which the region's suppliers will see increased business.

Tourism markets are growing. Hotel occupancy and room rates are rising. Plans for new construction and expansion are underway for hotels and the region's world class theme park attractions.

Future

The region has emerged from a major transition in its economic base. The defense and financial sector restructuring are almost complete.

Opportunities in industries where Southern California has a clear leadership position — foreign trade, entertainment and tourism, fashion and design — will create gains in jobs, income and population.

Construction should move into a period of strong growth based on increases in jobs, population, and households. CCSCE projects that total jobs will grow by 1 million (nearly 150,000 per year) or 14.6% between 1998 and 2005. The Basin will match the state growth rate and outperform the nation in the decade ahead.

1990-1994: Four Straight Years of Decline

The Los Angeles Basin had the largest economic decline in California. At the low point in 1993 the region had lost over 500,000 jobs. In addition, real income spending and construction all fell sharply.

Defense, construction, and retail spending declines explain the region's severe recession. The Los Angeles Basin was the location of most of the state's large job losses in the aircraft, space, defense sector. Construction fell between 50% and 75% in regional markets from 1989 to 1993. Real consumer spending fell by 15% between 1990 and 1993.

The region's share of total U.S. job peaked at 5.7% in 1989. By 1995 the Los Angeles Basin had only 5.1% of national jobs — the lowest share since 1972.

The share losses in manufacturing were even larger. From a high of 6.5% in 1986, the Basin by 1995 had fallen to just 5.2% of U.S. total manufacturing jobs.

Residents and economists feared that these figures indicated a persistent and irreversible loss of regional competitiveness. CCSCE wrote in 1993 and 1994 that this interpretation was not justified and the strong recovery that began in 1995 confirms our reading of the evidence.

There is no doubt about the size and persistence of the downturn in aircraft, space, and defense jobs. Between 1990 and 1994 nearly 120,000 direct jobs were lost. In addition, other related manufacturing jobs, for example, in metal products, were lost as a result of declining military and civilian aircraft orders. The pessimism was fueled by the fact that aerospace/defense job losses were continuing. In fact, another 16,000 jobs were lost between 1994 and 1997 before the sector posted a small job gain in 1998.

In 1989 over 115,000 residential building permits were issued in the region. By 1993 the number had declined to 28,700 — a 75.3% decline. The total value of all construction fell from $27.1 billion in 1989 to $11.3 billion in 1993 — adjusted for inflation. The region lost 68,000 jobs in construction and another 30,000 in related industries like wood products, furniture and stone, clay and glass.

Another major component of the region's sharp economic downturn was retail spending. Inflation adjusted taxable sales fell from $155.5 billion in 1990 to $132.2 billion in 1993 — a decline of 15% in just three years. As a result, retail trade jobs fell by nearly 100,000 by the end of 1993.

Financial restructuring was the final major contributor to regional job losses. Bank mergers, a decline in construction activity, and a move to greater use of technology reversed the long trend of job growth and led to substantial layoffs.

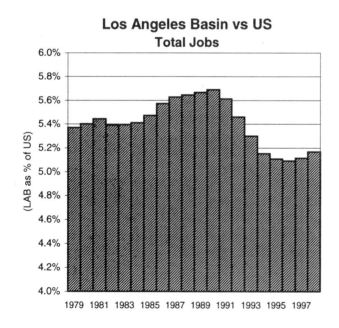

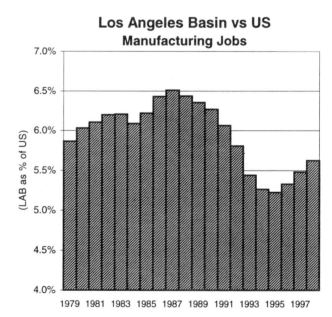

At the peak, more than 550,000 total jobs were eliminated in the Los Angeles Basin.

Los Angeles Basin Nonagricultural Wage & Salary Jobs (Thousands; Seasonally Adjusted)		
March 1990	6,307	
November 1993	5,752	
Difference	555	-8.8%

Source: EDD; Seasonally adjusted by CCSCE

However, as we see below, none of these factors destroyed the fundamental long term strengths of the regional economic base.

1994-1998: The Region Recovers

Record levels of foreign trade and motion picture production, a recovery in tourism, and gains in light manufacturing activities like apparel and toys are leading an economic recovery in the Los Angeles Basin.

Job levels in Orange County, the Riverside-San Bernardino metro area, and Ventura County are all now far ahead of pre-recession peaks. Only Los Angeles County remains with job losses – going above the 4 million level in November 1998 but still nearly 200,000 jobs below the pre-recession peak.

Orange County added more than 45,000 nonfarm jobs per year in both 1997 and 1998 (+3.5%/yr.). The strongest gains are in business and professional services and tourist related sectors. Manufacturing job levels have risen by 15,000 jobs since 1995.

The Inland Empire (Riverside and San Bernardino counties) showed continuing job gains while the rest of the region economy was in recession. The Inland Empire has benefited from gains in manufacturing and warehousing as well as continued migration from Los Angeles County and the associated growth in population serving jobs. The Inland Empire, since 1990, has grown faster than the national average.

Los Angeles County has now recovered approximately 80% of the 500,000 jobs lost after 1990. The rebound in construction and continuing gains in diversified manufacturing are raising job levels and the pre-recession peak should finally be exceeded in 1999.

Positive factors in the Los Angeles County economy include the strong gains in 1) motion pictures, 2) foreign trade, and 3) apparel and toy manufacturing.

Los Angeles Basin
Nonagricultural Wage & Salary Jobs
(Thousands; Seasonally Adjusted)

Metro Area	March 1990	November 1993	November 1997	November 1998
Los Angeles	4,187	3,676	3,913	4,003
Orange	1,181	1,113	1,247	1,293
Riverside-San Bernardino	711	736	858	899
Ventura	227	227	246	255
Los Angeles Basin	6,306	5,752	6,265	6,451

Source: EDD, seasonally adjusted by CCSCE

Income and spending have rebounded strongly since 1994 (see tables in Section 7). Total personal income, adjusted for inflation, reached $423 billion in 1998 exceeding the pre-recession high of $376 billion. Average household income is 6% above 1990 levels while per capita income surpassed the pre-recession peak (adjusted for inflation) by 1% in 1998.

Spending fell sharply between 1990 and 1994 — far exceeding the drop in income. By 1998 taxable sales at $164.1 billion finally passed the 1990 level of $161.3 billion (in 1998$).

Taxable sales grew throughout the region between 1994 and 1997 and early 1998 data suggest a continuation of strong growth last year. The region-wide gain of 16.0% is substantial when compared to the 6% increase in consumer prices.

Los Angeles Basin
Taxable Sales
($Millions)

County	1994	1997	Percent Change
Imperial	$1,041.1	$1,051.3	1.0%
Los Angeles	76,898.7	86,397.9	12.4%
Orange	28,276.3	34,921.4	23.5%
Riverside	9,814.5	11,972.4	22.0%
San Bernardino	11,843.5	14,005.0	18.2%
Ventura	6,026.2	7,042.7	16.9%
Los Angeles Basin	**$133,900.2**	**$155,390.6**	**16.0%**

Source: California Board of Equalization

Nonfarm Wage and Salary Jobs
Los Angeles Basin
March 1990-November 1998

Nonfarm Wage and Salary Jobs
Los Angeles County
March 1990-November 1998

Nonfarm Wage and Salary Jobs
Orange County
March 1990-November 1998

Nonfarm Wage and Salary Jobs
Riverside-San Bernardino
March 1990-November 1998

What is driving the region's economic base? Four contributors stand out:

- The motion picture industry is booming. Film starts in California surged in 1996 and 1997 and remained near record levels in 1998. Since January 1995 more than 50,000 wage and salary jobs (probably close to 90,000 total jobs) have been added in the industry.

- Foreign trade, especially exports, have risen throughout the recession and recovery. Trade volumes increased by 8% per year from 1990 through 1997 before the impact of Asian economic troubles hit in 1998.

- Southern California is the nation's leader in multimedia (see page 5-24), and the region has added nearly 30,000 software jobs during the recovery.

- The Basin is adding jobs in diversified manufacturing — with the largest gains in apparel, textiles and toys. Approximately 100,000 jobs were added between 1994 and 1998 as the Basin far outpaced nationwide growth

The regional economy is in transition. New sectors are emerging with the size and growth to replace defense and move the regional economy forward in the decade ahead. We turn to this story now.

The Los Angeles Basin Economy In Transition

It is no longer correct to think of the Los Angeles Basin as an economy dependent on defense. This means that the future of the regional economy will depend on what happens in other sectors. The key question is: Does the region possess the strengths to participate in the four fast growing sectors in California's economic base?

The changing structure of the Basin's economic base is shown graphically on the next page.

In 1972 there were three jobs in aircraft for every job in motion picture production. In 1998 there are 60,000 more jobs in motion pictures than in aircraft. Both sectors pay high wages (aircraft — $56,400; motion pictures — $64,900 in 1997) but the motion picture industry has, by far, the stronger growth potential.

LA Basin Economic Base in Transition

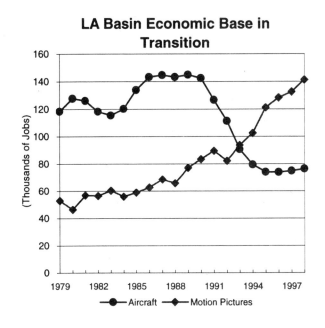

LA Basin Economic Base in Transition

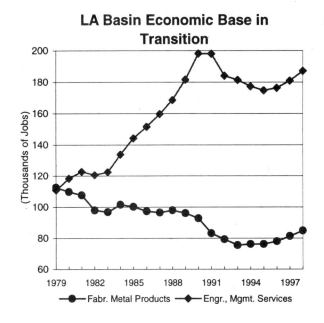

LA Basin Economic Base in Transition

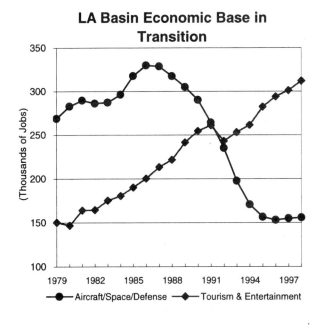

LA Basin Economic Base in Transition

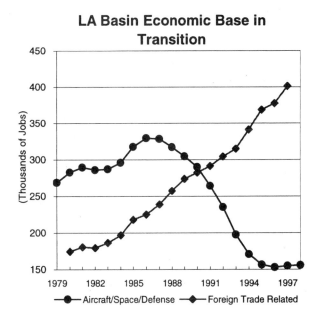

In 1972 there were two jobs in fabricated metal products for every job in the engineering and management services sector. In 1998 there are more than twice as many jobs in engineering and management services. The engineering and management service industries (average pay $52,600 in 1997) have strong growth potential.

In 1972 there were nearly 2½ jobs in the aircraft, space, defense sector for every job in tourism and entertainment. By 1998 the roles have reversed. There are more than twice as many jobs in tourism and entertainment than in aircraft, space and defense. The aerospace jobs do pay more, on average, but there are many high paying jobs in tourism and entertainment and that is where the growth will be.

In 1980 there were more jobs in aircraft, space, and defense than were associated with handling (not producing) the region's foreign trade. By 1997 there were more than twice as many jobs associated with handling foreign trade.

The transitions are producing a different economic base in the Los Angeles Basin.

In 1998 the region's 2.6 million basic jobs are distributed throughout CCSCE's seven categories. The largest share (31.2%) is in (professional diversified manufacturing services). The second largest sector, with over 577,000 jobs, is diversified manufacturing.[1]

Aircraft, space, and defense accounted for only 155,800 jobs — 6.1% of the Basin's economic base and 175,000 jobs below the 1986 peak levels. Tourism and entertainment had 317,900 jobs — far more than were in aerospace.

The Los Angeles Basin Economic Base — Past Performance and Future Prospects

The Los Angeles Basin possesses formidable long term strengths as evidenced in the strong recovery since 1994.

- A large diverse manufacturing base — despite the permanent loss of some aerospace jobs. The region possesses great strength in design and fashion which has led to gains in apparel and toy manufacturing as well as in other sectors such as textiles and furniture.

- The nation's largest tourism & entertainment complex. More than half of the nation's films are made in Los Angeles. The region possesses attractions for visitors from the state, nation and world.

---

[1] Note: The regional professional services category is defined more narrowly than in previous editions as described on p. 7-15.

Los Angeles Basin
Major Sector in Economic Base
1998

	Jobs (Thousands)	Change Since 1990
High Tech Manufacturing	107.7	-19.6
Diversified Manufacturing	796.7	-0.6
Textiles	22.5	8.9
Apparel	128.7	23.1
Furniture	44.4	-0.3
Printing, Publishing	74.2	-13.9
Chemicals	39.5	-0.6
Rubber & Plastic Products	55.5	-1.7
Fabr. Metal Products	84.9	-7.9
Non High Tech Machinery	129.1	-2.8
Aircraft/Space/Defense	155.8	-134.4
Aircraft	76.4	-66.1
Missiles & Space	12.4	-20.6
Search & Navig. Equipment	45.6	-33.8
Federal Civilian Defense	19.1	-13.4
Resource Based	71.7	-15.7
Transp.–Wholesale Trade	588.4	20.5
Trucking	75.3	11.0
Air Transportation	67.7	9.3
Wholesale Trade	425.2	-2.6
Professional Services	526.6	15.9
Computer Services	75.9	33.6
Legal Services	58.7	-9.4
Engr. & Mgmnt. Services	187.1	-11.0
Tourism & Entertainment	311.9	57.4
Hotels	77.1	-8.4
Motion Picture Production	141.3	57.8
Amusements	93.5	7.9
Total Economic Base	2,558.8	-76.4
Total Jobs	7,175.9	231.6

Source: CCSCE estimates based on January through October EDD data. See Appendix Chart A-2 for a list of regional basic industries.

- The Nation's largest port and airport complex located next to two fast growing market areas — Mexico and the Pacific Rim.

- The nation's second largest high tech and biotech complex built around Southern California's educational institutions, large pool of skilled labor and growing pool of venture capital funding.

- A large financial services complex serving both domestic and international markets.

- A growing number of new, small and medium size businesses. The region has been attractive to immigrant entrepreneurs who are bringing energy, innovation and international connections to the Basin's economic base.

The region has another great advantage: Diversity of locations for living and working. As one part of the region sees prices for housing and work space surge ahead, activity shifts to less expensive areas. The Los Angeles Basin has been able to offer alternative locations within its own regional boundaries.

Decentralization has allowed the region to accommodate substantial job and population growth. Whereas most jobs used to be located in Los Angeles County and northern Orange County, job nodes are now springing up in the Antelope Valley, western San Bernardino County around Ontario, and the Irvine area in Orange County. As population growth has shifted north and east to find affordable housing, new areas (such as the Ontario area) are now centrally located to large numbers of potential workers.

Diversified Manufacturing – The Los Angeles Basin has the nation's largest diversified manufacturing sector – a sector on the rebound after sharp losses associated with the declines in aerospace and construction markets. The sector surpassed 1990 job levels early in 1998 and continued to grow throughout the year. Moreover, the Basin has recaptured most of the share losses since 1986 and should reach a record high share of U.S. diversified manufacturing activity in 1999 or 2000.

Moreover, there is a substantial transition in the composition of the region's diversified manufacturing base away from heavy industry sectors towards industries which depend more on design, fashion, and craft skills and which are driven by newer, smaller, more entrepreneurial firms.

In the 1970s and early 1980s diversified manufacturing was a source of strength in the regional economy. The Basin boasted steady increases in its share of U.S. jobs and production.

The diversified manufacturing sector went into decline in the late 1980s — after defense spending started to fall but before the region's deep recession. The sector lost more than 100,000 jobs and fell from 5.4% of the nation's diversified manufacturing jobs in 1986 to less than 4.7% in 1994. The impact of construction declines should not be overlooked on sector job losses. Declines of 60% and more in construction spending led to declines in furniture; wood products; stone, clay and glass and other related manufacturing jobs.

A strong turnaround is now underway. Between 1994 and 1998 the region added both jobs and share. Four events account for the turnaround.

- The aerospace and construction declines have ended.

- U.S. economic growth averaged more than 3% per year.

- Foreign trade increased for diversified manufacturing products.

- Some sectors, notably textiles, apparel and toys are adding jobs by capturing new markets. As a result, the region's share of U.S. diversified manufacturing jobs has rebounded to almost 5.2% – near the mid 80s record levels.

The largest diversified manufacturing industry is apparel with 136,700 jobs in 1998. The Basin has 80% of the state's apparel and textile industry. Textiles account for another 22,500 jobs. Wholesale trade activities related to apparel account for another 25,000 jobs.

Los Angeles Basin Share of US Diversified Manufacturing

Apparel Jobs LA Basin vs United States

Los Angeles is a world leader in fashion design. The "Southern California look" is desired worldwide in women's and beach attire.

The apparel industry has grown in the region while declining nationwide. The Basin has added jobs and production while the national industry has shed more than 500,000 jobs since 1979.

The apparel industry retains future growth opportunities for four principal reasons.

- The design component gives Southern California a definite competitive advantage.

- Regional labor costs, while higher than foreign producers of "commodity" apparel, are actually much lower than European design competitors.

- The quick response time of the region's entrepreneurs is an advantage in the "just in time" retailing environment of discounters like Wal-Mart.

- There is a large base of family owned small businesses. The region's strong base of hard working immigrant entrepreneurs has created a set of businesses with the potential for forming networks and alliances to compete in a rapidly changing industry with strong international connections.

Continuing apparel industry growth faces new challenges. One challenge is to keep the cost gap narrow while foreign competitors remain fixed on lowering costs. Another challenge is to maintain the region's fashion advantage through joint industry/education training programs. Moreover, there is pressure for the industry to comply better with INS and EDD regulations.

These opportunities also require action on the part of the local industry. Recently the Los Angeles Basin apparel industry has been organizing to respond to future challenges. Initiatives sponsored by the industry itself, by a Southern California Edison led collaboration, and by the California Economic Strategy Panel were begun in 1997.

Southern California has a strong position in the biotech industry. In terms of public companies, the region ranks higher. The region ranks either first or second and has a significant share of national public companies according to a recent Ernst & Young report.

Southern California is the leader in biotech employees in public companies with 22,000 in 1997 or 23% of the national total. The region is also 1st in public company sales with $3.3 billion or 31% of the national total in 1997. Amgen is the national and regional leader in sales, sales per employee, and R&D expenditures.

	Public Biotech Companies ($Billions)					
	Employees		**Product Sales**		**R & D**	
	1997	**1994**	**1997**	**1994**	**1997**	**1994**
Bay Area	21,371	12,970	$2.6	$1.2	$2.0	$1.0
Los Angeles-Orange	22,000	6,940	3.3	1.9	.6	.3
New England	12,426	9,135	1.2	1.0	1.0	.7
San Diego	5,865	4,095	.4	.4	.6	.4
Total U.S.	94,492	52,675	$10.6	$5.2	$5.6	$3.8

Source: Ernst & Young

Toy manufacturing is a growth niche in the Basin. More than 6,000 jobs have been added since 1993 and the regional industry now boasts 28,900+ jobs. The sector is growing led by immigrant entrepreneurs who, like their apparel counterparts, find Los Angeles a good place to design and manufacture new products.

The Basin possesses large clusters in printing and publishing, plastics, chemicals, machinery, and petroleum. These sectors are projected to grow in production nationwide though job growth will be limited.

Because the diversified manufacturing sector is so large (796,700 jobs in 1998), its future competitive position is an important consideration in assessing the future of the Basin's economic base.

CCSCE projects that the region will add about 10,000 diversified manufacturing jobs by 2005 while job levels in the nation continue to decline. By 1998 the region's share of U.S. diversified manufacturing jobs had rebounded to over 5.1% – the highest level in the 1990s. The Basin's share should rise to record levels each year until 2005. CCSCE considers these projections to be conservative.

Positive factors that could push growth higher include:

- Strength in apparel, textiles, toys and biotech

- Projected growth in construction which will help the wood products and furniture industries

- Progress in implementing market based approaches to air quality by the SCAQMD (South Coast Air Quality Management District)

- Proximity to Pacific Rim markets, which remain the world's future leading growth markets despite the current turmoil

There are, however, negative factors in the region's competitive position. These include:

- Relatively high labor costs

- Relatively high housing costs despite very rapid rises in prices in other Western metro areas

- Questions about the region's quality of life (crime, schools, air quality, congestion)

The region's firms, as in other sectors, will compete mainly on the basis of technology and entrepreneurship — not as a low wage, low cost environment.

Foreign Trade — The region's ports and airports have posted a twenty year record of double digit gains in the volume of trade handled — between 1975 and 1997 trade volume grew by 12.8% annually. The growth in foreign trade supports job gains in professional services (like construction design and engineering), and financial services, wholesale trade, manufacturing, and tourism and entertainment.

Between 1987 and 1997 the volume of trade handled by the Basin's ports and airports grew from $77.6 billion to $185.9 billion — an average annual growth of 9.1%. By comparison the nation's trade grew by 8.9% per year. Trade volume has grown throughout the recession rising by more than 75% between 1990 and 1997.

Los Angeles Basin Foreign Trade Value of Exports and Imports 1987-1997 ($Billions)			
	Exports	**Imports**	**Total**
1987	$23.7	$53.9	$77.6
1990	$42.1	$64.6	$106.7
1997	$74.0	$111.8	$185.9
Average Annual Growth Rate 1987-1997			
Los Angeles	12.1%	7.6%	9.1%
California	12.7%	9.0%	10.3%
United States	10.5%	7.8%	8.9%

Source: U.S. Department of Commerce

Trade in services is important to the regional economy. Travel, the largest category of service exports, directly supports jobs in the Basin's large tourist cluster. Much of the nation's film and entertainment exports originate in the region and film export volumes have surged as discussed on page 5-29.

The graphs below show the rise of foreign trade passing through the region's customs districts. While the dollar volume of trade was surging, the region's share of U.S. trade also rose. Sharp gains in the 1980s pushed the region's share of total U.S. trade to near 12%. The 12% share has been maintained throughout the region's long recession – declining slightly from the impact of the Asian economic slowdown

Total Trade
LA Customs District

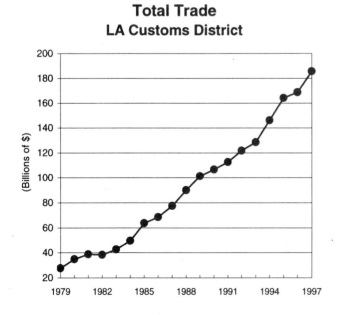

LA Basin Share of
US Foreign Trade

Exports produced in the region are surging. Between 1993 and 1997 exports produced by the region's firms rose from $27.4 billion to $37.8 billion — an increase of 38%. In addition all metro areas posted export gains in 1997.

Los Angeles Basin Exports Produced in the Region 1997 ($Billions)					
Destinations	Los Angeles	Orange	Riverside San Bernardino	Ventura	Los Angeles Basin
Mexico	$2.1	$1.4	$0.2		$3.7
Canada	2.8	1.0	0.3	0.2	4.3
Japan	5.9	1.4	0.3	0.1	7.7
Other Asia	7.3	2.3	0.7	0.3	10.6
Europe	4.7	2.0	0.4	0.3	7.4
Industries					
Transp. Equipment	8.4	0.6			
Ind. Mach & Computers	3.4	2.2			
Electronic Equipment	2.8	2.9			
Instruments	1.7	0.9			
Total Exports	**$25.8**	**$8.8**	**$2.1**	**$1.1**	**$37.8**

Source: International Trade Administration

Los Angeles County is the second largest goods export production center in the state. The county's $25.8 billion in 1997 exports ranked fifth behind San Jose and New York ($29.1 billion), Seattle and Detroit. Orange County's $8.8 billion ranks fourth in the state behind San Jose, Los Angeles, and San Francisco metro areas. Riverside-San Bernardino and Ventura trailed in export production but recorded the highest regional growth rates since 1993.

Los Angeles Basin Exports Produced in the Region ($Billions)			
Metro Area	1993	1997	Percent Change
Los Angeles	$20.0	$25.8	29.0%
Orange	5.7	8.8	55.6%
Riverside-San Bernardino	1.1	2.1	89.1%
Ventura	0.6	1.1	76.3%
Los Angeles Basin	**$27.4**	**$37.8**	**38.0%**

Source: International Trade Administration. Percentages calculated for unrounded data.

Most of the region's exports go to Asian countries. In 1996 Japan bought $8.6 billion from the region and other Asian countries accounted for another $9.8 billion. Europe was the next largest market ($7.0 billions) followed by Canada ($3.8 billion) and Mexico ($3.0). Exports to Mexico were up 50% since 1993.

Transportation equipment (primarily aircraft and parts) were still the leading export industry in 1996. High tech industries were the next three leading export sectors in the region.

The future for trade continues to be bright. Pacific Rim markets remain the world's growth leaders and approximately 40% of the nation's Pacific Rim trade goes through California ports and airports. See Section 3 for a discussion of the impact of recent developments in Asia. National and international trade agreements of recent years support the continued growth in this trade:

- The opening of Asian markets for financial and professional services

- Extension of most favored nation status to China

- The passage of the GATT and NAFTA agreements

- Progress on trade relationships with Japan and South Korea

- Relaxation of restrictions on technology exports

U.S. policy continues to support increasing market access around the world but especially with Pacific Rim countries. The opening of markets for financial and professional services will help Southern California firms. Negotiations for intellectual property right protection will be a big plus, if successful, for the region's entertainment and software/multimedia industries. In addition, the rapid growth of discretionary income in the Pacific Rim will support continued gains in tourism for Southern California destinations.

The passage of NAFTA should be a long run positive for the region. Trade with Canada and Mexico has increased substantially since the passage of NAFTA.

The Los Angeles Customs District (Los Angeles and Long Beach ports) is the largest port complex in the United States. It accounts for 25% of the nation's waterborne trade by volume.

The Los Angeles Customs District is the third largest container complex in the world. It ranks behind Hong Kong and Singapore but ahead of Rotterdam and the major port complex in South Korea.

These ports will play a larger role in future trade because world trade is being consolidated. Hub ports, able to unload increasingly large cargo ships of the future, are gaining share.

The Los Angeles and Long Beach ports are the preferred sites for west coast shipments destined for the rest of the nation. The Basin's ports, with an active construction program to accommodate an increasing number of large vessels, ship 40% of incoming cargo to destinations east of the Rockies.

Foreign Trade Volume in 1997

The region's ports and airports are continually challenged to expand capacity and technology. The ports are spending over $2 billion on internal port expansions and improvement. Los Angeles International Airport is in the process of selecting the preferred major expansion option to provide capacity for the region's growing passenger and air freight demands.

The Alameda Corridor, another $2 billion project, will link the ports to the national rail system in downtown Los Angeles. This project will increase the capacity to handle trade volume and reduce the associated traffic congestion. Final funding for the project has been approved and local communities are now negotiating final arrangements with the ports and key private sector participants.

Professional Services — Professional and other basic services are the third largest component of the region's economic base in terms of jobs. Professional services added over 180,000 jobs between 1979 and 1990 but have added only 15,900 jobs since 1990 as a result of the region's sharp recession.

As noted throughout the report, the relationship between manufacturing and service jobs is more complex in the 1990s than it was in the 1970s. First, manufacturing has a much larger contribution from service sector inputs — design, engineering, software. Second, some manufacturing job "losses" are really the result of contracting out services that were formerly done in house — accounting, software, data management, engineering.

The end result is that there is a closer link between professional services and manufacturing. Contract manufacturing is included in engineering services. The region is no longer an auto production center but is the location of one of the world's leading auto design clusters.

Software and multimedia (discussed in more detail in the Professional Services part of section 5) are the fastest growing high wage components of the professional services sector in the Los Angeles Basin. There is a close connection between these sectors and the Basin's entertainment complex discussed below.

Engineering and management services jobs increased from 111,000 in 1979 to 198,100 in 1990 before declining to 180,000 during the recession. Engineering and management services jobs recovered to 187,100 in 1998 and will be a major growth sector in the decade ahead.

Computer services are the fastest growing high wage sector in the region's economic base. Computer services (including software and Internet related jobs) increased from 20,100 in 1979 to 42,300 in 1990 and 75,900 in 1998. Legal services jobs more than doubled from 29,000 in 1979 to 58,700 in 1998 but are still below the 1990 peak.

Construction related services are becoming a growing national and export market. Additional professional services jobs that serve national and world markets exist in the financial sector but are not included in CCSCE's category.

Tourism & Entertainment — Tourism and entertainment jobs increased by over 100,000 between 1979 and 1990 and another 57,400 jobs were added since 1990. The sector accounts for more than twice as many jobs (311,900) as aerospace and defense (155,800) in 1998.

The California film industry was described above in *The California Economy to 2005* Section. Over 95% of the industry is located in the Los Angeles Basin.

The strong recent growth in production activity has brought nearly 50,000 new wage and salary jobs to the region since January 1995. The Los Angeles Basin remains the world center for most segments of the film industry. Recent developments indicate that the region is taking steps to maintain competitiveness in this fast growing high wage basic industry.

Newly published EDD estimates indicate that motion picture job growth continued in 1998 despite the slowdown in production growth. The region added nearly 8,000 production jobs to pass the 140,000 level in 1998.

Several new Southern California developments are underway which lay the foundation for future growth.

- The DreamWorks proposal for 1 million square feet of studio and sound stage developments in Playa Vista moved close to initiation.

- NBC has plans for an additional 1 million square feet of facilities in Burbank.

- The Motion Picture Association also reports recent and planned expansions by CBS, 20th Century Fox and Warner Brothers.

One major recent trend is the growing connection between the creative talent of Southern California and the technology base in Silicon Valley. Through joint efforts California is expanding the state's leadership position in new multimedia and animation projects.

Amusement job growth has been restrained since 1990 with gains of fewer than 10,000 jobs. On the other hand, major new developments are planned or underway including:

- the opening of the Getty Center

- large planned expansions of Universal City

- completed and future expansion at Disneyland

- new attractions – the Disney concert hall in Los Angeles and Aquarium of the Pacific in Long Beach

- major renovations for Dodger Stadium and the Anaheim Convention Center.

Major visitor, job, and spending growth is anticipated on the Basin during the next ten years.

Hotel employment is still below 1990 levels but occupancy and room rates are surging in 1998. The average hotel rate in Los Angeles County was $109.16 in October 1998 – up 9% from a year earlier with occupancy rates between 75% and 80% in recent months. Orange County room rates are also up 9% to $105 while occupancy is between 72% and 75%.

Aircraft, Space, Defense

The aircraft, space, and defense industry is covered in *The California Economy to 2005* section. Most of the manufacturing industry part of the sector is located in the Basin.

Job levels in the Basin have declined almost 50% since 1990. The 1998 job base of 155,800 accounts for only 6.1% of the region's economic base.

Los Angeles Basin Aircraft, Space, Defense Jobs 1986-2005 (Thousands)				
	1986	1990	1998 Est.	2005
Aircraft	143.2	142.5	76.4	78.5
Shipbuilding	5.2	2.8	2.3	2.2
Missiles, Space	30.0	33.0	12.4	9.5
Search & Navig. Equip.	116.3	79.4	45.6	36.0
Federal Civilian Defense	34.9	32.5	19.1	18.0
Total Sector	**329.6**	**290.2**	**155.8**	**144.2**

Source: EDD, CCSCE

In CCSCE's conservative projections aircraft, space, and defense jobs are projected to fall another 11,600 jobs by 2005 primarily all in the defense electronics (SIC 381) sector. There are a number of efforts underway to boost jobs in these industries like advanced transportation systems and information technology. The prospects for success are uncertain at this time.

It is, however, likely that renewed U.S. defense investment in technology will occur by the year 2005 which could boost employment in the region. For more discussion see the related material in Section 5.

Economic Base Projections to 2005

The region has good growth prospects in the four sectors of California's economic base that will lead the state's growth in the decade ahead. Foreign trade, professional services, tourism and entertainment, and high tech manufacturing will prosper in the region if CCSCE's California projections are on track.

Job growth in the region's economic base will be led by professional services (+92,500) jobs), transportation and wholesale trade (+60,300 jobs), and tourism and entertainment (+108,200 jobs).

However, maintenance of a strong position in the region's manufacturing base will be an important determinant of overall growth. The goal in diversified manufacturing is to make a transition to the high productivity manufacturing technology and operating systems of world class industries. For example, Germany exports textile products and machinery while paying wages higher than in the United States.

The main approach is to upgrade the technology of existing industries. The industry is examining collaborative efforts to develop high productivity approaches in the apparel and textile industry — an industry where the Los Angeles Basin has successfully captured a steadily growing share of the U.S. industry.

The idea of examining how the region's industry clusters can compete successfully in the 1990s has begun on an industry by industry basis under the leadership of regional public-private partnerships. The Regional Economic Strategies Consortium (RESC) is working with public and private groups in developing collaborative industry efforts. The California Economic Strategy Panel is also working with specific industry groups.

The region's industries and leaders are moving to respond both to the transition of the past four years and the opportunities facing the region in the decade ahead.

Los Angeles Basin Jobs By Major Basic Industry Group 1990-2005 (Thousands)						Change	
	1990	1994	1998	2005	1990-1994	1994-1998	1998-2005
High Tech Manufacturing	127.3	100.3	107.7	104.3	-27.0	7.4	-3.4
Diversified Manufacturing	797.3	706.0	796.7	809.5	-91.3	90.7	12.8
Aircraft, Space, Defense	290.2	170.7	155.8	144.4	-119.5	-14.9	-11.4
Resource Based	87.4	80.5	71.7	61.7	-6.9	-8.8	-10.0
Transp. & Wholesale Trade	567.8	519.5	588.4	648.7	-48.3	68.9	60.3
Professional Services	570.7	479.7	526.6	619.1	-31.0	46.9	92.5
Tourism & Entertainment	254.5	261.4	311.9	420.1	6.9	50.5	108.2
Total Basic Jobs	**2,635.2**	**2,318.1**	**2,558.8**	**2,807.7**	**-317.1**	**240.7**	**248.9**

Source: 1990, 1994, and 1998 —EDD, CCSCE; 2005—CCSCE

Jobs By Major Industry Group

The Los Angeles Basin had nearly 7.2 million jobs in 1998. The Basin accounts for half of the state's total economic activity. The Services sector is the region's largest major industry category. Services, led by business and health services, accounted for over 2 million jobs — more than a quarter of the Basin's total jobs.

Trade was the second largest sector with 1.5 million jobs. Manufacturing had more than one million jobs. The Los Angeles Basin still has over 50% of California's manufacturing activity. Also the region has the highest share of total jobs in the manufacturing sector (14.7%) among the state's economic regions.

Projections to 2005

Jobs in the Los Angeles Basin are projected to increase by more than 1.0 million between 1998 and 2005. In terms of absolute growth in jobs and production the Basin will show the largest regional expansion nationwide in the coming decade. The Basin's growth rate will also be higher than the projected job gain in the U.S.

					Change		
Los Angeles Basin							
Jobs By Major Industry Group							
1990-2005							
(Thousands)							
	1990	**1994**	**1998**	**2005**	**1990-1994**	**1994-1998**	**1998-2005**
Agriculture	59.7	54.8	50.9	41.2	-4.9	-3.9	-9.7
Mining	12.7	10.8	9.0	7.8	-1.9	-1.8	-1.2
Construction	258.4	202.8	248.8	270.3	-55.6	46.0	21.5
Manufacturing	1,196.5	964.9	1,052.9	1,052.9	-231.6	88.0	0.0
Transp., Pub. Utilities	294.1	290.7	320.9	370.9	-3.4	30.2	50.0
Trade	1,490.7	1,358.4	1,477.4	1,675.4	-132.3	119.0	198.0
Fin., Ins., & Real Estate	416.2	372.4	370.6	428.6	-43.8	-1.8	58.0
Services	1,720.0	1,750.1	2,004.9	2,625.1	30.1	254.8	620.2
Government	860.3	863.4	925.3	987.8	3.1	61.9	62.5
Self Employed	636.0	684.3	715.2	761.9	48.3	30.9	46.7
Total Jobs	**6,944.3**	**6,552.4**	**7,175.9**	**8,222.0**	**-391.9**	**623.6**	**1,046.1**

Source: 1990 and 1994—EDD with CCSCE estimate of self employed; 1998—CCSCE based on January-October EDD data; 2005—CCSCE

Nearly all the job gains will be in the broadly defined service economy. Services and Trade will be the two major industry groups and will account for more than three-quarters of the region's new jobs. Remember, however, that many of these jobs are in basic industries, and are a major part of the reason that the Basin will continue to have faster economic growth than the nation.

Income and Spending

The Los Angeles Basin represents half of the California market and over 5% of the national market in terms of income and spending. In 1998 the income earned by Basin residents reached $423.0 billion. The region would rank as the world's 12th largest economy measured in terms of total output and income.

Real (i.e., inflation adjusted) income and spending declined in the Los Angeles Basin between 1990 and 1994. The decline in taxable sales was far more severe than the drop in real total income.

A recovery in income and spending began in 1994. By 1998 real total personal income was more than 10% above 1990 levels. However, per capita income and real spending just regained 1990 levels after four years of economic recovery.

Gains in income and spending will continue in the decade ahead. Total real personal income is projected to rise 3.5% per year in the Basin between 1998 and 2005 — well above the anticipated 2.6% annual growth nationally.

Los Angeles Basin Income and Taxable Sales 1990-2005 (1998$)				
	Per Capita Income	Average HH Income	Total Personal Income (Billions)	Taxable Sales (Billions)
1990	$25,546	$76,282	$376.3	$161.6
1994	$23,277	$71,297	$364.1	$142.6
1998	$25,783	$81,132	$423.0	$164.1
2005	$29,198	$91,136	$538.6	$206.2
Average Annual Growth Rates				
1990-1994	-2.3%	-1.7%	-0.8%	-3.1%
1994-1998	2.6%	3.3%	3.8%	3.6%
1998-2005	1.8%	1.7%	3.5%	3.3%
California	1.8%	1.6%	3.5%	3.3%
United States	1.8%	1.6%	2.6%	

Source: U.S. Department of Commerce, California Board of Equalization

Spending growth for taxable sales has lagged behind income gains for two main reasons. First, the share of income spent on taxable items declined in the 1970s and 1980s as spending on housing and services (non taxable items) rose more quickly. Second, there was a clear decline in consumer confidence in the region after 1990. People held back on spending from concern about their future job and income security as well as the existing downturn.

Spending on taxable sales should grow more in line with income in the decade ahead. Regional spending on taxable items by households is projected to grow from $161.6 billion in 1998 to $206.2 billion in 2005 all in 1998$. This represents an annual spending growth of 3.3% — nearly the same as for total personal income.

Regional per capita income at $25,546 in 1998 is now below the national average. If the national economy produces productivity gains in the decade ahead as projected, per capita income in the Los Angeles Basin will grow by 1.7% per year and reach $29,198 by 2005 (in 1998$).

Per capita income will remain below the national average in 2005, primarily because region households have a large number of children. Household incomes, on the other hand, will remain above the national average.

Average household income in the Basin was $81,132 in 1998 — 15% above the national average. The Basin has larger households and more workers per household compared to the nation.

Average household income will increase by 1.7% per year and reach $91,136 in 2005 — 16% above the national average.

In general, income and spending in the Basin will keep pace with statewide growth rates and grow faster than projected national rates.

Construction Activity

A strong recovery in building activity is underway in the Basin. New building valuation rose by 42% between 1996 and 1998 led by gains in nonresidential construction. Existing home prices have rebounded and new residential construction is up modestly in 1998.

The fundamental determinants of long term construction growth — jobs, population, households, and affordability — continue to look solid in the decade ahead. The rebound in both residential and nonresidential construction should accelerate in 1999.

Construction: A Large and Cyclical Industry

The value of new building construction activity (excluding public works) in the Los Angeles Basin averaged $14.7 billion per year between 1970 and 1998 measured in 1998 prices. At the peak in 1988 and 1989 the new construction market reached over $27 billion or 8% of the region's total output. However, construction levels dropped to near $10 billion before recovering to the long term regional average in 1998.

An average of 76,400 new homes were built each year since 1970. The peak year for units was 1986 when total construction reached a record 161,300 units. The peak year for residential valuation ($17.2 billion) was 1989 when the high occurred for single family construction. However, residential building remained under 45,000 units per year since 1991.

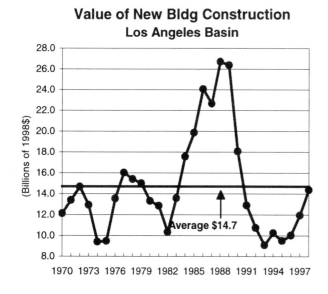

Value of New Bldg Construction
Los Angeles Basin

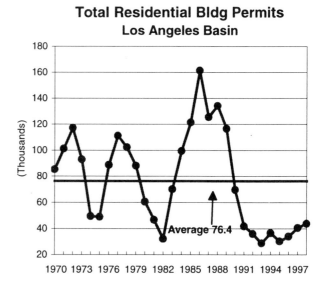

Total Residential Bldg Permits
Los Angeles Basin

Construction cycles are normal in the region. The Basin's construction cycles have coincided with periods of recession in the national economy — 1974/75, 1981/82, and 1990/91. The current downturn has, however, been extended while national residential construction markets have recovered.

Recent Construction Market Trends

There was a sharp decline in construction activity after 1989 throughout California. The Los Angeles region construction market has sustained the sharpest declines in the state. These declines are one reason why the Southern California economy had the most severe recession in the state.

Total annual new building construction in 1998 ($14.4 billion) showed a 44% increase from 1996 levels but remained 45% below 1989 levels. Los Angeles County is the most depressed market with 1998 construction levels less than one-half of 1989 valuation. Orange County now has the strongest rebound led by nonresidential building but is still 25% below 1989 levels.

The Inland Empire counties (Riverside and San Bernardino) posted nearly 50% gains in building since 1996 — also led by increases in nonresidential construction. 1998 construction levels in both counties, however, remain almost 50% below the 1989 spending.

| | Los Angeles Basin Construction Trends (Billions of 1998$) | | | | | |
| | New Building Construction | | | Residential Permits (Thousands) | | |
	1989	1993	1998	1989	1993	1998
Imperial	$0.1	$0.1	$0.1	0.8	0.6	0.4
Los Angeles	13.2	4.4	5.7	48.3	7.3	10.2
Orange	4.5	1.7	3.4	16.6	6.4	10.9
Riverside	4.1	1.2	2.3	25.7	7.3	12.3
San Bernardino	3.3	1.1	1.7	20.0	5.9	6.0
Ventura	1.1	0.5	1.0	5.0	1.4	3.4
Los Angeles Basin	**$26.4**	**$9.1**	**$14.2**	**116.4**	**28.8**	**43.1**

Source: Construction Industry Research Board; 1998 estimates by CCSCE based on Jan-Oct CIRB data

The low levels of residential permits since 1994 leave the region far below 1989 building levels. The Inland Empire counties had 18,800 permits in 1998, down 60% from the 45,700 permits issues in 1989. Los Angeles County had just over

10,000 permits — down nearly 80% from the 48,300 residential permits issues in 1989.

Orange County, aided by strong job growth, saw increased residential construction in both 1996 and 1997. Total permits were more than 11,000 in 1997 and near 11,000 in 1998 (aided by the region's strongest multi-family unit market) and are down only 25% from 1989 levels.

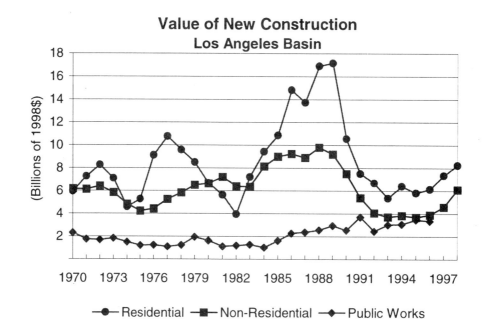

Value of New Construction
Los Angeles Basin

Affordability and Household Growth: The Foundations for a Housing Recovery

Interest rate declines, renewed job and population growth, and a move towards equilibrium with housing prices in other areas are laying the groundwork for a stronger residential construction market in the years ahead. The first signs of recovery appeared in 1997 with a rebound in resale prices throughout the region.

Even with income growth slowed by the recession, home prices and incomes have moved back towards balance since 1989. Moreover, home mortgage rates have fallen by more than 3 percentage points since 1989. Mortgage rates which used to be over 10% are now below 7%.

Affordability indices have rebounded in all regional submarkets. From the lows established in 1989, by the end of 1998 the median priced house will be affordable to nearly 40% of Los Angeles and Orange County households and 56% of all households in the Inland Empire, as calculated by the California Association of Realtors. Affordability is probably higher because the Realtor's index does not fully take recent income gains into account.

CCSCE expects that affordability will remain high in 1999. Income gains in 1998 and 1999 combined with low mortgage rates will push affordability up even with modest increases in median resale prices.

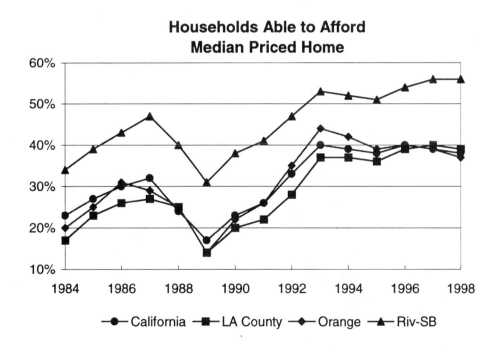

**Households Able to Afford
Median Priced Home**

Prices in competing western housing markets moved much closer to Southern California prices in the 3rd Q of 1998. Median resale prices in the Inland Empire ($125,000) are now lower than in Denver ($149,100), Las Vegas ($130,600), Portland ($160,600), Salt Lake City ($133,100), and Seattle ($200,600) and are close to third quarter 1997 median prices in Phoenix ($121,900). Median prices in Los Angeles County ($197,400) are closer to competing areas than at any time in the past 20 years and only Orange County median prices ($273,000) remain substantially above those in competing markets.

Job growth and demographic trends point to higher household formation in the region. Job growth should average near 150,000 per year (comparable to 1980s levels) and much above the low growth levels of the 1990-1998 period. As a result, household growth is projected to average 93,000 per year between 1998 and 2005.

The projected household growth will support new residential construction averaging around 100,000 units per year from 1998 to 2005. Even though it remains difficult to envision in today's depressed market, the demographic projections and positive affordability trends point to a strong residential market in the Los Angeles Basin in the years ahead.

Nonresidential Construction: Analysis and Outlook

Total nonresidential new construction in the Basin (excluding public works) peaked in 1988 and 1989 at near $10 billion in 1998 prices. In 1998 total nonresidential valuation had recovered to $6 billion (a 60% recovery from the 1993 low) — excluding public works because the Construction Industry Research Board has temporarily suspended publications of spending estimates for this category.

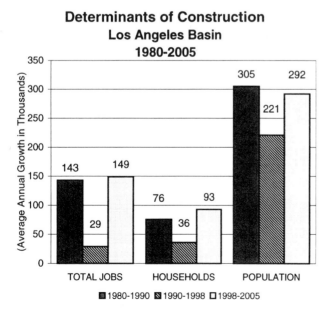

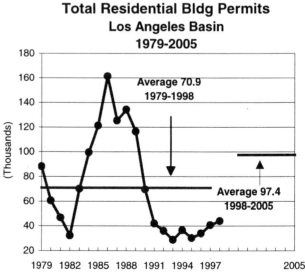

It is helpful to disaggregate the nonresidential market in order to understand what has happened in the current downturn and to assess the prospects for recovery. The declines in commercial and industrial construction are well known to anyone who follows the California economy.

Los Angeles Basin Nonresidential Construction (Billions of 1998$)			
	1989	**1993**	**1998**
Commercial	$4.5	$1.1	$2.5
Industrial	1.1	0.2	0.9
Other Nonresidential	0.9	0.5	0.6
Alterations/Additions	2.6	1.9	2.2
Heavy Construction	2.9	3.0	
Total Building Construction	**$9.1**	**$3.7**	**$6.2**
Total (incl Heavy)	**$12.0**	**$6.7**	

Source: Construction Industry Research Board

Commercial construction includes office buildings, retail stores, and hotels as well as parking garages, recreation facilities, and service stations. After averaging $4 to $5 billion per year in new construction in the mid 1980s, overbuilding and recession combined to reduce commercial valuation to $1.1 billion in 1993. A strong recovery to $2.5 billion in 1998 still left commercial building levels 45% below the previous peak.

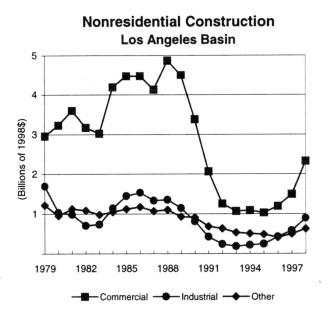

Nonresidential Construction
Los Angeles Basin

—■—Commercial —●—Industrial —◆—Other

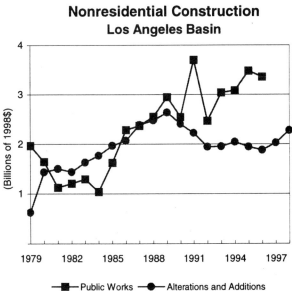

Nonresidential Construction
Los Angeles Basin

—■—Public Works —●—Alterations and Additions

Industrial construction rose sharply in 1997 with large gains in Orange, Riverside, and San Bernardino counties. The industrial market is currently the tightest construction market in the region and 1998 permit levels reached nearly $1 billion – still below mid 1980s levels.

Two categories of nonresidential construction gained significantly between 1979 and 1998. The value of alterations and additions grew steadily to 1989 and plateaued at $2 billion per year until rising again in 1998. It is the second largest category of nonresidential building in the 1990s to date. Alterations and additions are related to upgrading the existing stock of buildings. The size of the existing stock of buildings has always grown even when new construction slows down.

Heavy construction ("public works") has grown to where it is now the largest category of nonresidential building in the Los Angeles Basin — averaging over $3 billion in the 1990s.

Outlook for Future Growth

Total nonresidential construction activity should expand in the years ahead. CCSCE projects that the fundamental determinants of construction activity — job and household growth — will recover in the region and reach levels last experienced in the 1980s.

Commercial building should increase as higher job levels fill existing space. Office vacancy rates are falling in most parts of the region and office job levels are reaching record levels.

Public works construction will be very strong in the years ahead.

- The Alameda corridor construction is near, expansion plans are being developed for LAX and other regional airports and expansions are planned for both of the region's major ports

- There is a major expansion of federal transportation funding

- School enrollment increases and class size reductions will create demand for new facilities and the $9.2 billion state bond issue and locally passed bonds will fund a surge in new construction

- New facilities, e.g., the downtown LA sports arena, Disney concert hall, and the entertainment industry expansions are in process

As available industrial and commercial space is filled by growing jobs, population, and tourists, the nonresidential construction rebound that began in 1997 should continue and expand in the period ahead.

SAN FRANCISCO BAY AREA

SAN FRANCISCO BAY AREA

Summary

The San Francisco Bay Area, with a population of 6.8 million residents, is the fifth largest metropolitan market in the United States. With a 1998 regional gross product of $283 billion, the Bay Area is the world's 19th largest economic market.

Per capita income levels in the Bay Area are the highest in California. Moreover, per capita and household incomes are now more than 30% above the national average. The Bay Area is the wealthiest regional market of comparable size anywhere in the world.

The Bay Area has emerged from the early 1990s recession with a surge of economic growth based primarily on the region's technology base. Four examples show the strength of the Bay Area economy in 1997:

- Bay Area job growth between 1994 and 1998 was 13.3% — outpacing both the state (+11.1%) and national (+9.2%) job increases.

- Venture capital funding will increase nearly 20% in 1998 to reach approximately $4.4 billion — the ninth straight year of increase and one-third of the national total.

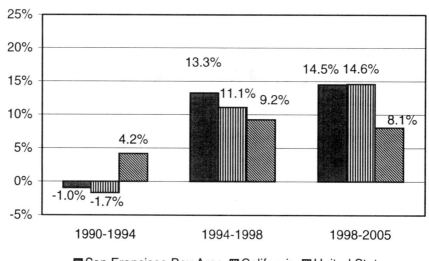

Past and Future Job Growth
San Francisco Bay Area

■San Francisco Bay Area Ⅲ California ◩United States

- Silicon Valley average wages increased 5.7% in 1996 to reach $44,819 — the second highest metro area in the nation. The Bay Area average wage gained 4.9% to $37,966 — the second highest regional average nationwide.

- Silicon Valley recorded the largest increase in exports ($12.9 billion) of any metropolitan area in the United States between 1993 and 1997 — all in high tech manufacturing sectors. Silicon Valley's $29.1 billion in 1997 tied the area with New York as the largest export producing metro area in the nation — all of this despite an Asia related decline in exports in 1997.

The Bay Area's economic base is solidly positioned to participate in the four high growth sectors identified by CCSCE. The region's strength in these sectors — high technology, foreign trade, tourism and entertainment, and professional services — should increase the already large gap in average income levels between the Bay Area and the nation.

Two future growth markets — multimedia and tools to access and use the Internet — symbolize the Bay Area's bright opportunities for long term growth. Silicon Valley is acknowledged as the world leader in many segments of both markets.

The Bay Area will grow faster than the nation but more slowly than other regions of California in the decade ahead. The Bay Area will add an average of 73,300 jobs per year to 2005.

The pressures of growth are occurring first in the Bay Area. Traffic is increasing, vacancies are low, and home prices and rents are rising. Continuing economic gains are raising concerns and challenges of growth last heard in the booming late 1980s. The issues of land use, quality of life and economic growth are explored further in Section 6.

1994-1998: A Region Surges Ahead

The Bay Area economy has outpaced the nation in job growth since 1994. Job levels in the Bay Area increased by 13.3% between 1994 and 1998 compared to a 9.2% gain in the nation and 11.1% gain in California.

The region has been led by strong job gains in Silicon Valley. Job levels in Santa Clara County (San Jose Metro Area) are now 130,000 above pre-recession peaks having added 35,000 jobs per year for the past four years.

All metro areas in the region reached record job levels in 1998. The East Bay and Sonoma County posted the largest growth rates. The San Francisco metro area joined the recovery in 1996 and has a 2% job growth rate in 1998.

Silicon Valley job growth slowed dramatically in mid 1998. During the first four months of 1998 Silicon Valley job levels were 42,000 (4½%) above 1997 levels. For the four months ending in November year over year job gains had dropped to an average of 14,000 (+1½%).

| San Francisco Bay Area Nonagricultural Wage & Salary Jobs (Thousands: Seasonally Adjusted) | | | | |
Metro Area	March 1990	January 1994	November 1997	November 1998
Oakland	883	874	965	989
San Francisco	954	901	997	1,016
San Jose	822	794	944	953
Santa Rosa	138	138	168	172
Vallejo-Napa	141	144	153	159
Bay Area	2,938	2,851	3,227	3,289

Source: EDD, CCSCE seasonal adjustment to EDD data

Income and spending have grown rapidly since 1994. Real per capita income in the Bay Area leads California both in terms of ① the highest level statewide and ② the largest increase since 1994. Bay Area per capita income at $35,381 in 1988 is 33% above the national average and 31% above the state average. The Bay Area has also outpaced both the state and nation in real income growth.

Per Capita Income (1998$)			
	1994	1998	Percent Change
Los Angeles Basin	$23,277	$25,783	10.8%
San Francisco Bay Area	31,849	35,381	11.1%
San Diego Region	23,451	26,003	10.9%
Sacramento Region	24,759	27,230	10.0%
California	24,425	26,982	10.5%
United States	24,285	26,466	9.0%

Nonfarm Wage and Salary Jobs
San Francisco Bay Area
March 1990-November 1998

Nonfarm Wage and Salary Jobs
Oakland Metro Area
March 1990-November 1998

Nonfarm Wage and Salary Jobs
San Francisco Metro Area
March 1990-November 1998

Nonfarm Wage and Salary Jobs
Santa Clara County
March 1990-November 1998

Income growth and a surging business sector are leading to spectacular gains in taxable sales. Taxable sales in the Bay Area reached $89 billion in 1997 — up nearly 30% over 1994 levels. Consumer prices increased by less than 8% during those three years. The region was led by strong business related taxable sales in Santa Clara County. The early data for 1998, cited in Section 3, suggest that growth in taxable sales is continuing.

San Francisco Bay Area Taxable Sales ($Millions)			
County	1994	1997	Percent Change
Alameda	$14,164.1	$18,523.6	30.8%
Contra Costa	7,818.2	9,277.4	18.7%
Marin	2,564.6	3,108.2	21.2%
Napa	1,024.2	1,327.1	29.6%
San Francisco	8,798.3	10,966.2	24.6%
San Mateo	8,172.6	10,733.8	31.3%
Santa Clara	19,633.2	29,651.5	37.3%
Solano	2,754.9	3,254.6	18.1%
Sonoma	3,951.9	4,989.9	26.3%
San Francisco Bay Area	$68,882.2	$89,132.3	29.4%

Source: California Board of Equalization

The Region's Economic Base

The San Francisco Bay Area has a diversified economic base. The 1.3 million jobs in the Bay Area's economic base are distributed throughout CCSCE's seven major categories as shown on page 9-7. The region has a comparatively small exposure in the slow growing resource and aircraft, space, defense sectors.

The Region's Emerging Economic Base — The San Francisco Bay Area possesses a number of strengths which will be the foundation for job growth in the decade ahead:

- A large and highly skilled labor force. The Bay Area has one of the nation's largest concentrations of scientific, professional and managerial talent and the state's most highly educated workforce

San Francisco Bay Area
Major Sectors in Economic Base
1998

	Jobs (Thousands)	Change Since 1990
High Tech Manufacturing	204.4	20.1
Computers	58.7	-2.4
Electronic Components	88.3	14.6
Instruments	57.7	7.8
Diversified Manufacturing	265.9	18.5
Food Products	38.5	0.3
Apparel & Textiles	19.8	0.2
Printing & Publishing	36.9	0.1
Chemicals	20.4	-1.7
Non High Tech Machinery	67.9	18.6
Aircraft/Space/Defense	28.5	-43.2
Resource Based	35.7	-0.9
Transportation – Wholesale Trade	272.9	20.0
Trucking	32.8	4.6
Air Transportation	47.9	8.1
Wholesale Trade	183.8	10.1
Professional Services	434.2	87.6
Computer Services	126.3	79.2
Legal Services	34.8	-2.1
Engr. & Mgmnt. Services	130.2	21.1
Tourism & Entertainment	91.7	18.4
Hotels	44.1	1.1
Amusements	43.2	14.6
Total Economic Base	1,331.8	119.0
Total Jobs	3,617.4	392.5

Source: CCSCE estimates based on January through October EDD data. See Appendix Chart A-2 for a list of regional basic industries.

- Leading educational institutions, such as Stanford University and the University of California in Berkeley, with world class programs in science and engineering

- One of the nation's largest concentrations of technology and related venture capital firms

- A leading position in new growth sector — biotech, multimedia, and providing access to information

- A highly attractive quality of life including outstanding climate and proximity to unique environmental and outdoor recreation opportunities

High Technology — The Bay Area is well known for its high technology manufacturing companies. In 1998 the major high tech manufacturing industries employed 204,400 workers. Most of the industry is located in Silicon Valley (Santa Clara County) although recent trends have pushed more high tech manufacturing into the East Bay. New industries such as biotech, Internet tools, and advanced telecommunications are being added to the region's base in computers, semiconductors and instruments.

In a real sense the future of the Bay Area high tech complex is tied to national trends — the success of the U.S. industry in worldwide competition in the 1990s. Two major trends — 1) rapid growth in sales, exports, profits, and wages and 2) more modest opportunities for job growth as a result of strong productivity gains — were covered in *The California Economy to 2005* section.

For the Bay Area economy the key question is — is the Bay Area losing its competitive position? Is the region positioned to fully participate in these high growth markets?

High tech has remained a high and rising portion of Silicon Valley's manufacturing base. Over 60% of Silicon Valley manufacturing is in high tech (and the share is growing) compared with 9% nationwide. For the Bay Area as a whole, nearly 40% of manufacturing jobs are in high tech. **Silicon Valley and Bay Area manufacturing remains concentrated in future high growth areas!**

The Bay Area had 7.2% of U.S. high tech manufacturing jobs in 1975. The Bay Area share rose to 10.2% in 1984. The region's share of national high tech jobs has remained steady for over a decade before hitting a record 11.6% share in 1997.

The region's share of the nation's high tech jobs remained at record levels in 1998 despite the region's relatively high share of U.S. Asian export losses. This confirms CCSCE's finding that the 1998 impacts reflected what happened to a big customer (Asia) and did not indicate a long term weakness in the region's competitive position.

Losses of electronics assembly jobs to other regions has been fully offset by the growth in high wage R&D and startup manufacturing jobs. Far from losing share, the Bay Area is poised to gain even a larger future share based on the surge in start ups and IPOs in the region.

Data for 1997 and 1998 confirm that Silicon Valley high tech manufacturing remains very competitive.

- Sales of the 150 largest high tech firms hit a record $185.3 billion in 1997, up 8.7% from 1996 and nearly double 1993 levels.

- Profits reached a record $15.4 billion, up 15% from 1996 and more than triple 1993 levels.

- Nearly 90% of the companies' sales and profits are related to high tech.

- Venture capital funding reached a new record in 1998 ($4.4 billion) continuing to lay the foundation for future high tech job growth.

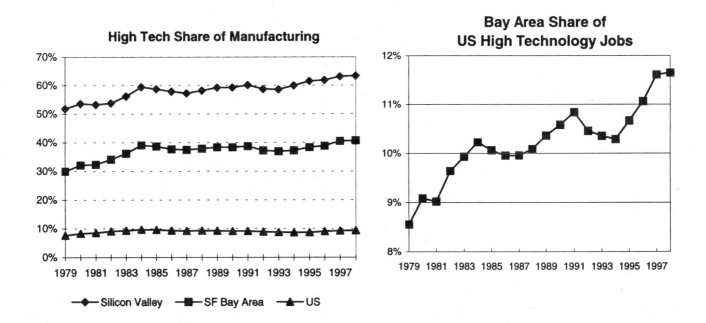

		Silicon Valley			
		150 Largest Companies			
		($ Millions)			
Sector	Number of Companies	1997 Revenue	1997 Profits	1993 Revenue	1993 Profits
Computers	6	$61,997	$2,931	$37,779	$442
Semiconductors	28	39,791	7,799	16,505	2,876
Disk Drives	8	16,681	782	9,203	-117
Other Technology	16	10,841	739	5,810	176
Software	24	13,746	1,055	4,989	149
Other Non-Technology	19	12,140	375	6,737	132
Networking	6	12,188	1,122	2,641	301
Semiconductor Mfg. Equip.	13	8,540	468	2,270	166
Telecommunications	10	2,499	128	1,271	55
Retailing	7	3,061	120	2,307	39
Peripherals	6	1,870	63	1,957	87
Medical/Pharmaceuticals	7	1,933	167	3,454	322
Total	**150**	**$185,288**	**$15,415**	**$94,923**	**$4,628**

Source: San Jose Mercury News, April 19, 1998

The Bay Area is the nation's biotechnology capital. A recent Ernst and Young survey identified 61 public biotech firms in the Bay Area — tops in the nation. These firms are pushing the genetic frontier to make new products for health care, agriculture, and environmental markets. Leading firms in the region include Genentech (3,200 employees), Chiron (1,900 employees) and Alza (1,000 employees) – three of the nation's five largest biotech firms.

Public Biotechnology Industry in 1997 Number of Firms	
San Francisco Bay Area	61
New England	54
San Diego	33
New Jersey	22
New York	20
Los Angeles—Orange County	14

Source: Ernst & Young

In terms of public companies, the Bay Area also ranks first or second on most biotech indicators. The Bay Area ranks first in R&D expenditures and assets, and second in product sales and the number of employees as shown below.

| | **Employees** | | **Product Sales** | | **R & D** | |
	1997	**1994**	**1997**	**1994**	**1997**	**1994**
Bay Area	21,371	12,970	$2.6	$1.2	$2.0	$1.0
Los Angeles-Orange	22,000	6,940	3.3	1.9	.6	.3
New England	12,426	9,135	1.2	1.0	1.0	.7
San Diego	5,865	4,095	.4	.4	.6	.4
Total U.S.	94,492	52,675	$10.6	$5.2	$5.6	$3.8

Public Biotech Companies
($Billions)

Source: Ernst & Young

The industry has steadily expanded in firms, employment, and sales. However, as yet there has not been the rapid increase in jobs associated with the early growth phase in semiconductors or computers.

The products of bioscience offer possibilities for major changes in areas ranging from drug therapies to agriculture to environmental cleanup. While the dimensions of future job and income growth are still uncertain, the Bay Area retains a leadership position and will participate fully in future growth.

Two new areas have emerged in recent years — multimedia and services related to the Internet.

Multimedia is a "fusion technology" that reflects the integration of several different industries, including design, software, publishing, computers, communications equipment, and consumer electronics. Multimedia reflects the increasing importance of information based technologies and industries.

The Bay Area and Hollywood are developing the world's strongest multimedia alliance. These alliances merge the technology base of Silicon Valley with the creative talent of Hollywood. A good example of this merger is the recent collaboration of Silicon Graphics and DreamWorks to create the first end-to-end digital studio. Lucas Arts and Broderbund Software represent Bay Area leaders in other segments of the multimedia cluster.

The Bay Area is a major player in the U.S. multimedia sector (the second largest industry concentration following Southern California).

The Bay Area is the home of the Internet access industry. Netscape, developer of the most popular Internet browser, is headquartered in Mountain View. Collabra and Netcom represent other segments of the Internet market.

Technology Focus on R&D — The Bay Area has been accomplishing what other regions yearn for. The Bay Area is identified as the place to be for the high paying, high value added segment of the growing technology market.

The region's labor force, university base, venture capital cluster, and high quality of life are the economic foundations that have attracted record levels of venture capital to new technology startups. Both in Internet tools and more traditional areas the region's firms specialize in the development of new ideas and new products.

The focus on providing an environment for world class R&D facilities has allowed the region to maintain high incomes and offset the worldwide decline in technology assembly and routine manufacturing jobs. Business leaders now realize that quality of life is a critical determinant of continued economic success. Recent reports by the Bay Area Council and Joint Venture: Silicon Valley Network clearly state that land use, housing and environmental quality decisions are linked to the potential for continued high tech growth in the Bay Area.

Foreign Trade — San Francisco has a fast growing foreign trade cluster. The volume of trade expanded by 11.5% per year between 1987 and 1997. Customs district volume growth far exceeded the 10.3% annual state growth and the 8.9% annual gains in the nation.

San Francisco Foreign Trade Value of Exports and Imports 1987-1997 ($Billions)			
	Exports	**Imports**	**Total**
1987	$14.3	$21.8	$36.0
1990	$23.1	$28.1	$51.3
1997	$48.2	$58.8	$107.0
Average Annual Growth Rate 1987-1997			
San Francisco	12.9%	10.5%	11.5%
California	12.7%	9.0%	10.3%
United States	10.5%	7.8%	8.9%

Source: U.S. Department of Commerce

In 1997 custom district export volume was $48.2 billion and total trade volume was $107 billion. Bay Area export volume began to slow in 1997 and 1998 as high exports leveled off. Recent trends are discussed in Section 3.

The Bay Area's export growth has been led by high tech exports to Pacific Rim countries. Export statistics released by the International Trade Administration show Silicon Valley had the largest value of exports produced in 1997 ($29.1 billion tied with New York) among U.S. metropolitan areas.

Over 90% of Silicon Valley's exports are in high tech and all the growth is occurring in these sectors. Asian markets are accounting for the largest share of Bay Area exports. Silicon Valley exports increased 80% since 1993 and recorded the largest dollar gain nationwide despite a decline in 1997 trade volumes.

Destination	Oakland	San Francisco	San Jose	Santa Rosa	Vallejo-Napa	SF Bay Area
San Francisco Bay Area Exports Produced in the Region 1997 ($Billions)						
Mexico	$0.2	$0.5	$0.8			$1.4
Canada	0.8	.3	3.4			4.5
Japan	1.3	2.1	4.8	.2		8.4
Other Asia	2.8	2.9	11.7	.2	.1	17.7
Europe	1.4	2.9	6.8	.3	.1	11.5
Industries						
Elec. Machinery	$2.1	$2.2	$11.9			
Ind. Mach. & Computers	1.8	1.7	13.0			
Instruments	.5	.8	2.7			
Food Products	.5	.8	.1			
Transp. Equipment	.2	1.7	.2			
Total Exports	**$6.9**	**$10.0**	**$29.1**	**$.9**	**$.4**	**$47.3**

Source: International Trade Administration

Bay Area exports increased by 56% between 1993 and 1997. At $47.3 billion the Bay Area far surpasses the Los Angeles region in exports produced. The Oakland metro area posted strong export gains while exports produced in the San Francisco metro area rebounded in 1998 (+$1.4 billion) to move slightly ahead of 1993 levels.

The Oakland metro area followed the Silicon Valley pattern of high tech exports to Asian markets.

San Francisco Bay Area Exports Produced in the Region 1993-1997 ($Billions)			
Metro Area	**1993**	**1997**	**Percent Change**
Oakland	$4.2	$6.9	65.5%
San Francisco	9.3	10.0	7.7%
San Jose	16.2	29.1	79.7%
Santa Rosa	.4	.9	109.3%
Vallejo-Napa	.2	.4	124.1%
SF Bay Area	**$30.3**	**$47.3**	**56.1%**

Source: International Trade Administration; Percentages based on unrounded data.

Tourism and Entertainment — The Bay Area attracts tourists from around the world. Attractions like San Francisco, Point Reyes, Monterey, the Wine Country and the entire northern coastal region offer unique opportunities for recreation and relaxation.

California benefits from locations close to fast growing Pacific Rim markets. The Bay Area participates in these growing markets. International travel is rising based on growing worldwide discretionary income.

Professional Services — Professional services are another of the Bay Area's economic strengths. The legal, software and engineering/management service clusters provide services to the region's high tech firms, other Bay Area industries, and export markets throughout the nation and the world. **Much of the job growth associated with expanding technology industries shows up in service sector jobs.**

As in other regions, professional services have and will provide the largest number of new high paying jobs in the Bay Area's economic base. The relationship between professional services and the Silicon Valley technology complex is an important component of Silicon Valley's success in attracting new firms.

San Francisco Bay Area Growth in Computer Service Jobs (Thousands)			
Metro Area	July 1993	1st Q 1998	Percent Change
San Jose	27.3	58.9	116%
San Francisco	18.0	36.7	104%
Oakland	11.3	22.0	95%
Santa Rosa	0.6	1.1	83%
Vallejo-Napa	0.3	0.8	167%
Bay Area	**57.5**	**119.5**	**108%**

Source: EDD

Software jobs are the region's largest high wage growth sector. Recent data show that the Bay Area added more than 60,000 software jobs between 1993 and 1998 and by the end of 1998 had more than 120,000 software jobs. While Silicon Valley is the nation's software growth leader, other Bay Area subregions are participating in the growth. The San Francisco metro area has added nearly 20,000 jobs — many associated with San Francisco's growing multimedia sector.

Software jobs have increased by 108% in the past five years in the region.

These jobs pay an average of $75,000 in the East Bay, $80,000 in San Francisco and $90,000 in Silicon Valley firms.

Internet services and multimedia jobs are often classified in SIC 737 – Computer Services and it is difficult to identify each industry segment separately. The Bay Area is home to industry leaders like Netscape, Yahoo, and Excite; Pixar (computer animation), E-Trade (on-line brokerage services) and 3DO (interactive multimedia products).

Economic Base 1990-1998: The Surge Back from Recession

The Bay Area's economic base has led the state out of recession. Following a loss of 40,000 jobs between 1990 and 1994, the Bay Area added 175,000 basic jobs (+13.2%) during the past three years. High tech manufacturing, discussed above, added 32,000 jobs — a 20% gain.

The region also saw growth in diversified manufacturing jobs — led by gains in capital goods in the non high tech machinery industries. The diversified manufacturing sector is still larger than high tech with 265,900 jobs in 1998 — near the all time high set in the late 1970s. Diversified manufacturing had a 10% job gain during the past four years.

Professional services led the growth surge adding 74,500 jobs since 1994. The largest additions were in computer services, discussed above, and engineering and management services (+21,100) — both high paying sectors.

Wholesale trade and trucking have rebounded from recession lows — aided by the growth in regional foreign trade and high tech sales. Tourism has also rebounded by adding more than 13,000 jobs since 1994.

The region's aircraft, space, and defense sector has continued to decline since 1994. However, the sector is now such a small part of the region's economic base that the past 1994 job losses did not prevent the region from growing 50% faster than the nation has since 1994.

Projections to 2005

The Bay Area has a well positioned economic base concentrated in world leading growth industries. As a result, the region should easily outpace the nation in job growth in the decade ahead.

There are three major keys to the future growth of the Bay Area's economic base. First, the region's growth will depend on the world and national outlook for the products of high tech manufacturing. Moreover, the region will be challenged to retain its position as the world class technology leader.

Second, the region's growth will depend on continued increases in the volume of international trade and financial services between California and the rest of the world.

Finally, the region will need to come to grips with issues of job/housing balance and infrastructure which are being articulated with increasing frequency in Bay Area communities. The successful resolution of these issues is necessary to preserve one of the region's major economic drawing cards — the usually high quality of life experienced in the Bay Area.

San Francisco Bay Area
Jobs By Major Basic Industry Group
1990-2005
(Thousands)

	1990	1994	1998	2005	Change 1990-1994	Change 1994-1998	Change 1998-2005
High Tech Manufacturing	184.3	162.7	204.4	203.6	-21.6	41.7	-0.8
Diversified Manufacturing	247.4	241.4	265.9	278.2	-6.0	24.5	12.3
Aircraft, Space, Defense	71.7	45.8	28.5	26.0	-25.9	-17.3	-2.5
Resource Based	36.6	35.0	34.2	31.7	-1.6	-0.8	-2.5
Transp. & Wholesale Trade	255.6	236.7	272.9	297.4	-16.2	36.2	24.5
Professional Services	346.6	359.7	434.2	542.8	13.1	74.5	108.6
Tourism & Entertainment	73.3	78.7	91.7	112.1	5.4	13.0	20.4
Total Basic Jobs	**1,212.8**	**1,160.0**	**1,331.8**	**1,491.8**	**-52.8**	**171.8**	**160.0**

Source: 1990, 1994, and 1998 —EDD, CCSCE; 2005—CCSCE

The outlook for high tech manufacturing is positive as indicated earlier in this report. The output of high tech industries is expected to grow well above the average rate of growth in both U.S. and world economies. The application of technology in the production and distribution processes of the major economies of the world is certain to be a "growth industry".

Business and public leaders in the Bay Area are taking strong steps to enhance the region's competitive position in specific technology market segments. The most widespread organizational effort is Joint Venture: Silicon Valley Network (JV:SV). For JV:SV, Silicon Valley extends throughout the technology firms in the broader region and is not confined to Santa Clara County. JV:SV has launched a number of initiatives in the industry networking and public policy areas.

Public policy initiatives have already been successful in improving the foundations for regional growth. On the regulatory side, the recent development of more uniform local building permit procedures for all the cities in Santa Clara County is another in a series of regulatory streamlining initiatives.

The Bay Area Economic Forum which includes the entire nine county region, also is moving ahead with initiatives to solidify the region's economic competitiveness. The Bay Area Economic Forum is taking a regional leadership position in base re-use issues and in providing an organizational framework for the region's multimedia cluster.

The linkage between high tech production and where the job growth occurs has become more complex. Jobs formerly located in major manufacturing firms are increasingly contracted out to firms in other sectors like business and engineering and management services. This makes manufacturing job totals lower but doesn't really diminish the job creation potential of large high tech production gains.

As a result, most of the basic job growth shows up in the professional services category which will account for 80% of the job growth in the Bay Area's economic base to 2005. High tech jobs are difficult to project given the very high rates of productivity growth. CCSCE would not be surprised if the number of high tech jobs in the region grew in the decade ahead.

The aircraft, space, defense sector will not be a large component of the Bay Area's economic base in the future. More jobs will be lost primarily from base closures. Most Bay Area bases are situated in desirable locations. Base re-use, while challenging in the near term, offers a great opportunity in a region where large tracts of land close to the region's labor force are scarce.

The Bay Area will be the first region to face the necessity to plan for future growth. Already the current economic surge is leading to more congestion and rapidly rising housing prices. These pressures threaten both the region's quality of life **and** the ability to attract the workforce required for continued world market leadership.

The conflicts of economic growth (more jobs raise prosperity but negatively impact the quality of life) are probably the Bay Area's greatest challenge entering the 21st century. CCSCE discusses growth issues in more detail in Section 6.

Jobs By Major Industry Group

The San Francisco Bay Area had more than 3.6 million jobs in 1998. The Bay Area accounted for about 23% of the state's total jobs. The Services sector is the region's largest major category. Services, led by business and health services, accounted for 1,072,400 jobs — slightly more than a quarter of the Bay Area's total jobs in 1998.

Trade was the second largest sector with over 698,300 jobs. Manufacturing had over 498,000 jobs and was the region's third largest major industry category.

The Bay Area has the second highest share of jobs in manufacturing, behind the Los Angeles Basin, among all California regions.

Finance, Insurance and Real Estate (FIRE) accounted for 214,000 jobs. The FIRE sector in the Bay Area represented 5.9% of the region's total jobs — the highest FIRE share among California regions.

The Outlook to 2005

Jobs in the San Francisco Bay Area are projected to grow by 14.5% between 1998 and 2005 to reach a level of more than 4.1 million. The region's growth rate will be below the state average but above the projected 8.1% national gain. Two major groups — Trade and Services — will account for about 80% of the job gains. Smaller gains are projected for most other sectors.

The regional growth should continue to move north, east and south within the Bay Area and to adjacent counties. How the decentralization process is handled – both for jobs, housing and transportation – will be a critical factor in determining the health of the regional economy in the years ahead.

San Francisco Bay Area Jobs By Major Industry Group 1990-2005 (Thousands)					Change	
	1990	1994	1998	2005	1990-1994	1994-1998	1998-2005
Agriculture	22.5	22.6	23.0	20.5	0.1	0.4	-2.5
Mining	5.0	4.5	3.9	3.7	-0.5	-0.6	-0.2
Construction	124.5	109.0	156.1	149.1	-15.5	47.1	-7.0
Manufacturing	480.7	436.9	498.4	508.1	-43.8	61.5	9.7
Transp., Pub. Utilities	167.8	168.0	182.9	213.2	0.2	14.9	30.3
Trade	669.9	632.2	698.3	789.2	-37.7	66.1	90.9
Fin., Ins., & Real Estate	205.0	201.3	214.0	238.2	-3.7	12.7	24.2
Services	807.1	872.3	1,072.4	1,384.9	65.2	200.1	312.5
Government	458.4	444.5	449.9	488.1	-13.9	5.4	38.2
Self Employed	284.1	302.4	318.5	347.6	18.3	16.1	29.1
Total Jobs	**3,224.9**	**3,193.6**	**3,617.4**	**4,142.6**	**-31.3**	**423.8**	**525.2**

Source: 1990 and 1994—EDD with CCSCE estimate of self employed; 1998—CCSCE based on January-October EDD data; 2005—CCSCE

Income and Spending

The San Francisco Bay Area represents over one quarter of the California market and over 3% of the national market in terms of income and spending. In 1998 the income earned by Bay Area residents reached $238.9 billion.

The Bay Area is the nation's wealthiest region of comparable size. Despite the recent recession, per capita and average household incomes in the region are more than 30% above the national average and will continue to grow faster than the national average.

During the 1990-1994 recession real (i.e., inflation adjusted) income and spending remained relatively constant. However, between 1994 and 1998 real income and spending surged, leading the state in growth. Total income (in 1998$) grew by 4.2% annually and taxable sales, led by business spending, increased at 5.5% per year.

Total real personal income is projected to rise by 3.2% per year in the region between 1998 and 2005 — above the anticipated 2.6% annual growth nationally.

San Francisco Bay Area Income and Taxable Sales 1990-2005 (1998$)				
	Per Capita Income	Average HH Income	Total Personal Income (Billions)	Taxable Sales (Billions)
1990	$32,304	$87,050	$195.5	$81.1
1994	$31,849	$87,649	$202.7	476.7
1998	$35,381	$100,647	$238.9	$95.0
2005	$40,067	$112,685	$297.3	$116.7
Average Annual Growth Rates				
1990-1994	-0.4%	0.2%	0.9%	-1.4%
1994-1998	2.7%	3.5%	4.2%	5.5%
1998-2005	1.8%	1.6%	3.2%	3.0%
California	1.8%	1.6%	3.5%	3.3%
United States	1.8%	1.6%	2.6%	

Source: U.S. Department of Commerce, California Board of Equalization, CCSCE

Regional per capita income, which surged to $35,381 in 1998, is nearly 34% above U.S. levels. If the national economy produces productivity gains in the decade ahead as projected, per capita income in the Bay Area will grow by 1.8% per year and reach $40,067 by 2005 (in 1998$)

Average household income in the Bay Area was $100,647 in 1998 — 43% above the national average. The average household income will increase by 1.6% per year and reach $112,685 in the Bay Area by 2005.

Total income and spending growth in the Bay Area will trail the state average slightly as a result of slow rates of population growth. Regional growth will exceed the national average. Per capita and average household income will grow in line with the state average and grow faster than the national growth rate.

The region will remain the nation's wealthiest area of more than 1 million people in 2005.

Spending fell in real dollars by more than 5% during the recession. However, taxable sales rose sharply since 1996 to reach $95.0 billion in 1998.

Spending on taxable items, which rose more slowly than income in the 1980s and early 1990s, will rise more in line with income in the decade ahead. Regional spending on taxable items by households is projected to grow from $95.0 billion in 1998 to $116.7 billion in 2005 all in 1998$. This represents an annual spending growth of 3.0%.

Construction Activity

A surge in job growth made Silicon Valley and the Bay Area the best construction market in California in 1997. More modest gains followed in 1998 pushing regional construction to $10 billion for the first time ever.

Since 1994 the Bay Area has experienced the sharpest gains in housing prices and rents. Moreover, the Bay Area has the lowest industrial vacancy rates and highest rents for industrial and R&D space.

Bay Area real estate markets are the tightest in California. New job creation is far outpacing residential building and, simultaneously, creating the demand for new nonresidential space. The fundamentals (job, population and household growth) support a continuation of the strong Bay Area construction markets.

Construction: A Large and Cyclical Industry

The value of new building construction in the San Francisco Bay Area (excluding public works where the data series has been suspended by CIRB) averaged $7.3 billion a year between 1970 and 1998 measured in 1998 prices. At the previous peak in 1986 the new construction market reached just over $9 billion. Construction levels remained under the long term average between 1990 and 1995 before surging to record levels in 1997 and 1998.

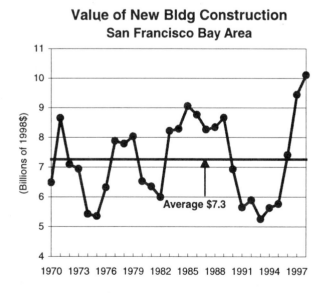

Value of New Bldg Construction
San Francisco Bay Area

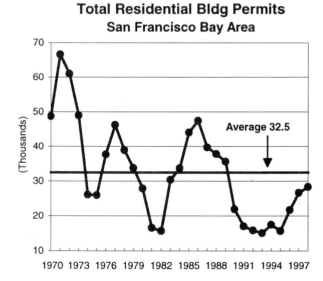

Total Residential Bldg Permits
San Francisco Bay Area

An average of 32,500 new homes were built each year since 1970. The peak year for units was 1971 with 68,000 units and the recent peak was 1986 with over 47,000 units. The peak year for residential valuation ($5.6 billion) was in 1989 but a new record will be set in 1998 or 1999. Permit levels have been near 15,000 in the early 1990s before rebounding to above 25,000 in 1997 and 1998. However, residential building levels are still below the long term average despite continuing strong job growth.

Recent Construction Market Trends

Silicon Valley led a surge in Bay Area construction since 1993. Although a regional record for total building valuation was set in 1998, not all Bay Area markets participated.

Total building valuation fell from $8.7 billion in 1989 to $5.3 billion (in 1998 prices) at the low in 1993 before rebounding to a record $10.1 billion in 1998. Santa Clara and Alameda counties led the recovery, accounting for $5.7 billion of the 1998 regional total and far surpassing 1989 valuation levels. Solano County remains the furthest below previous peaks with Contra Costa, San Francisco, San Mateo and Sonoma back near 1989 building levels.

The recovery has been led by nonresidential building in response to rapid job gains and declining vacancy rates in the region's high tech centers.

Residential building is still below 1989 levels in most of the region. However, Santa Clara and Alameda have seen a surge in both single family and apartment construction in response to rising rents and tiny vacancy rates. The two counties accounted for over 50% of the Bay Area's residential permits in 1997 and 1998.

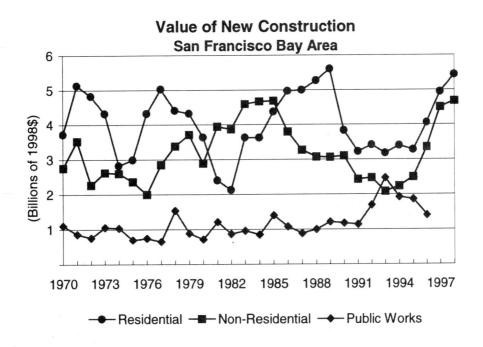

Value of New Construction
San Francisco Bay Area

—●— Residential —■— Non-Residential —◆— Public Works

San Francisco Bay Area
Construction Trends
(Billions of 1998$)

	New Building Construction			Residential Permits (Thousands)		
	1989	**1993**	**1998**	**1989**	**1993**	**1998**
Alameda	$1.6	$1.0	$2.3	6.0	2.6	5.9
Contra Costa	1.4	.9	1.0	7.7	3.4	4.1
Marin	.4	.2	.3	1.4	.3	.6
Napa	.3	.1	.2	1.0	.4	.5
San Francisco	.8	.6	.9	1.5	1.0	3.1
San Mateo	.9	.4	1.0	2.4	.5	2.0
Santa Clara	1.7	1.3	3.2	4.9	3.4	7.7
Solano	1.0	.3	.4	6.2	1.5	2.0
Sonoma	.7	.4	.6	4.5	1.9	2.7
Total	**$8.7**	**$5.3**	**$10.0**	**35.6**	**15.1**	**28.5**

Source: Construction Industry Research Board; 1998 estimates by CCSCE based on Jan-Oct CIRB data.

The Outlook for Housing

The Bay Area's job growth is far outpacing residential building. From 1994 through 1998 the region has added 425,000 jobs and began construction on 92,000 residential units. Since 1990 the Bay Area has added 92,000 residents per year and added just barely 20,000 houses and apartments annually.

As a result prices and rents have soared. During the past three years median home prices in Silicon Valley have risen more than 40% to $370,000 and in the region have risen more than 25% to $325,000 – highest in the state.

Apartment rents have soared also. In less than two years average rents have risen 25% in the region and more than 30% in Silicon Valley. Rising prices and rents have led to increases in new building but still at levels below the addition of new jobs and residents.

Moreover, the Bay Area is the one part of California where housing affordability is falling again. While mortgage rates are near 20 year lows and income growth is the highest in California, housing prices are rising faster. As a result, affordability has dropped to near 30% in the region. While affordability levels are still higher than in the late 1980s, fewer households in the Bay Area can afford a median priced home than anywhere else in the state.

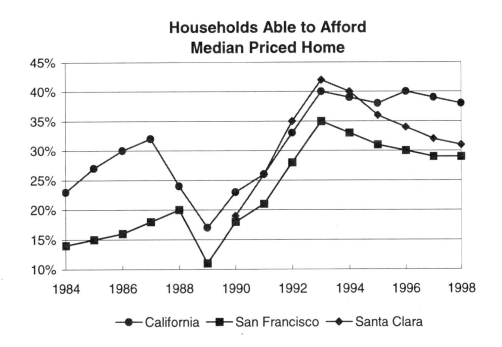

Households Able to Afford
Median Priced Home

Future job and population growth will provide a firm foundation for increased housing demand in the Bay Area. Job growth is projected at 73,000 per year to 2005 – lower than in 1997 and 1998 but higher than the 1980s average. Population growth will average 95,000 annually – slightly higher than in recent years.

The projected job and population growth will support nearly 37,000 new residential units per year both to meet new demand and make up for recent low levels of housing production.

There are two big questions about these housing projections. The first is whether any of these new units will be built outside the region in adjacent counties like San Joaquin (Stockton area), Merced, or San Benito. It is likely that some of the demand attributable to Bay Area job growth will be satisfied by spillout and long commutes.

The other question is whether an expansion of new building can hold prices and rents within affordable limits for the new households. Since the rising prices signal strong demand and desire to live in the region, there is no easy answer to when and if affordability will become a barrier to job and housing growth in the Bay Area.

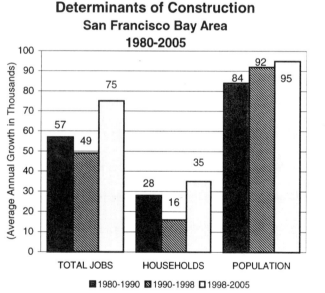

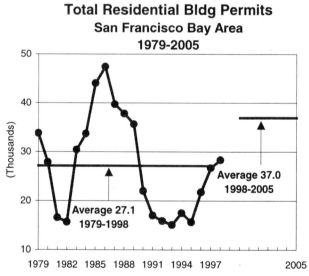

Nonresidential Construction – Analysis and Outlook

Nonresidential building surged in 1996 and 1997 and registered additional gains in 1998 in response to the Bay Area's large job gains and the previous five years of low building levels. Nonresidential building (excluding pubic works construction) nearly reached $4.6 billion in 1998 – the highest level since 1985's record $4.8 billion (in 1998$).

Commercial construction, led by a tripling in office building, reached $1.6 billion in the region in 1997. The surge was led by new construction in Silicon Valley but San Mateo, Alameda, and San Francisco also posted large gains. Commercial building declined slightly in 1998 to around $1.2 billion.

Industrial building has been rising for four consecutive years. Industrial construction probably reached $1 million in 1998 – nearly equal to the 1979 and 1984 record levels.

San Francisco Bay Area Nonresidential Construction (Billions of 1998$)			
	1985	1993	1998
Commercial	$2.2	$0.4	$1.2
Industrial	0.6	0.2	1.0
Other Nonresidential	0.3	0.2	0.3
Alterations/Additions	1.5	1.4	2.0
Heavy Construction	1.4	2.5	
Total Bldg. Constr.	**$4.8**	**$2.2**	**$4.6**
Total (Incl. Heavy)	**$6.2**	**$4.7**	

Source: Construction Industry Research Board; 1998 estimates by CCSCE based on Jan-Oct CIRB data

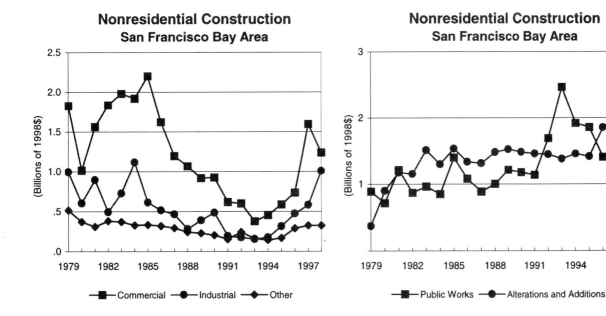

Nonresidential Construction
San Francisco Bay Area

Nonresidential Construction
San Francisco Bay Area

During the long construction decline two building types — 1) alterations and additions and 2) public works (heavy construction) became the leading construction sectors in the region and throughout the state. Spending on alterations and additions surged to near $2 billion (in 1998$) in 1996, 1997, and 1998.

In most years since 1990 public works construction accounted for the largest dollar contribution to nonresidential building in the Bay Area averaging near $2 billion annually in the mid 1990s. The Construction Industry Research Board (CIRB) has temporarily suspended reporting of public works valuation so no 1997 estimate is currently available.

Outlook for Future Growth

All signs point to record levels of new construction in the Bay Area in the years ahead.

Housing construction should continue to increase following the expected job and population growth. Rising unit volume combined with the demand for larger and more expensive units should finally produce record residential valuation levels.

The Bay Area should have at least another year or two of strong nonresidential building to catch up with the job surge. Beyond that continuing job gains should support a steady high level of building.

Public works building is set to surge in the years ahead. Bay Area communities are raising taxes and tolls to finance an expansion of transportation and education infrastructure. Major projects include

— BART extension to San Francisco International Airport

— Continuing bridge repair including a major Bay Bridge renovation

— Expansion of light rail and rail commute capacity including track and train upgrades for the Peninsula's Caltrain routes

— School repair and expansion to meet the needs of class size reduction and enrollment growth

Recent passage of the 1998 federal Transportation Equity Act (TEA 21) increases funding levels by 40% for the next six years and gives priority to funding in urban area. Recent passage of the $9.2 billion state education facilities bond package and numerous Bay Area local school bond elections provide new capital funding for schools.

SAN DIEGO REGION

SAN DIEGO REGION

Summary

The San Diego region included more than 2.8 million residents and 1.2 million jobs in 1998. With a gross regional product of $87 billion, the region ranks as the world's 38th largest economy. Moreover, the region's size expands significantly when considered in combination with the Tijuana area contiguous to San Diego across the Mexican border.

Between 1990 and 1994 the San Diego economy was in a long recession. Job levels declined by less than the state average, but were well behind the national economic performance. Real income, spending and construction levels fell. The aerospace manufacturing base shrunk by over 50%.

San Diego has been in a sustained economic recovery since 1994. Job growth during the past four years (12.6%) outpaced the state (11.1%) and national average (9.2%). The region posted record levels of total jobs, foreign trade, and tourism in 1998. Sustained job gains have led to a return of large population increases in 1997 and 1998 – averaging 60,000 people per year.

CCSCE projects that San Diego will be the fastest growing region in California and one of the fastest growing large regional economies in the nation. Between 1998 and 2005 job levels are projected to increase by more than 20% as compared with 14.6% in California and 8.1% in the nation.

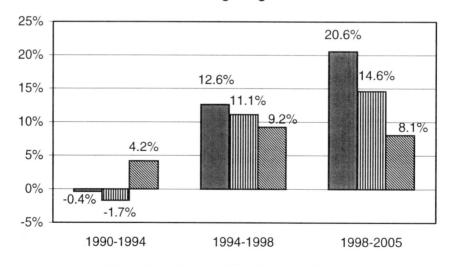

Past and Future Job Growth
San Diego Region

The post NAFTA period has brought large trade gains with Mexico and a rapid expansion in maquiladora jobs and related activities in San Diego. Manufacturing jobs are growing despite continued aerospace job declines since 1994. New industries such as telecommunications and biotech are slowly transforming the region's economic base.

The region's economic base is undergoing a long term transition away from aircraft, space, defense and into the four high growth sectors of California's economic base. The region's strength in these areas — high tech, foreign trade, tourism & entertainment, and professional services — is the reason for the relatively strong growth projected to 2005.

The region's economic transition is well understood by business and public sector leaders. A number of public–private partnership initiatives are underway in the San Diego–Tijuana region. These initiatives aim to give San Diego the organizational and infrastructure foundations to capitalize on the region's leading economic base sectors.

One looming challenge is that the region is rapidly using up the presently zoned residential land. Although the current economic growth has not been limited by land use constraints, the San Diego region (like the Bay Area) will soon confront the close connection between economic growth, land use polices, and quality of life challenges.

1990-1998: Recession and Recovery

The San Diego economy has overcome sharp declines in construction and defense related manufacturing. Total jobs will reach approximately 1,225,000 in 1998 setting a new high for jobs in the region. Below is a summary of the key factors in San Diego's recession and recovery.

The 1990's brought sharp jobs losses in the region's defense manufacturing base. Aircraft and missile/space job levels fell by 75% with the loss of more than 25,000 jobs between 1990 and 1998.

There was no recovery in the aircraft, space, defense sector when the San Diego economy turned up in 1994. Another 4,000 manufacturing jobs were lost after 1994. On the other hand, San Diego's military bases escaped most of the California base closures and contractions. Civilian DOD base jobs remained steady near 22,500 throughout the 1990's and now account for the majority of the sector's total jobs.

The region's recovery marked the transition into CCSCE's four major economic base growth areas.

Defense Related Jobs in San Diego (Thousands)				
	1980	**1990**	**1994**	**1998**
Aircraft & Missiles	19.3	27.2	11.3	6.2
Shipbuilding & Repair	9.6	7.3	5.8	6.7
Search & Navigation Equipment	5.0	4.7	2.5	2.5
Defense Related Manufacturing	33.9	39.2	19.6	15.4
Federal Civilian DOD	23.2	23.7	22.6	22.4
Total Sector	57.1	62.9	42.2	37.8

Source: EDD, CCSCE

Most of the basic job gains were in professional services — led by a 5,700 gain in computer services since 1994 and 10,300 new jobs in engineering and management services. Non defense manufacturing made a comeback with gains in telecommunications, other high tech machinery and toys.

Job growth brought new highs in real income. Per capita and average household income reached record levels in 1998 (adjusted for inflation) and spending also rebounded to a new high.

Taxable sales had fallen 8% in real dollars between 1990 and 1994 contributing to the long recession. By 1998 taxable sales reached a record $29.8 billion with real (i.e., inflation adjusted) annual growth of 5.6% per year since 1994 to lead the state's spending recovery.

Construction declines of more than 50% also contributed to the early 1990's recession. By 1997, as discussed in detail later in this section, construction markets were rebounding and will contribute positively to the regions future growth.

The Region's Economic Base

The San Diego region has a diversified economic base. The 395,600 jobs in San Diego's economic base in 1998 are distributed throughout CCSCE's seven major categories as shown below.

The Region's Emerging Economic Base

The San Diego region possesses a number of strengths which will be the foundation for job growth in the 1990s:

San Diego Region Major Sectors in Economic Base 1998		
	Jobs **(Thousands)**	**Change** **Since 1990**
High Tech Manufacturing	26.3	-4.3
Computers	6.4	0.1
Electronic Components	9.9	-0.3
Medical Instruments	4.3	0.2
Other Instruments	5.7	-4.3
Diversified Manufacturing	82.0	18.2
Apparel	5.1	1.9
Printing & Publishing	12.9	0.4
Chemicals Including Drugs	4.6	1.5
Non High Tech Machinery	24.8	6.4
Misc. Manufacturing	8.6	5.1
Aircraft/Space/Defense	38.2	-24.7
Aircraft	6.2	-8.8
Shipbuilding	6.7	-0.6
Missiles/Space	0.4	-11.8
Federal Civilian Defense	22.4	-1.3
Resource Based	11.8	-0.4
Transportation – Wholesale Trade	59.9	2.8
Professional Services	131.6	26.9
Computer Services	15.9	8.7
Engr. & Mgmnt. Services	51.5	17.0
State Education	22.0	4.0
Tourism & Entertainment	45.8	9.0
Hotels	25.2	2.5
Amusements	19.8	6.4
Total Economic Base	395.6	27.6
Total Jobs	1,222.1	132.5

Source: CCSCE estimates based on January through October EDD data.
See Appendix Chart A-2 for a list of regional basic industries.

- San Diego is one of California's three major port complexes — gateway to the Pacific Rim.

- San Diego is located adjacent to the Mexican border. The advantages of this location include

  - Participation in Mexico's growing economy and the benefits of NAFTA

  - Spinoffs from the maquiladora program which is growing rapidly

  - Access to the broader labor and retail market areas of the greater San Diego-Tijuana metro area

- World class university research programs. The U.C. campus at LaJolla is a world leader in biotech and other areas. The CSU system has multiple campuses in the region and there are private universities and colleges as well.

- A broad base in technology from computers and electronics to the developing telecommunications industry cluster. The region has a depth of business and labor force talent and experience.

- San Diego is a major tourism site for national, worldwide and state visitors. The convention business is an important and growing sector.

Foreign Trade — San Diego has one of the nation's fastest growing foreign trade sectors. The volume of trade expanded by 18.0% per year between 1987 and 1997 — far outpacing state and national growth rates. In fact trade volumes in San Diego grew at **twice the national average** since 1987.

In 1997 trade volume reached $23.0 billion up from $15.0 billion in 1995 benefiting from the recovery in Mexico. Moreover, total trade was up another 15.7% in the first nine months of 1998 – the only region in California to post trade gains in 1998.

Exports produced in the region reached $7.8 billion in 1997 — up 80% from 1993 export levels. Exports to Mexico ($3 billion in 1996) account for nearly half of total exports.

San Diego Customs District Value of Exports and Imports 1987-1997 ($Billions)			
	Exports	**Imports**	**Total**
1987	$1.7	$2.7	$4.4
1990	$3.4	$4.4	$7.8
1997	$9.0	$14.0	$23.0
Average Annual Growth Rate 1987-1997			
San Diego	18.1%	18.0%	18.0%
California	12.7%	9.0%	10.3%
United States	10.5%	7.8%	8.9%

Source: U.S. Department of Commerce

San Diego Exports Produced in the Region 1993-1997 ($Billions)			
Destinations			**1993-1997 Percent Change**
	1993	**1996**	**1997**	
Mexico	$1.8	$3.0	$3.4	82.0%
Canada	.4	.6	.8	97.7%
Japan	.3	.5	.6	95.5%
Other Asia	.6	1.0	1.0	72.6%
Europe	.9	1.2	1.4	48.7%
Industries				
Electronic Machinery	$1.1	$2.5	$3.1	172.6%
Ind. Mach. & Computers	.9	1.2	1.3	48.3%
Instruments	.5	.6	.6	21.7%
Misc. Manuf. (Toys)	.2	.4	.4	200.7%
Total Exports	**$4.4**	**$6.7**	**$7.8**	79.2%

Source: International Trade Administration; percentages calculated from unrounded data.

San Diego's exposure to Asian economic turmoil is less than in other regions. Even with rapid growth since 1993, exports to Asia ($1.6 billion in 1997) were close to the level traded with Europe and far behind the NAFTA countries in dollar volume.

High tech dominates San Diego's exports with $3.1 billion in electrical machinery including telecommunications and $1.3 billion in industrial machinery including computers. Miscellaneous manufacturing (including toys) is the fourth largest goods export sector.

Tourism is an important services export sector in the region.

High Technology — The technology sector in San Diego is changing as well as growing.

Newly emerging growth areas include biotech, medical instruments, software, and telecommunications. The region has the nation's third largest concentration of public biotech firms according to a recent Ernst & Young survey.

Public Biotechnology Industry in 1997 Number of Firms	
San Francisco Bay Area	61
New England	54
San Diego	33
New Jersey	22
Mid Atlantic Region	20
Los Angeles—Orange County	14

Source: Ernst & Young

The region's biotech cluster has grown from research at UCSD and one original company, Hybritech, which was formed in the 1970s to develop diagnostic tests. More than 20 companies, many formed in the past ten years, have grown out of this foundation.

The San Diego biotech sector is made up of many smaller companies. As a result, the region ranks high in the number of companies but relatively lower in total revenues. However, regional companies did rank third in R&D expenditures with $620 million in 1997 as shown on the Ernst & Young tabulation.

Public Biotech Companies
($Billions)

	Employees		Product Sales		R & D	
	1997	1994	1997	1994	1997	1994
Bay Area	21,371	12,970	$2.6	$1.2	$2.0	$1.0
Los Angeles-Orange	22,000	6,940	3.3	1.9	.6	.3
New England	12,426	9,135	1.2	1.0	1.0	.7
San Diego	5,865	4,095	.4	.4	.6	.4
Total U.S.	94,492	52,675	$10.6	$5.2	$5.6	$3.8

Source: Ernst & Young

The largest companies, according to a San Diego Business Journal compilation, are Agouron Pharmaceuticals (860 employees in 1998) which makes products to fight cancer and AIDs and Gen-Probe (466 employees) which makes DNA probe tests for diagnosing human diseases.

Bioscience jobs have nearly doubled from 1991 through 1998 to reach a level of more than 22,000 as shown below.

San Diego Bioscience Jobs

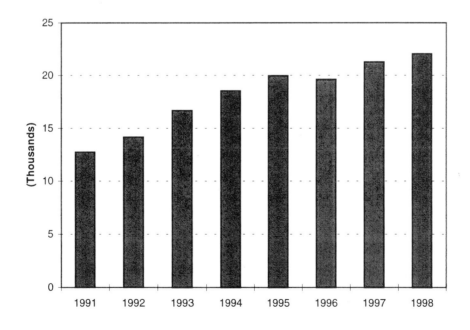

Companies and the research community in the region have organized to support the competitiveness of San Diego's biotech industry. CONNECT, an offshoot of the UCSD program in technology and entrepreneurship and BIOCOM — the San

Diego Biocommerce Association are working to create the private and public sector foundations for future growth. A current project by the California Trade and Commerce Agency has provided a link between regional and state economic strategy efforts.

Advanced telecommunications is a new technology growth sector for the San Diego region. Wireless communication is becoming a world class regional specialty niche.

Qualcomm is the industry leader. The Qualcomm standard for wireless communications has been adopted as the industry standard by the regional Bell operating companies. Qualcomm developed specialized wireless communication for the nation's trucking industry. Area firms have produced the technology used by Wal-Mart to co-ordinate inventory management and purchases.

Qualcomm with over 10,000 employees in 1998 is the region's largest high tech employer. Qualcomm added more than 6,000 workers during the past three years. New ventures include a recently announced joint venture with Microsoft (Wireless Knowledge) to give consumers mobile access to e-mail and Internet using wireless technology and a Qualcomm spin-off for global wireless markets.

Regional companies hope to go beyond a research leadership role to provide manufacturing job opportunities. The joint effort of Qualcomm and Sony to design and manufacture digital cellular phone equipment in the region is an example. The phones are built in Sony's San Diego facilities using Qualcomm technology.

Qualcomm's industry leadership has made San Diego a leading telecommunications technology center. Other companies include Nokia Mobile Phones, Sprint PCS, and Uniden Mobile Phones. Science Applications International Corp. (SAIC) is the region's third largest technology employer (behind Qualcomm and Sony) with nearly 4,000 employees and a growing position in the telecommunications applications industry.

Tourism & Entertainment — San Diego's tourism and entertainment sector is now larger than the aircraft, space, defense sector in terms of total jobs.

Visitor spending in 1997 reached $4.4 billion and accounts for 5% of the gross regional product according to data from the San Diego Convention and Visitors Bureau. The hotel and amusement sectors provided 45,000 jobs in 1998 — a gain of 10,000 jobs since 1990.

Additional jobs were created in the retail and restaurant sectors. Tourist spending accounts for 127,400 jobs in the regional economy according to the San Diego Chamber of Commerce.

San Diego has world class beach and recreation facilities and major attractions such as the San Diego Zoo, Sea World, the Wild Animal Park, and the Old Town Historical Park. Moreover, the region benefits from the easy access to Tijuana and the Baja peninsula. Visitor attendance and aircraft arrivals set records in 1997 and hotel occupancy and room rates moved sharply higher in 1998.

Professional and Other Basic Services — Professional services are the largest and fastest growing sector of San Diego's economic base. Professional and other basic services accounted for 131,600 jobs in 1997 — equal to 33% of San Diego's economic base.

Basic service jobs such as business services, engineering and management services, and legal services do serve local as well as statewide and national markets. These three industries also serve business markets in the region. As in Silicon Valley much of the job growth associated with expanding technology industries shows up in service jobs supplying inputs to technology firms.

Engineering and management services are the largest sector in professional services. San Diego engineering and management services sector had 51,500 jobs in 1998 up 3,000 from a year earlier and a gain of 17,000 jobs since 1990. Computer service job levels doubled from 1990 to reach 15,900 in 1998 and state education posted 22,000 jobs primarily from the UC and CSU campuses.

Diversified Manufacturing — The diversified manufacturing sector has been a star performer in San Diego's economic base. Jobs in diversified manufacturing industries increased during the 1980s (when the nation lost two million diversified manufacturing jobs) and increased by another 18,200 jobs between 1990 and 1998 — continuing to grow during the recession.

The largest sector is machinery (excluding high tech) which now has 24,800 jobs. Color TV assembly is included in this sector and Sony, the largest firm, now has 4,000 San Diego employees.

San Diego boasts two former Fortune Magazine's 100 fastest growing companies — Calloway Golf and Thermotrex. Thermotrex manufactures a laser based hair removal system and has had a 52% annual sales growth rate from 1993 through 1997 ending with nearly $300 million in 1997 sales. Callaway Golf was the region's 5th largest public company in 1997 with over $800 million in sales, and more than 2,500 employees.

Printing and publishing is the next largest cluster with 12,900 jobs in 1997. Apparel jobs have been increasing steadily and now total more than 5,100. The region has also expanded employment in chemicals (which includes new biotech companies) and plastics.

Miscellaneous manufacturing jobs have more than doubled since 1990 – rising from 3,500 to 8,600 in 1998. The region's toy industry is tied to opportunities for joint manufacturing presented by the maquiladora industry across the border.

The maquiladora industry is one reason for the success of the region's manufacturing base. Under the maquiladora process, firms can have products assembled across the border in Mexico and returned, duty free, to the U.S. for final production and distribution. The labor costs in Mexico are a fraction of those in the San Diego area.

Total employment in maquiladora located in Baja California surpassed 200,000 in 1998. Since 1990 maquiladora jobs have more than doubled according to data compiled for the Institutio Nacional de Estadistica. Maquiladora production in Baja California (and particularly in Tijuana) also supports an increase in economic activity in San Diego. Some maquiladoras feed San Diego manufacturing activity and all support wholesale and foreign trade growth.

A list of some of the largest maquiladoras in Tijuana is shown below.

Largest Maquiladoras in Tijuana		
Parent Firms	Jobs in 1997	Product
Sony	5,200	Color TVs, Computer Monitors
Sanyo	4,500	Refrigerators, Color TVs
Matsushita	2,300	Televisions
Samsung	2,300	Electronics
Hasbro	1,600	Toys
Tohoku Pioneer	1,600	Stereo Auto Speakers
Leviton	1,300	Electronic Devices
Scripto - Takai	1,300	Consumer Goods
Hitachi	1,300	Televisions
Mattel	1,200	Toys
Hyundai	1,250	Trailer Chassis

Source: Twin Plant News, September 1997

Maquiladora Jobs in Baja California

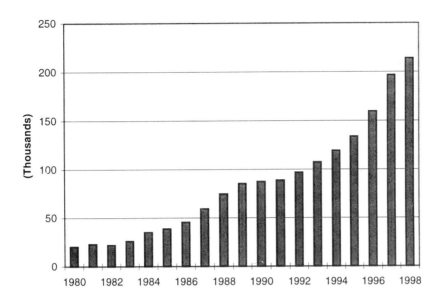

Projections to 2005 — Economic Base

Jobs in San Diego's economic base are projected to increase by more than 65,000 jobs (+16.8%) to 2005 — far outpacing the national increase.

The largest gains are expected in professional services following statewide and national trends. Most other job gains will be in diversified manufacturing, tourism & entertainment and wholesale trade.

The rapid growth in foreign trade will be felt in all sectors: 1) pushing up jobs in transportation and wholesale trade, 2) providing markets for manufacturing **and** services exports, and 3) supporting growth in San Diego's tourism industry.

High technology will grow in terms of production and profits. Job gains will depend on 1) how rapidly new technology clusters take off and 2) the race between output and productivity gains. High technology has already passed the aircraft, space, defense sector in terms of manufacturing jobs and sales and the gap will increase.

The region is in the midst of a transition in its technology base. The movement is away from defense related activities to the newer biotech and communications sectors. Industry, research, and community organizations are working to build the foundations for success but success is by no means guaranteed.

San Diego Region Jobs By Major Basic Industry Group 1990-2005 (Thousands)					Change		
	1990	1994	1998	2005	1990-1994	1994-1998	1998-2005
High Tech Manufactur.	30.6	24.2	26.3	27.8	-6.4	2.1	1.5
Diversified Manufactur.	63.8	68.4	82.0	94.9	4.6	13.6	12.9
Aircraft, Space, Defense	62.9	42.2	38.2	37.1	-20.7	-4.0	-1.1
Resource Based	12.2	12.2	11.8	11.3	0.0	-0.4	-0.5
Transp. & Whsle. Trade	57.7	53.2	59.9	69.6	-3.6	6.5	9.7
Professional Services	104.7	113.6	131.6	164.4	8.9	18.0	32.9
Tourism & Entertain.	36.8	40.5	45.8	57.0	3.7	5.3	11.2
Total Basic Jobs	**367.9**	**354.6**	**395.6**	**462.3**	**-13.4**	**41.1**	**66.7**

Source: 1990, 1994, and 1998—EDD, CCSCE; 2005—CCSCE

The diversified manufacturing sector is expected to grow in terms of production and may post a small increase in jobs. San Diego is still benefiting from the movement and expansion of firms from the Los Angeles Basin. Foreign investment and growing markets in Mexico and the Pacific Rim will also influence the pace of growth in diversified manufacturing.

The maquiladora process is helping the region's diversified manufacturing base. In industries like toys and TV manufacturing, new plants in the region are being established to take advantage of twin plants across the border in Mexico.

The aircraft, space and defense sector will remain close to current levels. The defense manufacturing component has already shrunk significantly. Future job gains or losses will depend on U.S. defense spending policy after 2000. For the moment, San Diego has not been adversely affected by the base closures although continuing reductions may eventually hit the region.

Jobs By Major Industry Group

The San Diego region has more than 1.2 million jobs in 1998 — about 8% of the state total. Job levels are now 12.1% above pre-recession totals.

Projections to 2005: Major Industry Groups

The region should add close to 250,000 jobs by 2005. San Diego will lead California in job gains — growing by 20.6% compared to the projected 14.6% state growth. San Diego will be one of the fastest growing large metropolitan areas nationally — far outpacing the projected 8.1% national job growth rate.

Job gains will be highest in Services (+116,300) and Trade (+51,400). This is similar to the pattern of the 1980s and to projected statewide trends.

					Change 1990-1994	Change 1994-1998	Change 1998-2005
San Diego Region **Jobs By Major Industry Group** **1990-2005** **(Thousands)**							
	1990	1994	1998	2005	1990-1994	1994-1998	1998-2005
Agriculture	10.8	10.6	10.8	10.3	-0.2	0.2	-0.5
Mining	0.7	0.4	0.4	0.4	-0.3	0.0	0.0
Construction	51.6	40.6	55.3	61.6	-11.0	14.7	6.3
Manufacturing	134.1	114.1	124.7	139.3	-20.0	10.6	14.6
Transp., Pub. Utilities	36.0	36.4	41.8	51.9	0.4	5.4	10.1
Trade	236.7	227.0	246.0	297.4	-9.7	19.0	51.4
Fin., Ins., & Real Estate	63.9	59.1	62.7	75.2	-4.8	3.6	12.5
Services	266.3	296.1	354.1	470.4	29.8	58.0	116.3
Government	177.4	181.5	199.3	220.0	4.1	17.8	20.7
Self Employed	112.2	119.4	127.0	146.8	7.2	7.5	19.8
Total Jobs	**1,089.6**	**1,085.3**	**1,222.1**	**1,473.4**	**-4.3**	**136.7**	**251.3**

Source: 1990 and 1994—EDD with CCSCE estimate of self employed; 1998—CCSCE based on January-October EDD data; 2005—CCSCE

The manufacturing sector will grow in terms of sales and profits. San Diego is expected to record a small gain in manufacturing jobs in contrast to job losses nationwide. The magnitude of manufacturing job growth will depend on 1) the region's success in establishing new growth industries and 2) trends in productivity growth.

Income and Spending

The San Diego region represents 8% of the California market and 1% of the national market in terms of income and spending. In 1998 the income earned by San Diego residents reached $73.3 billion.

The San Diego market is growing faster than the nation. Between 1980 and 1990 real (i.e. inflation adjusted) income grew by 4.5 % annually in the region — fastest in the state and exceeding the national 2.4% annual growth rate. During the recession most measures of real income and spending fell slightly.

In 1998 real income, total personal, per capita and average household income reached new record levels for the second straight year.

Total real personal income is projected to rise by 3.9% per year in the San Diego region between 1998 and 2005 — well above the anticipated 2.6% annual growth nationally. Real personal income grew by 4.2% from 1994 through 1998 to lead the state.

	Per Capita Income	Average HH Income	Total Personal Income (Billions)	Taxable Sales (Billions)
San Diego Region Income and Taxable Sales 1990-2005 (1998$)				
1990	$24,299	$68,768	$61.0	$26.1
1994	$23,451	$67,213	$62.2	$24.0
1998	$26,003	$77,039	$73.3	$29.8
2005	$29,447	$85,496	$95.8	$38.0
Average Annual Growth Rates				
1990-1994	-0.9%	-0.6%	0.5%	-2.0%
1994-1998	2.6%	3.5%	4.2%	5.6%
1998-2005	1.8%	1.5%	3.9%	3.9%
California	1.8%	1.6%	3.5%	3.3%
United States	1.8%	1.6%	2.6%	

Source: U.S. Department of Commerce, California Board of Equalization, CCSCE

Regional per capita income, temporarily depressed in the early 1990s, is now slightly below the U.S. average. Rapid gains between 1994 and 1998 regained all of the earlier losses and brought regional per capita income 7% ahead of 1990 levels measured in 1998$. If the national economy produces productivity gains in the decade ahead as projected, per capita income in the region will grow by 1.8% per year and reach $29,447 by 2005 (in 1998$) — almost equal to the national average.

Average household income in the San Diego region was $77,039 in 1998 — 9% above the national average. The average household income will increase by 1.5% per year and reach $85,496 in 2005.

Real taxable sales declined by nearly 10% between 1990 and 1994 before rebounding strongly since 1996. Taxable sales in 1997 ($29.1 billion) have finally exceeded the pre-recession peak by 14%.

Spending on taxable items will rise in line with income in the decade ahead. Regional spending on taxable items by household is projected to grow from $29.8 billion in 1998 to $38.0 billion in 2005 all in 1998$. This represents an annual spending growth of 3.9%.

In general, San Diego will be one of the fastest growing regions in California in terms of income and spending growth and will grow much faster than projected national rates.

Construction Activity

In 1998 San Diego had the best construction year since 1989. The value of new building construction reached $3.5 billion — exceeded only by building levels in the 1984-89 boom years.

Residential building has remained low despite the region's economic recovery. Permit levels reached near 12,500 in 1998 but remain well below the long term average. Nonresidential building levels have risen each year since 1994 and are now approaching the record mid 80s levels of $1.5 billion annually.

The longer term fundamentals continue to look strong in San Diego. Growth in jobs, population and income should lead to a substantial rebound in residential and nonresidential markets in the decade ahead.

Construction: A Large and Cyclical Industry

The value of new building construction activity in the San Diego region averaged $3 billion per year between 1970 and 1998 measured in 1998 prices — excluding public works construction where the data series was temporarily suspended in 1997. At the peak in 1986 the new construction market reached over $5.5 billion or 14% of the region's total output. An upturn in 1997 and 1998 brought construction valuation back to above the long term average.

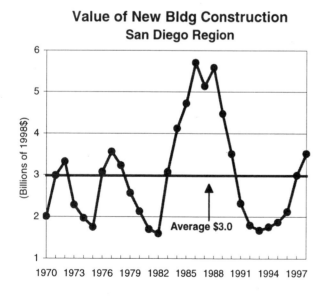

Value of New Bldg Construction
San Diego Region

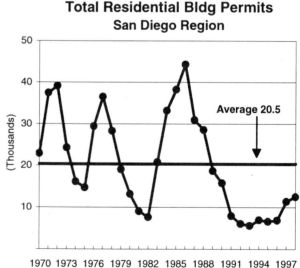

Total Residential Bldg Permits
San Diego Region

An average of 20,500 new homes have been built each year since 1970. The peak year for units was 1986 with a record 44,300 units. The peak years for residential valuation ($4.2 billion) were in 1986 and 1988. Residential permits have remained below the long term average for 10 straight years.

San Diego has participated in the state's long construction recession. Despite recent gains, total annual new construction since 1994 remains below the late 1980s peak levels. Residential building valuation rebounded to near $2.3 billion in 1998 with the rise in new units. In contrast, residential building valuation was in the $3-4 billion range throughout the mid 1980s.

Nonresidential building has increased led by public works construction. In 1998 nonresidential building is up by 25% in the region led by gains in industrial and office building. Nonresidential valuation approached $1 billion in 1997 and surged to near $1.2 billion in 1998 – the highest level since 1990 but still below the $1.5 billion average of the mid 1980s.

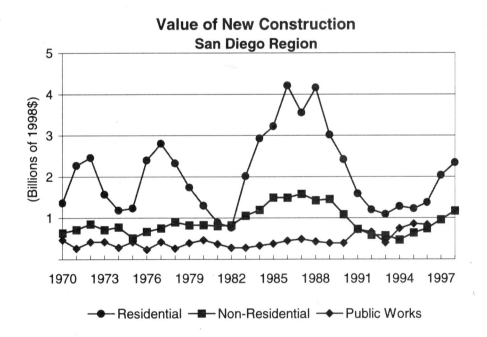

Value of New Construction
San Diego Region

The Outlook for Housing

Continuing job growth led to increases in housing construction in 1996, 1997 and 1998. The resale housing market picked up steam in 1997 as median resale prices regained the price losses of the early 1990s. Median resale prices rose to well over $200,000 in 1998 reaching record levels for several months in a row.

The fundamentals for continued residential building increases are good. Annual job gains will average 35,900 — near levels in the 1980s and three times the yearly gains of the early 1990s. Population growth will also move back towards 1980s levels.

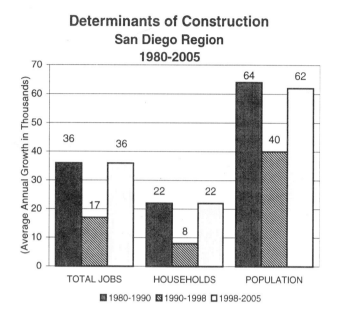

Determinants of Construction
San Diego Region
1980-2005

■ 1980-1990 ◪ 1990-1998 □ 1998-2005

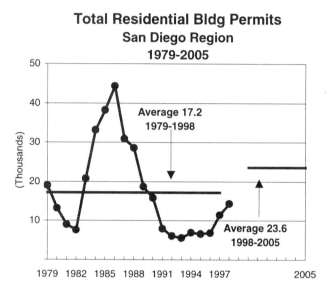

Total Residential Bldg Permits
San Diego Region
1979-2005

Average 17.2
1979-1998

Average 23.6
1998-2005

As a result residential construction levels should average 23,700 units per year to 2005 — more than double the yearly additions so far in the decade.

The affordability outlook in the region is good. Income gains have outpaced housing price appreciation since 1990. Moreover, San Diego region resale prices are much more competitive with other regions than a few years ago.

For example San Diego median resale prices have climbed back to the $200,000 level in 1998. Between 1990 and 1998 median resale prices in Denver rose from $86,000 to $150,000; in Portland from $80,000 to $159,000; and in Salt Lake City from $70,000 to $131,000.

Moreover, mortgage rates are near 20 year lows again. Mortgage rates which were over 10% just six years ago are now below 7%. One question mark is the availability of land zoned for residential building. SANDAG (the San Diego Association of Governments) forsees a shortage of residential land beginning after 2000. However, local zoning decisions are not unchangeable and the region does possess sufficient vacant land overall to support the projected housing gains and more.

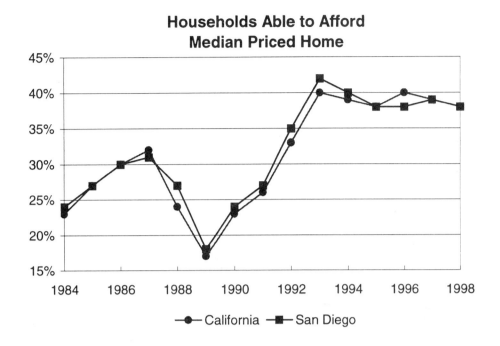

Households Able to Afford Median Priced Home

Legend: California, San Diego

Nonresidential Construction: Analysis and Outlook

Nonresidential building construction (excluding public works) was still below record levels in 1998 although the region posted two straight years of strong growth. Total nonresidential valuation was $1.2 billion versus a record of $1.5 billion in the mid 1980s.

Commercial construction has rebounded slowly despite the recent job gains. Commercial building valuation was near $400 million in 1998 down from highs near $800 million in the mid 1980s.

Two building types — 1) alterations and additions and 2) public works have provided the majority of construction spending in recent years. The volume of alterations and additions has averaged $300 million in the 1990s. By 1998 spending on alterations and additions neared $400 million – close to the 1986 record.

Public works spending had been, by far, the largest category of nonresidential building in the 1990s. Public works accounted for between $700 million and $900 million since 1991. The Construction Industry Research Board temporarily suspended publishing estimates of public works spending in 1997.

San Diego Region Nonresidential Construction (Billions of 1998$)			
	1989	1993	1998
Commercial	$0.8	$0.2	$0.4
Industrial	0.2	*0.0	0.3
Other Nonresidential	0.1	0.1	0.1
Alterations	0.3	0.3	0.4
Heavy Construction	0.4	0.4	
Total Bldg. Constr.	**$1.5**	**$0.6**	**$1.2**
Total (Incl. Heavy)	**$1.9**	**$1.0**	

Source: Construction Industry Research Board; *Under $50 million

Outlook for Future Growth

Total nonresidential building should expand in the years ahead. CCSCE projects that the fundamental determinants of construction growth — job and household increases — will recover in the region.

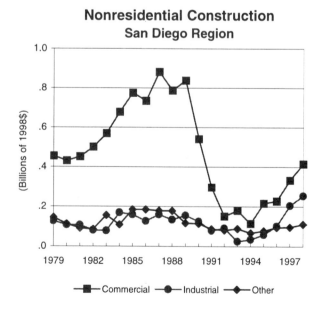

Nonresidential Construction
San Diego Region

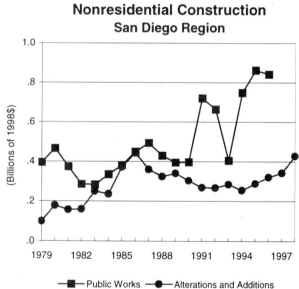

Nonresidential Construction
San Diego Region

Nonresidential building should show continued growth and reach record levels in the near future. Three factors support the positive long term outlook:

- Infrastructure spending should surge. The 1998 election brought passage of support for a new downtown stadium, $1.5 billion in local school bonds, and a $9.2 billion state school bond package. San Diego's transportation funding will grow under the 1998 federal Transportation Equity Act (TEA - 21).

  Airport and light rail expansion will augment infrastructure spending.

- Strong job growth and tightening commercial and industrial space markets will lead to continued growth in commercial and industrial building.

- Future job and population growth will also support a steady rise in spending to upgrade existing facilities.

San Diego's expected status as California's fastest growing region will translate into new records in nonresidential construction in the near future.

SACRAMENTO REGION

SACRAMENTO REGION

Summary

The Sacramento region included 800,000 jobs and 1.7 million residents in 1998. Jobs and income grew between 1990 and 1994 when the rest of the state was in recession. The region outpaced the nation in job growth and kept pace with the state growth rate during the past four years and in 1998 reached a gross regional product of $55 billion.

The Sacramento region was one of the nation's fastest growing metropolitan area economies in the 1980s. Total jobs increased by nearly 50% between 1979 and 1990 — an average growth rate of 3.7% per year. The region's economy expanded nearly twice as fast as the state and national economies.

The 1990s brought a rapid expansion of high tech manufacturing into the Sacramento region. Major domestic and foreign producers like Packard Bell, Apple, Intel, Hewlett Packard and NEC located or expanded manufacturing and research facilities in the region — bringing nearly 10,000 new jobs since 1990.

CCSCE projects that the region will again outperform the nation in economic growth in the decade ahead. Jobs will increase by 17.4% between 1998 and 2005 — well below the 1980s trend, but above expected state (14.6%) and national (8.1%) growth rates.

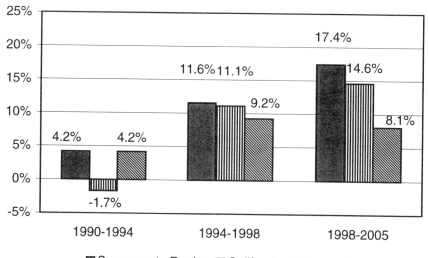

Past and Future Job Growth
Sacramento Region

■ Sacramento Region ▥ California ▨ United States

Positive regional factors include 1) the continued rapid growth in high technology firms, 2) the regional position as a retail center for surrounding counties and 3) Sacramento's competitive housing prices and quality of life. Moreover, state government employment is poised to expand in the decade ahead pushed by higher revenues and broad new mandates in welfare reform and workforce development — programs turned over to the states by the federal government.

The Region's Economic Base

The Sacramento region possesses a number of strengths which will be the foundation for job growth in the decade ahead:

- Sacramento is the center of state government in California – a state which will add 5 million residents and nearly 1 million students by 2005.

- The region has successfully developed a high tech complex which continues to attract new firms and expansions.

- The region is a major distribution node on the I-80 corridor which serves Rocky Mountain and Midwest markets.

- The region serves as a retail and service center for several smaller northern California county areas.

- Sacramento continues to provide a low cost in-state alternative to the Los Angeles, San Francisco and San Diego regions. There has been a strong movement of people within California to the Sacramento region.

The Sacramento region economic base contains one "industry" that is much larger than all others. State Government, including general government and education activities, employed 94,700 workers in 1998. This one sector accounts for over 33% of the region's economic base. Major employers are the State Government, University of California at Davis, and California State University at Sacramento.

The professional services sector dominates the region's economic base with more than half of all basic jobs. Besides state government, the leading industries in 1998 are computer services with 9,900 jobs and engineering and management services with 20,100 jobs.

The high tech manufacturing sector, though small, has attracted a lot of attention in the region. This brings hope for future job gains. By mid 1998, the computer and electronic components industries employed nearly 7,800 and 7,600 workers respectively in the region.

Sacramento Region
Major Sectors in Economic Base
1998

	Jobs (Thousands)	Change Since 1990
High Tech Manufacturing	17.0	9.7
Diversified Manufacturing	30.5	2.3
Food Products except Canning	4.7	0.5
Lumber, Wood Products	4.5	-1.2
Printing, Publishing	6.0	-0.5
Aircraft/Space/Defense	10.6	-11.1
Missiles/Space	2.0	-1.5
Federal Civilian Defense	8.3	-9.6
Resource Based	12.4	-1.7
Agriculture	9.0	0.1
Pres. Fruits Vegetables	2.3	-0.8
Transportation – Whsle. Trade	46.5	2.4
Wholesale Trade	32.4	2.4
Professional Services	141.6	19.6
Computer Services	9.9	5.5
Engr. & Mgmnt. Services	20.1	5.4
State Government	72.5	8.1
State Education	22.2	1.4
Tourism & Entertainment	19.2	5.2
Hotels	6.9	-0.3
Amusements	12.0	5.4
Total Economic Base	277.8	26.4
Total Jobs	803.1	112.0

Source: CCSCE estimates based on January through October EDD data. See Appendix Chart A-2 for a list of regional basic industries.

There are now 17,000 high tech manufacturing jobs in the region – up from 7,300 in 1990. Apple's Laguna West facility has added workers throughout 1998 to keep up with surging iMac orders. Apple now employs 1,700 workers with more hiring planned. Hewlett Packard is the largest high tech employer in the region with 5,500 jobs followed closely by Intel with 5,200 jobs.

Packard Bell is the third largest high tech employer. Recent layoffs in response to declining PC sales have pushed job levels down to 3,000 from 4,000 a year earlier. In June 1998 NEC, currently with 1,800 jobs, announced another Sacramento area expansion.

Oracle (software) has begun operations in the region with a 300 job software facility in Rooklin.

The Sacramento region is still able to add significant numbers of moderately priced homes. This advantage plus the proximity to Silicon Valley gives Sacramento a competitive edge for high tech expansions in California – offering the cost and quality of life advantages of out of state locations while being 90 miles from Silicon Valley.

The region has absorbed the loss of over 11,000 defense related jobs since 1990 **and still managed to post total job gains**. Most of the job cuts related to the closure of Mather Air force Base and the Sacramento Army Depot have already occurred. The region now faces the realignment of activities at McClellan Air Force Base. Approximately 3,000 jobs have been lost and another 3,400 jobs will be eliminated in 1999.

There are approximately 30,000 jobs in the region's diversified manufacturing sector. The largest industries in 1998 were printing and publishing with 5,900 jobs and lumber and wood products with 3,800 jobs. The next leading industries were food products (except canning) with 4,700 jobs and non high tech machinery with 3,700 jobs.

Economic Base Growth: 1990-1998

The region's economic base actually grew during the long California recession. Gains in business services and high tech offset losses in other manufacturing.

High tech jobs expanded rapidly after 1994 led by the Packard Bell relocation. The region has added 9,700 high tech manufacturing jobs since 1990. Professional services and state government also led the region's economic base to a gain of 19,600 jobs in the 1994-1998 period.

Jobs in Sacramento's economic base increased by 112,000 or 16.2% between 1990 and 1998 — the largest gain among California's major economic regions.

Exports produced in the region increased from $1.1 billion in 1993 to $1.7 billion in 1997 — a gain of 55.2%. Japan was the largest single market with $361 million in 1997 exports. European countries accounted for $637 million and other Asian countries bought $352 million from the Sacramento region. Canada and Mexico accounted for less than $250 million in 1997 sales.

Declines in exports to Asia and Europe caused a decline in total exports in 1997. Exports to Canada and Mexico rose and partially offset the other declines.

Sacramento Region Exports Produced in the Region 1993-1997 ($Millions)				
Destination	**1993**	**1996**	**1997**	**Percent Change**
Mexico	$34.5	$65.5	$69.9	102.7%
Canada	82.0	114.7	169.5	106.7%
Europe	427.1	637.0	530.7	24.3%
Japan	206.9	470.2	360.6	74.3%
Other Asia	214.7	439.5	351.6	63.7%
Total Exports	**$1,075.6**	**$1,908.6**	**$1,669.5**	53.2%

Source: International Trade Administration; percentages calculated from unrounded data.

Projections to 2005 — Economic Base

The region's economic base will continue to grow rapidly based on four factors.

1. Renewed growth in state government employment. First, there will be strong demographic pressures. The state's population will grow again based on expected job gains. School age population (K-12 and higher education) will increase faster than the general population.

    Second, the revenue picture has improved. Economic growth is being translated into sustained increases in revenues.

    Third, the state will begin implementing broad new mandates in designing and administering welfare reform and workforce preparation programs. The movement to return federal power to the states may also extend to Medicaid in the coming years.

    Finally, renewed prosperity and growth will bring increased demands for public services and infrastructure improvements. While there is still no consensus on long term budget priorities, the outlook for resolving California's budget gridlock has improved.

2. Growth in high tech output and jobs. The region's high tech production will expand rapidly in the decade ahead. This surge will lead to continued job

gains in related sectors such as business and engineering and management services.

CCSCE projects a gain of 4,200 high tech jobs by 2005. Previous CCSCE long term projections were exceeded in 1997 by the region's strong growth. With low vacancy rates and rising land/lease prices in Silicon Valley, the Sacramento region could again exceed CCSCE's projections by capturing Silicon Valley expansion and relocations. The land price advantage of the region increased substantially in 1998 for both residential and non residential uses.

3. Professional services job growth will certainly continue strong. Business and engineering/management services growth is tied both to serving the region's high tech and state government base.

   The seat of government for the world's seventh largest economy has drawn a surge of law, accounting and other specialized professional services and regional headquarter offices.

4. The region serves as both a regional center for rural northern California and a gateway to the Midwest along the I-80 corridor. These locational advantages will result in job growth in trucking and wholesale trade as well as in the sectors listed above.

Sacramento Region
Jobs By Major Basic Industry Group
1990-2005
(Thousands)

	1990	1994	1998	2005	Change 1990-1994	1994-1998	1998-2005
High Tech Manufacturing	7.3	9.6	17.0	21.2	2.3	7.4	4.2
Diversified Manufacturing	28.2	27.3	30.5	33.0	-0.9	3.2	2.5
Aircraft, Space, Defense	21.7	13.6	10.6	9.7	-8.1	-3.0	-0.9
Resource Based	14.1	12.5	12.4	11.5	-1.6	-0.1	-0.9
Trans. & Wholesale Trade	44.1	41.6	46.5	54.0	-2.5	4.9	7.5
Professional Services	122.0	128.9	141.6	165.4	6.9	12.7	23.8
Tourism & Entertainment	14.0	15.8	19.2	24.5	1.8	3.4	5.3
Total Basic Jobs	**251.4**	**249.3**	**277.8**	**319.3**	**-2.1**	**28.5**	**41.5**

Source: 1990, 1994, and 1998 —EDD, CCSCE; 2005—CCSCE

As a result, basic jobs are projected to grow by 41,500 or over 15% between 1998 and 2005. These gains will make Sacramento one of the leading growth areas nationwide.

Jobs By Major Industry Group

The Sacramento region had more than 803,100 total jobs in 1998. The region contains 5% of all jobs in California.

The Government sector is the region's largest major industry category. Government (local, state and federal) accounted for 198,100 jobs in 1998 — roughly one-quarter of Sacramento region jobs. The Sacramento area is the only economic region in California where Government is the largest sector.

Other large sectors are Trade and Services. Manufacturing had only 6.6% of the region's jobs compared to 12.7% statewide. The Services sector is the second largest major industry category in the Sacramento region; it ranks first in the other regions.

Sacramento Region Jobs By Major Industry Group 1990-2005 (Thousands)							
						Change	
	1990	1994	1998	2005	1990-1994	1994-1998	1998-2005
Agriculture	8.9	8.4	9.0	7.9	-0.5	0.6	-1.1
Mining	0.6	0.6	0.3	0.5	0.0	-0.3	0.2
Construction	35.5	29.4	42.9	42.3	-6.1	13.5	-0.6
Manufacturing	43.8	42.5	52.9	59.3	-1.3	10.4	6.4
Trans., Pub. Utilities	28.2	30.4	32.0	39.5	2.2	1.6	7.5
Trade	147.4	146.6	159.1	183.0	-0.8	12.5	23.9
Fin., Ins., & Real Estate	39.8	44.3	47.0	53.3	4.5	2.7	6.3
Services	138.9	161.2	190.3	255.1	22.3	29.1	64.8
Government	184.3	188.7	198.1	219.2	4.4	9.4	21.1
Self Employed	63.7	67.8	71.5	83.2	4.1	3.7	11.7
Total Jobs	**691.1**	**719.9**	**803.1**	**943.2**	**28.8**	**83.2**	**140.1**

Source: 1990 and 1994—EDD with CCSCE estimate of self employed; 1998—CCSCE based on January-October EDD data; 2005—CCSCE

The Services industry category has contributed the most new jobs in the Sacramento region since 1990 — 51,400. The Government sector accounted for 13,800 additional jobs. Trade, which was restrained by stagnant retail sales, added 11,700 jobs between 1990 and 1998.

Projections to 2005

Jobs in the Sacramento region are projected to grow by 17.4% to reach 943,200 in 2005.

Three major industry groups — Services, Trade and Government — will account for most of the growth. These three sectors will contribute over 80% of the region's job growth. A portion of the growth in Services will be in sectors included in the region's economic base such as business services. Government jobs will account for a larger share of the regional growth than in the period since 1990.

In 2005 Services will be the largest major industry category in the Sacramento region with 255,100 jobs — more than one-quarter of the regional total. Trade and Government will also each account for roughly 20% of the region's total jobs.

A small job gain is expected in Manufacturing and Construction.

A proportion of the growth in the Trade and Services sectors represents sales to residents of adjacent counties. Sacramento is the major regional center in California north and east of the Bay Area. Just as San Francisco serves markets up the north coast of California, so Sacramento serves markets in the Sacramento Valley and Mountain region counties.

The growth of Sacramento's economic base has drawn migrants from other areas of the state. In contrast to the Los Angeles and San Francisco regions, most new residents in Sacramento come from within California. They come to follow the job growth and for many of the same reasons: lower costs of land and housing and a less congested living environment.

Income and Spending

The Sacramento region represents 5% of the California market. In 1998 the income earned by Sacramento region residents reached $46.2 billion.

The Sacramento market is growing faster than the nation. Between 1980 and 1990 real (i.e. inflation adjusted) income grew by 4.3% annually in the region — far exceeding the national 2.4% annual growth rate. During the recession real income grew slowly while the size of other markets in the state shrank temporarily.

Real income and spending have surged since 1994. Total personal income is now more than 20% above 1990 levels. Real per capita and average household income have risen 7% in the 1990s and are now above the national average.

Total real personal income is projected to rise by 4.0% per year in the Sacramento region between 1998 and 2005 — well above the anticipated 2.6% annual growth nationally. The Sacramento market will be one of the fastest growing markets with more than one million residents in the state and nation.

	Per Capita Income	Average HH Income	Total Personal Income (Billions)	Taxable Sales (Billions)
Sacramento Region Income and Taxable Sales 1990-2005 (1998$)				
1990	$25,483	$68,370	$38.0	$17.6
1994	$24,759	$66,266	$39.6	$17.0
1998	$27,230	$73,577	$46.2	$19.6
2005	$30,836	$81,442	$60.7	$25.4
Average Annual Growth Rates				
1990-1994	-0.7%	-0.8%	1.0%	-0.9%
1994-1998	2.4%	2.7%	3.9%	3.6%
1998-2005	1.8%	1.5%	4.0%	3.8%
California	1.8%	1.6%	3.5%	3.3%
United States	1.8%	1.6%	2.6%	

Spending on taxable items grew along with income in the 1980s — in marked contrast to the slow growth of spending in other regions. Taxable sales increased by 4.0% per year in Sacramento until the recession began.

Real spending fell slightly between 1990 and 1994 before rebounding to a new high of $19.6 billion in 1998.

Spending on taxable items will rise in line with income in the decade ahead. Regional spending on taxable items by households is projected to grow from $19.6 billion in 1998 to $25.4 billion in 2005 all in 1998$. This represents an annual spending growth gain of 3.9% higher than the projected 3.3% annual statewide growth rate.

Regional per capita income at $27,230 in 1998 is now 3% above the U.S. average. If the national economy produces productivity gains in the decade ahead as projected, per capita income in the region will grow by 1.8% per year and reach $30,836 by 2005 (in 1998$) — slightly above the projected $29,990 per capita income in the nation.

Average household income in the Sacramento region was $73,577 in 1998 — 4% above the national average. The average household income will increase by 1.5% per year and reach $81,442 in 2005.

The Sacramento region will grow faster than both the state and nation in income and spending in the decade ahead.

Construction Activity

Construction levels in Sacramento remained near the long term average during the early 1990s — not dipping as much as in other regions. A strong rebound in nonresidential construction began in 1997 and residential building surged ahead in 1998. Total building valuation increased approximately 30% in 1998 to $3.0 billion while home building jumped by 50% to 15,000 units.

As a result, nonresidential construction was the highest since the record 1988-90 years and residential building finally rose above the region's long term average.

Construction activity should increase in the coming years. Sacramento will experience above average levels of growth in jobs and population. Land prices are among the lowest in California's major regions.

Construction: A Large Cyclical Industry

The value of new building construction activity in the Sacramento region averaged nearly $1.9 billion per year between 1970 and 1998 measured in 1998 prices. At the peak in 1989 the new construction market reached $3.5 billion. 1998 construction levels of $3 billion approached the mid 80s peak.

An average of 14,100 new homes have been built each year since 1970. The peak year for units was 1986 with a record 23,800 units. The peak year for residential valuation ($2.7 billion) was 1989 when the high occurred for single family units. Residential permits dropped to near 10,000 per year between 1991 and 1997 before rebounding last year.

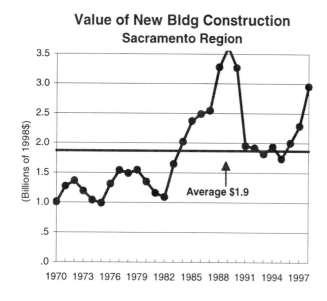

Value of New Bldg Construction
Sacramento Region

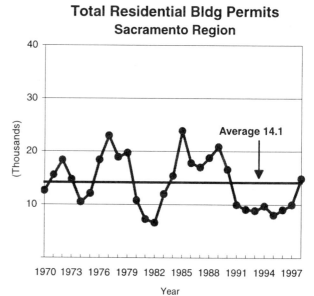

Total Residential Bldg Permits
Sacramento Region

Recent Construction Market Trends

About half of the sharp decline in residential building in the region since 1989 was recovered in 1998. Permit levels in Sacramento County remain 50% below 1989 construction levels. Residential building reached record levels in Placer County in 1998 but remain well below previous highs in El Dorado.

Total building valuation reached $3.0 billion in 1998 led by gains in residential construction. Nonresidential building led the 1997 gains. Placer County set new records in residential permits and total building valuation.

	Sacramento Region **Construction Trends** **(Billions of 1998$)**					
	New Building Construction			**Residential Permits** **(Thousands)**		
	1989	**1993**	**1998**	**1989**	**1993**	**1998**
El Dorado	$0.4	$0.2	$0.3	2.2	0.8	1.1
Placer	0.8	0.4	0.9	4.7	2.1	5.8
Sacramento	2.3	1.1	1.4	13.1	5.1	6.5
Yolo	0.2	0.1	0.3	0.8	0.9	1.7
Total Region	**$3.6**	**$1.8**	**$3.0**	**20.8**	**8.8**	**15.1**

Source: Construction Industry Research Board; 1998 estimates by CCSCE based on Jan-Oct CIRB data

Affordability and Household Growth: The Foundations for Housing Recovery

Price decreases, interest rate declines, strong population growth, and a move towards equilibrium with housing prices in other areas are laying the groundwork for a stronger residential construction market in the years ahead.

Affordability indices have rebounded in the region. From the lows established in 1989, by the end of 1998 the median priced house will be affordable to more than 60% of Sacramento region households as calculated by the California Association of Realtors. This is the highest affordability ratio in California.

CCSCE expects that affordability will continue to remain high in 1999. Real incomes are growing and the median resale price remains below previous peaks. Moreover, mortgage rates are below 7% versus 10% in the early 1990s.

Median prices in the Sacramento region are now well below prices in most major western markets. Recent median prices of near $125,000 compare with 3rd quarter 1998 medians of $150,000 in Denver, $125,400 in Las Vegas, $159,000 in Portland and $131,000 in Salt Lake City. Sacramento, with access to the state capitol and the region's growing high tech complex, offers very competitive land prices for both residential and nonresidential development.

Job growth and demographic trends point to higher household formation in the region. Job, population, and household growth are expected to reach 1980s levels between 1998 and 2005.

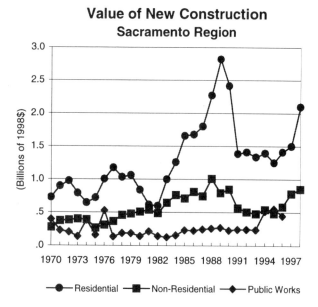

Value of New Construction
Sacramento Region

— Residential — Non-Residential — Public Works

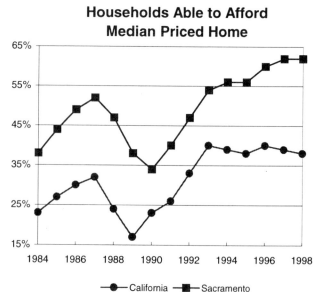

Households Able to Afford
Median Priced Home

— California — Sacramento

The projected household growth will support new residential construction averaging around 16,400 units per year from 1998 to 2005. The demographic projections and positive affordability trends point to a strong residential market in the Sacramento region in the years ahead.

Nonresidential Construction: Analysis and Outlook

Commercial construction rebounded to near $400 million in 1997 led by gains in new office building.

Industrial building rebounded strongly in 1997 before easing in 1998 but remains in the $100 million range and below record levels.

Two building types — 1) alterations and additions and 2) public works (heavy construction) accounted for most regional nonresidential construction during the 1990s. Nonresidential alterations and additions were a relatively stable $200 annually through 1996 before rising to near $250 million in 1998.

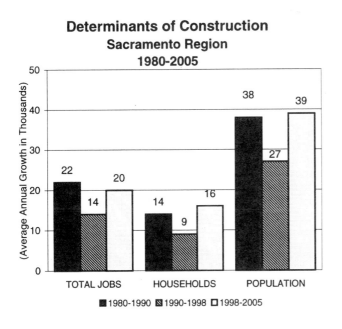

Determinants of Construction
Sacramento Region
1980-2005

■1980-1990 ◪1990-1998 ☐1998-2005

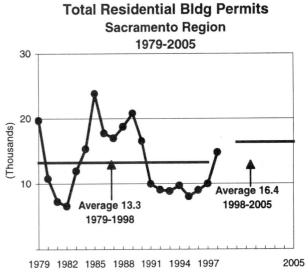

Total Residential Bldg Permits
Sacramento Region
1979-2005

Average 13.3
1979-1998

Average 16.4
1998-2005

Public works spending accounted for half of all nonresidential building in 1994, 1995 and 1996. 1997 spending estimates are unavailable because the Construction Industry Research Board has temporarily suspended reporting the public works estimates.

Sacramento Region Nonresidential Construction (Billions of 1998$)			
	1989	1993	1998
Commercial	$0.4	$0.2	$0.4
Industrial	0.2	0.0*	0.1
Other Nonresidential	0.1	0.1	0.1
Alterations/Additions	0.2	0.2	0.3
Heavy Construction	0.3	0.2	
Total Bldg. Constr.	$0.9	$0.5	$0.9
Total (incl. Heavy)	**$1.1**	**$0.8**	

Source: Construction Industry Research Board; *less than $50 million; 1998 estimates by CCSCE based on Jan-Oct CIRB data

Outlook for Future Growth

Several factors will support the growth of nonresidential construction in the Sacramento region.

1. Job growth will exceed the state average. High tech job growth should continue and new manufacturing and R&D facilities (already announced and prospective) will boost industrial spending.

2. State government will expand and there are announced plans for major future state office construction.

3. As a high growth area, the region will have an above average share of new school and transportation infrastructure.

4. The region will continue as a regional retail center and as a center for organizations doing business with the state government.

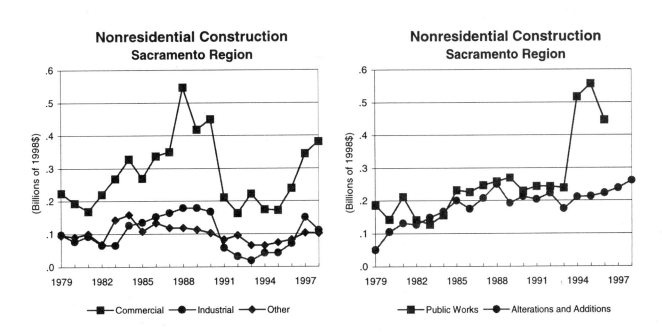

APPENDIX A

CHART A-1
California and United States
Basic Industries by Category

	SIC (1987 SIC Code)	Est. 1998 Jobs in California (Thousands)
Diversified Manufacturing		
Beverages	208	35.0
Knitting Mills	225	9.5
Floor Coverings	227	2.9
Other Textiles	22 exc 225,227	12.2
Apparel	23	154.6
Millwork	243	23.8
Other Wood Products	24 exc 241,2,3	19.6
HH Furniture	251	33.1
Partitions	254	8.8
Non HH Furniture	25 exc 251,254	17.3
Paperboard	265	19.6
Converted Paper	267	16.3
Paper Products	26 exc 264,265	4.5
Publishing	272-4	32.6
Synthetic Fibers	282	4.4
Drugs	283	30.3
Cleaning Products	284	13.9
Chemical Products	281,6,7,9	21.2
Plastic Products	308	63.2
Rubber Products	30 exc 308	13.7
Leather	31	7.1
Blast Furnaces	331	7.0
Iron and Steel Foundries	332	6.0
Nonferrous Rolling & Drawing	335	10.9
Nonferrous Foundries	336	6.5
Other Primary Metal Products	33 exc 331,2,3,5,6	3.9
Cutlery	342	12.4
Fab. Structural Metal Prod.	344	39.1
Screw Machinery Products	345	12.7
Metal Stampings	346	15.1
Coating & Engraving	347	23.7
Misc. Fabr. Metal Products	349	15.2
Farm Machinery	352	3.0
Construction Machinery	353	8.2
Metalworking Machinery	354	18.6
Special Industry Machinery	355	21.8
General Industrial Machinery	356	18.1
Service Industry Machinery	358	10.9
Other Nonelec Machinery	351,359	58.6
Elec. Trans & Distribution	361	6.0
Elec. Industrial Appliances	362	8.4
Household Appliances	363	2.9
Electrical Light & Wiring	364	21.0
TV-Radio Receivers	365	18.0
Misc. Electrical Products	369	15.5
Motor Vehicles	371	35.2
Misc. Transportation Equip.	374,5,9	9.2
Misc. Manufacturing	39	50.0

	SIC (1987 SIC Code)	Est. 1998 Jobs in California (Thousands)
High Technology		
Computers & Office Equip.	357	95.8
Communications Equipment	366	37.8
Electronic Components	367	159.0
Meas. & Contr. Instruments	382,387	71.0
Medical Instruments	384	44.8
Ophthalmic Equipment	385	5.3
Photo Equipment	386	4.8
Aircraft/Space/Defense		
Ordnance	348	**0.9**
Aircraft	372	87.4
Shipbuilding	373	11.1
Missiles & Space	376	25.2
Search & Navig. Equipment	381	57.3
Federal Defense		73.5
Resource Based		
Agriculture		384.4
Metal Mining	10	1.9
Coal Mining	11,12	0.0
Oil and Gas	13	22.1
Nonmetallic Mining	14	5.3
Pres. Fruits & Vegetables	203	46.9
Tobacco	21	0.0
Logging	241,2	14.2
Transportation and Wholesale Trade		
Railroads	40	14.5
Water Transportation	44	20.4
Airline Transportation	45	133.8
Pipeline Transportation	46	1.4
Wholesale Trade – Durables	50	473.8
Professional Services		
Computer Services	737	250.0
Legal Services	81	119.3
Engr. & Mgmnt. Services	87	448.2
Tourism & Entertainment		
Hotels	70	187.0
Motion Picture Film & Distr.	781,2	148.1
Amusements	79	197.0

Source: CCSCE based on January through October EDD data

CHART A-2
California and Economic Regions
Basic Industries by Category

	SIC (1987 SIC Code)	Est. 1998 Jobs in California (Thousands)
Diversified Manufacturing		
Other Food Products	20 exc 203	136.1
Textiles	22	24.6
Apparel	23	154.6
Other Lumber, Wood Products	24 exc 241,2	43.4
Furniture	25	59.2
Paper Products	26	40.4
Printing & Publishing	27	153.5
Chemicals	28	74.7
Petroleum Products	29	19.4
Rubber & Plastic Products	30	76.9
Leather	31	7.1
Stone, Clay, Glass	32	48.7
Primary Metal Products	33	34.3
Fabricated Metal Products	34	131.7
Other Non Electrical Mach.	35 exc 357	139.2
Other Electrical Machinery	36 exc 367	109.6
Motor Vehicles	371	35.2
Misc. Transportation Equip.	374,5,9	9.2
Misc. Manufacturing	39	50.0
High Technology		
Office, Computing Equip.	357	95.8
Electronic Components	367	159.0
Meas. & Contr. Instruments	382	71.0
Medical Instruments	384	44.8
Other Instruments	38 exc 382,384,381	10.1
Aircraft/Space/Defense		
Aircraft	372	87.4
Shipbuilding	373	11.1
Missiles & Space	376	25.2
Search & Navig. Equipment	381	57.3
Federal Defense		73.5
Resource Based		
Agriculture	01-09	384.4
Metal Mining	10-14	29.3
Pres. Fruits & Vegetables	203	46.9
Logging	241,2	14.2

	SIC (1987 SIC Code)	Est. 1998 Jobs in California (Thousands)
Transportation & Wholesale Trade		
Railroads	40	14.5
Truck Transportation	42	165.1
Water Transportation	44	20.4
Airline Transportation	45	133.8
Pipeline Transportation	46	1.4
Whsle. Trade – Durables	50	473.8
Whsle. Trade – Nondurables	51	322.2
Professional Services		
Computer Services	77	250.0
Legal Services	81	119.3
Engr. & Mgnmt. Services	87	448.2
Federal Civilian Employees		206.1
State Government		233.0
State Education		185.7
Tourism & Entertainment		
Hotels	70	187.0
Motion Picture Film & Distribution	781.2	148.1
Amusements	79	197.0

Source: CCSCE based on January through October EDD data